Queen of Great Britain Victoria

Speeches in Parliament from her accession to the present time

A compendium of the history of Her Majesty's reign

Queen of Great Britain Victoria

Speeches in Parliament from her accession to the present time
A compendium of the history of Her Majesty's reign

ISBN/EAN: 9783337150624

Printed in Europe, USA, Canada, Australia, Japan

Cover: Foto ©Suzi / pixelio.de

More available books at **www.hansebooks.com**

THE QUEEN'S SPEECHES
IN PARLIAMENT.

From Her Accession to the Present Time.

A COMPENDIUM OF THE HISTORY OF HER MAJESTY'S REIGN
TOLD FROM THE THRONE.

EDITED AND COMPILED BY

F. SIDNEY ENSOR,

AUTHOR OF "THROUGH NUBIA TO DARFOOR."

LONDON:
W. H. ALLEN & CO., 13 WATERLOO PLACE. S.W.
PUBLISHERS TO THE INDIA OFFICE.

1882.

LONDON :
W. H. ALLEN & CO., 13 WATERLOO PLACE, S.W.

CONTENTS.

PARLIAMENT I.

THE QUEEN'S SPEECHES
IN PARLIAMENT.

PARLIAMENT I.—SESSION I.

OPENING OF PARLIAMENT BY HER MAJESTY IN PERSON.

Date.—November 20th, 1837.

The Cabinet.—First Lord of the Treasury, Viscount Melbourne; Lord Chancellor, Lord Cottenham; President of the Council, Marquess of Lansdowne; First Lord of the Admiralty, Earl of Minto; Chancellor of the Duchy of Lancaster, Lord Holland; Lord of the Privy Seal and First Commissioner of Land Revenue, Viscount Duncannon; Home Secretary, Lord John Russell; Foreign Secretary, Viscount Palmerston; Colonial Secretary, Lord Glenelg; President of the Board of Control, Sir John Cam Hobhouse; Secretary at War, Viscount Howick; President of the Board of Trade, Right Hon. Charles Poulett Thomson; Chancellor of the Exchequer, Right Hon. Spring Rice.

The Queen's Speech.

My Lords and Gentlemen,

I have thought it right to assemble you for the transaction of public business at the earliest convenient period after the dissolution of the last Parliament.

1

It is with great satisfaction that I have received from all foreign Powers the strongest assurance of their friendly disposition, and of their earnest desire to cultivate and maintain with me the relations of amity; and I rejoice in the prospect that I shall be able to promote the best interests of my subjects by securing to them the advantages of peace.

I lament that civil war still afflicts the kingdom of Spain. I continue to exercise with fidelity the engagements of my Crown with the Queen of Spain, according to the stipulations of the Treaty of Quadruple Alliance.

I have directed a treaty of commerce which I have concluded with the United Republic of Peru and Bolivia to be laid before you, and I hope soon to be able to communicate to you similar results of my negotiations with other Powers.

I recommend to your serious consideration the state of the province of Lower Canada.

Gentlemen of the House of Commons,

The demise of the Crown renders it necessary that a new provision should be made for the Civil List. I place unreservedly at your disposal those hereditary revenues which were transferred to the public by my immediate predecessor, and I have commanded that such papers as may be necessary for the full examination of this subject shall be prepared and laid before you, desirous that the expenditure in this, as in every other department of the Government, should be kept within due limits. I feel confident that you will gladly make adequate provision for the support of the honour and dignity of the Crown.

The estimates for the services of next year are in course of preparation, and will be laid before you at the accustomed period. I have directed that the utmost economy should be enforced in every branch of the public expenditure.

My Lords and Gentlemen,

The external peace and domestic tranquillity which at present happily prevail, are very favourable for the consideration of such measures of reformation and amendment as may be necessary or expedient, and your attention will naturally be directed to that course of legislation which was interrupted by the necessary dissolution of the last Parliament.

The result of the inquiries which have been made into the condition of the poor in Ireland, has been already laid before Parliament, and it will be your duty to consult whether it may not be safe and wise to establish by law some well-regulated means of relief for the destitute in that country.

The municipal government of the cities and towns in Ireland calls for better regulation.

The laws which govern the collection of the tithe composition in Ireland require revision and amendment. Convinced that the better and more effectual administration of justice is amongst the first duties of a Sovereign, I request your attention to those measures which will be submitted to you for the improvement of the law.

You cannot but be sensible of the deep importance of these questions which I have submitted to you, and of the necessity of treating them in that spirit of im-

1 *

partiality and justice which affords the best hope of bringing them to a happy and useful termination. In meeting this Parliament, the first that has been elected under my authority, I am anxious to declare my confidence in your loyalty and wisdom. The early age at which I am called to the sovereignty of this kingdom, renders it a more imperative duty that, under Divine Providence, I should place my reliance upon your cordial co-operation, and upon the love and affection of my people.

Mover of Address in the Lords, The Duke of Sussex.
Seconder ,, ,, Lord Portman.
Mover of Address in the Commons, Lord Leveson.
Seconder ,, ,, Mr. Gibson Craig.

PROROGATION OF PARLIAMENT BY HER MAJESTY IN PERSON.

Date.—August 16th, 1838.

The Queen's Speech.

My Lords and Gentlemen,

The state of public business enables me to close this protracted and laborious Session.

I have to lament that the civil war in Spain forms an exception to the general tranquillity. I continue to receive from all foreign Powers the strongest assurances of their desire to retain with me the most amicable relations.

The disturbances and insurrections which have unfortunately broken out in Upper and Lower Canada have been promptly suppressed, and I entertain a confident hope that firm and judicious measures will empower you to restore a constitutional form of government, which unhappy events have compelled you for a time to suspend.

I rejoice at the progress which has been made in my Colonial possessions towards the entire abolition of Negro Apprenticeship.

I have observed with much satisfaction the attention which you have bestowed upon the amendment of the domestic institutions of the country. I trust that the mitigation of the law of Imprisonment for Debt will prove at once favourable to the liberty of my subjects, and safe for commercial credit, and that the Established Church will derive increased strength and efficiency from the restriction of the granting of Benefices in Plurality.

I have felt great pleasure in giving my assent to the Bill for the Relief of the Destitute Poor in Ireland. I cherish the expectation that its provisions have been so cautiously framed, and will be so prudently executed, that whilst they contribute to relieve distress, they will tend to preserve order and to encourage habits of industry and exertion.

I trust, likewise, that the Act which you have passed relating to the Composition for Tithe in Ireland, will increase the security of that property, and promote internal peace.

Gentlemen of the House of Commons,

I cannot sufficiently thank you for your despatch and liberality in providing for the expenses of my household, and the maintenance of the honour and dignity of the Crown. I offer you my warmest acknowledgments for the addition which you have made to the income of my beloved mother.

I thank you for the supplies which you have voted for the ordinary public service, as well as for the readiness with which you have provided means to meet the extraordinary expenses rendered necessary by the state of my Canadian possessions.

My Lords and Gentlemen,

The many useful measures which you have been able to consider, while the settlement of the Civil List, and the state of Canada, demanded so much of your attention, are a satisfactory proof of your zeal for the public good. You are so well acquainted with the duties which now devolve upon you in your respective counties, that it is unnecessary to remind you of them. In the discharge of them you may securely rely upon my firm support; and it only remains to express an humble hope that Divine Providence may watch over us all, and prosper our united efforts for the welfare of the country.

PARLIAMENT I.—SESSION II.

OPENING OF PARLIAMENT BY HER MAJESTY IN PERSON.

Date.—February 5th, 1839.

The Cabinet.—First Lord of the Treasury, Viscount Melbourne; Lord Chancellor, Lord Cottenham; President of the Council, Marquess of Lansdowne; First Lord of the Admiralty, Earl of Minto; Chancellor of the Duchy of Lancaster, Lord Holland; Lord Privy Seal and First Commissioner of Land Revenue, Viscount Duncannon; Home Secretary, Lord John Russell; Foreign Secretary, Viscount Palmerston; Colonial

Secretary, Lord Glenelg (on Friday, February 8th, Lord Glenelg resigned office) ; President of the Board of Control, Sir John Cam Hobhouse ; Secretary at War, Viscount Howick : President of the Board of Trade, Right Hon. Charles Poulett Thomson ; Chancellor of the. Exchequer, Right Hon. Thomas Spring Rice.

The Queen's Speech.

My Lords and Gentlemen,

I rejoice to meet you again in Parliament. I am particularly desirous of recurring to your advice and assistance at a period when many matters of great importance demand your serious and deliberate attention.

I continue to receive from foreign Powers gratifying assurances of their desire to maintain with me the most friendly relations.

I have concluded with the Emperor of Austria a Treaty of Commerce, which I trust will extend and improve the intercourse between my subjects and those of the Emperor.

I have also concluded a treaty of the same kind with the Sultan, calculated to place the commercial relations between my dominions and the Turkish Empire upon a better and more secure footing.

I have directed copies of those treaties to be laid before you.

I have been engaged—in concert with Austria, France, Prussia, and Russia—in negotiations, with a view to the final settlement of the differences between Holland and Belgium.

A definitive treaty of peace, founded upon anterior

arrangements, which have been acceded to by both parties, has, in consequence, been proposed to the Dutch and Belgian Governments. I have the satisfaction to inform you that the Dutch Government has already signified to the Conference its acceptance of that treaty, and I trust that a similar announcement from the Belgian Government will put an end to the disquietude which the present unsettled state of these affairs has necessarily produced.

The warranty of the Five Allied Powers affords satisfactory security for the preservation of peace.

I lament the continuance of the Civil War in Spain, which engages my anxious and undiminished attention.

Differences which have arisen have occasioned the retirement of my Minister from the Court of Teheran. I indulge, however, the hope of learning that a satisfactory adjustment of these differences will allow of the re establishment of my relations with Persia upon their former footing of friendship.

Events connected with the same differences have induced the Governor-General of India to take measures for protecting British interests in that quarter of the world, and to enter into engagements, the fulfilment of which may render military operations necessary. For this purpose such preparations have been made as may be sufficient to resist aggression from any quarter, and to maintain the integrity of my Eastern dominions.

The Reform and Amendment of the Municipal Corporations of Ireland are essential to the interests of that part of my dominions.

It is also urgent that you should apply yourselves to the prosecution and completion of those measures which

have been recommended by the Ecclesiastical Commissioners of England, for the purpose of increasing
the efficiency of the Established Church, and of confirming its hold upon the affection and respect of my
people.

The better enforcement of the law, and the more
speedy administration of justice, are of the first importance to the welfare of the community, and I feel
assured that you will be anxious to devote yourselves to
the examination of the measures which will be submitted
to you for the purpose of attaining these beneficial
results.

Gentlemen of the House of Commons,

I have directed the annual Estimates to be prepared and laid before you.

Adhering to the principles of economy, which it is
my desire to enforce in every department of the State, I
feel it my duty to recommend that adequate provision
be made for the exigencies of the public service. I
fully rely on your loyalty and patriotism to maintain
the efficiency of those Establishments which are essential
to the strength and security of the country.

My Lords and Gentlemen,

It is with great satisfaction that I am enabled to
inform you that, throughout the whole of my West
Indian possessions, the period fixed by law for the final
and complete Emancipation of the Negroes has been
anticipated by Acts of the Colonial Legislatures, and
that the transition from the temporary system of apprenticeship to entire freedom has taken place without any
disturbance of public order and tranquillity. Any

measures which may be necessary, in order to give full effect to this great and beneficial change, will, I have no doubt, receive your careful attention.

I have to acquaint you, with deep concern, that the province of Lower Canada has again been disturbed by insurrection, and that hostile incursions have been made into Upper Canada by certain lawless inhabitants of the United States of North America. These violations of the public peace have been promptly suppressed by the valour of my forces and the loyalty of my Canadian subjects. The President of the United States has called upon the citizens of the Union to abstain from proceedings so incompatible with the friendly relations which subsist between Great Britain and the United States.

I have directed full information upon all these matters to be laid before you, and I recommend the present state of these provinces to your serious consideration. I rely upon you to support my firm determination to maintain the authority of my Crown, and I trust that your wisdom will adopt such measures as will secure to those parts of my Empire the benefit of internal tranquillity and the full advantages of their own great national resources.

I have observed with pain the persevering efforts which have been made, in some parts of the country, to excite my subjects to disobedience and resistance to the law, and to recommend dangerous and illegal practices. For the counteraction of all such designs, I depend upon the efficacy of the law, which it will be my duty to enforce—upon the good sense and right disposition of my people—upon their attachment to the principles

of justice, and their abhorrence of violence and disorder.

I confidently submit all these great interests to your
wisdom, and I implore Almighty God to assist and
prosper your counsels.

Mover of Address in the Lords, Earl of Lovelace.
Seconder „ „ Lord Vernon.
Mover of Address in the Commons, Mr. E. Buller.
Seconder „ „ Mr. G. W. Wood.

PROROGATION OF PARLIAMENT BY HER MAJESTY IN
PERSON.

Date.—August 27th, 1839.

The Queen's Speech.

My Lords and Gentlemen,

The public business having been brought to a
close, I have now to perform the satisfactory duty of
releasing you from your long and laborious attendance
in Parliament.

I rejoice that a definitive treaty between Holland and
Belgium, negotiated by the mediation of the Five
Powers, has settled the differences between those two
countries, and has secured the peace of Europe from
dangers to which it had so long been exposed.

The same concord which brought these intricate questions to a peaceful termination prevails with regard to
the affairs of the Levant.

The Five Powers are alike determined to uphold the
independence and integrity of the Ottoman Empire, and
I trust that this union will ensure a satisfactory settlement of matters which are of the deepest importance to
the whole of Europe.

It has afforded me the sincerest pleasure to have been able to assist in effecting a reconciliation between France and Mexico. Intent upon preserving for my subjects the blessings of peace, I am highly gratified when I can avail myself of an opportunity of removing misunderstandings between other Powers.

I have recently concluded, with the King of the French, a convention calculated to put an end to differences which have arisen of late years between Great Britain and France. This convention, by removing causes of dispute, will tend to cement that union between the two countries which is so advantageous to both, and so conducive to the general interests of Europe.

I shall continue to pursue with perseverance the negotiations in which I am engaged to persuade all the powers of Christendom to unite in a general league for the entire extinction of the Slave Trade, and I trust that, with the blessing of Providence, my efforts in so righteous a cause will be rewarded with success.

I regret that the differences which led to the withdrawal of my Minister from the Court of Teheran have not yet been satisfactorily adjusted by the Government of Persia.

In order to fulfil the engagements announced to you at the opening of the present session, the Governor-General of India has moved an army across the Indus, and I have much satisfaction in being able to inform you that the advance of that expedition has been hitherto unopposed, and there is every reason to hope that the important objects for which these military operations have been undertaken will be finally obtained.

I have observed with much approbation the attention which you have bestowed upon the internal state and condition of the country. I entirely concur in the measures which you have framed for the preservation of order, the repression of crime, and the better administration of justice in this metropolis, and I have given a cordial assent to the Bills which you have presented to me for the establishment of a more efficient constabulary force in those towns which peculiarly required it, and for effecting the important object of generally extending and invigorating the civil power throughout the country.

Gentlemen of the House of Commons,

I thank you for the zeal and readiness with which you have voted the supplies for the service of the year.

It has been with satisfaction that I have given my consent to a reduction of the postage duties. I trust that the Act which has passed on this subject will be a relief and encouragement to trade, and that, by facilitating intercourse and correspondence, it will be productive of much social advantage and improvement. I have given directions that the preliminary step should be taken to give effect to the intention of Parliament as soon as the inquiries and arrangements required for this purpose shall have been completed.

The advantageous terms upon which a considerable amount of the unfunded debt has been converted into stock afford a satisfactory proof of the reliance placed on the credit and resources of the country, as well as on your determination to preserve inviolate the national faith.

My Lords and Gentlemen,

It is with great pain that I have found myself compelled to enforce the law against those who no longer concealed their design of resisting by force the lawful authorities, and of subverting the institutions of the country.

The solemn proceedings of courts of justice, and the fearless administration of the laws by all who are engaged in that duty, have checked the first attempts at insubordination; and I rely securely upon the good sense of my people, and upon their attachment to the Constitution, for the maintenance of law and order, which are as necessary for the protection of the poor as for the welfare of the wealthier classes of the community.

PARLIAMENT I.—SESSION III.

OPENING OF PARLIAMENT BY HER MAJESTY IN PERSON.

Date.—January 16th, 1840.

The Cabinet.—First Lord of the Treasury, Viscount Melbourne; Lord Chancellor, Lord Cottenham; President of the Council, Marquess of Lansdowne; First Lord of the Admiralty, Earl of Minto; Chancellor of the Duchy of Lancaster, Lord Holland; Lord of the Privy Seal, Earl of Clarendon; First Commissioner of Land Revenue, Viscount Duncannon; Home Secretary, Marquess of Normanby; Foreign Secretary, Viscount Palmerston; Colonial Secretary, Lord John Russell; President of the Board of Control, Right Hon. Sir John Cam Hobhouse, Bart.; Chancellor of the Ex-

chequer, Right Hon Francis Thornhill Baring; Chief
Secretary for Ireland, Viscount Morpeth.

The Queen's Speech.

My Lords and Gentlemen,

Since you were last assembled, I have declared
my intention of allying myself in marriage with the
Prince Albert of Saxe Coburg and Gotha. I humbly
implore that the Divine blessing may prosper this union,
and render it conducive to the interests of my people,
as well as to my own domestic happiness, and it will be
to me a source of the most lively satisfaction to find the
resolution I have taken approved by my Parliament.

The constant proofs which I have received of your
attachment to my person and family, persuade me that
you will enable me to provide for such an establishment
as may appear suitable to the rank of the Prince and
the dignity of the Crown.

I continue to receive from foreign Powers assurances
of their unabated desire to maintain with me the most
friendly relations.

I rejoice that the civil war, which has so long disturbed and desolated the Northern Provinces of Spain,
has been brought to an end by an arrangement satisfactory to the Spanish Government and to the people of
those provinces, and I trust that ere long peace and
tranquillity will be established throughout the rest of
Spain.

The affairs of the Levant have continued to occupy
my most anxious attention. The concord which has
prevailed amongst the Five Powers has prevented a
renewal of hostilities in that quarter, and I hope that

the same unanimity will bring these important and difficult matters to a final settlement in such a manner as to uphold the integrity and independence of the Ottoman Empire, and to give additional security to the peace of Europe.

I have not yet been enabled to re-establish my diplomatic relations with the Court of Teheran, but communications which I have lately received from the Persian Government inspire me with confident expectation that the differences which occasioned a suspension of those relations will soon be satisfactorily adjusted.

Events have happened in China which have occasioned an interruption of the commercial intercourse of my subjects with that country. I have given, and shall continue to give, the most serious attention to a matter so deeply affecting the interests of my subjects and the dignity of my Crown.

I have great satisfaction in acquainting you that the military operations undertaken by the Governor-General of India have been attended with complete success, and that in the expedition to the westward of the Indus the officers and troops, both European and Native, have displayed the most distinguished skill and valour.

I have directed that further papers relating to the affairs of Canada should be laid before you, and I confide to your wisdom this important subject.

I recommend to your early attention the state of the Municipal Corporations of Ireland.

It is desirable that you should prosecute those measures relating to the Established Church which have been recommended by the Ecclesiastical Commissioners of England.

Gentlemen of the House of Commons,

I have directed the Estimates for the services of the year to be laid before you. They have been framed with every attention to economy, and at the same time with a due regard to the efficiency of those establishments which are rendered necessary by the extent and circumstances of the Empire.

I have lost no time in carrying into effect the intentions of Parliament by the reduction of duties on Postage, and I trust that the beneficial effects of this measure will be felt throughout all classes of the community.

My Lords and Gentlemen,

I learn with great sorrow that the commercial embarrassments which have taken place in this and in other countries are subjecting many of the manufacturing districts to severe distress.

I have to acquaint you, with deep concern, that the spirit of insubordination has in some parts of the country broken out into open violence, which was speedily repressed by the firmness and energy of the magistrates, and by the steadiness and good conduct of my troops. I confidently rely upon the power of the law, upon your loyalty and wisdom, and upon the good sense and right feeling of the people, for the maintenance of order, the protection of property, and the promotion, as far as they can be promoted by human means, of the true interests of the Empire.

Mover of Address in the Lords, Duke of Somerset.
Seconder   „   „   Lord Seaford.
Mover of Address in the Commons, Hon. G. H. Cavendish.
Seconder   „   „   Sir Wm. Somerville.

2

PROROGATION OF PARLIAMENT BY HER MAJESTY IN
PERSON.

Date.—August 11th, 1840.

The Queen's Speech.

My Lords and Gentlemen,

      The state of public business enables me to close
this session of Parliament; and in releasing you from your
attendance, I have to thank you for the care and attention
with which you have discharged your important duties.

      I continue to receive from foreign Powers assurances
of their friendly disposition, and of their anxious desire
for the maintenance of peace.

      I congratulate you upon the termination of the civil
war in Spain. The objects for which the Quadruple
engagements of 1834 were contracted having now been
accomplished, I am in communication with the Queen
of Spain with a view to withdraw the naval force which,
in pursuance of those engagements, I have hitherto
stationed on the northern coast of Spain.

      I am happy to inform you that the differences with
the Government of Naples, the grounds and causes of
which have been laid before you, have been put into a
train of adjustment by the friendly mediation of the
King of the French.

      I rejoice also to acquaint you that the Government of
Portugal has made arrangements for satisfying certain
just claims of some of my subjects, and for the payment
of a sum due to this country under the stipulations of
the Convention of 1827.

      I am engaged, in concert with the Emperor of Austria,
the King of Prussia, the Emperor of Russia, and the

Sultan, in measures intended to effect the permanent pacification of the Levant, to maintain the integrity and independence of the Ottoman Empire, and thereby to afford additional security for the peace of Europe.

The violent injuries inflicted upon some of my subjects by the officers of the Emperor of China, and the indignities offered to an Agent of my Crown, have compelled me to send to the coast of China a naval and military force for the purpose of demanding reparation and redress.

I have gladly given my assent to the Act for the Regulation of Municipal Corporations in Ireland.

I trust that the law which you have framed for further carrying into effect the Reports of the Ecclesiastical Commissioners will have the beneficial effect of increasing the efficiency of the Established Church, and of better providing for the religious instruction of my people.

I have observed with much satisfaction the result of your deliberations on the subject of Canada. It will be my duty to execute the measures which you have adopted in such a manner as, without impairing the Executive authority, may satisfy the just wishes of my subjects, and provide for the permanent welfare and security of my North American Provinces.

The legislative bodies of Jamaica have applied themselves to the preparation of laws rendered necessary or expedient by the altered state of society. Some of those laws require revision and amendment ; but I have every reason to expect cordial assistance from the Assembly of Jamaica in the salutary work of improving the condition and elevating the character of the inhabitants of

2 *

that Colony   The conduct of the emancipated negroes throughout the West Indies has been remarkable for tranquil obedience to the law, and a peaceable demeanour in the relations of social life.

Gentlemen of the House of Commons,

I thank you for the supplies which you have granted for the service of the year.

I lament that it should have been necessary to impose additional burdens upon my people ; but I trust that the means which you have adopted for the purpose of meeting the exigencies of the public service, are calculated to press with as little severity as possible upon all classes of the community.

My Lords and Gentlemen,

In returning to your respective counties, you will resume those duties which you perform so much to the public benefit and advantage.   It is my anxious desire to maintain tranquillity at home and peace abroad.   To these objects, so essential to the interests of this country, and to the general welfare of mankind, my efforts will be sincerely and unremittingly directed ; and feeling assured of your co-operation and support, I humbly rely upon the superintending care and continued protection of Divine Providence.

PARLIAMENT I.—SESSION IV.

OPENING OF PARLIAMENT BY HER MAJESTY IN PERSON.

Date.—January 26th, 1841.

The Cabinet.—First Lord of the Treasury, Viscount Melbourne ; Lord Chancellor, Lord Cottenham ; Presi-

dent of the Council, Marquess of Lansdowne; First
Lord of the Admiralty, Earl of Minto; Lord of the
Privy Seal and Chancellor of the Duchy of Lancaster,
Earl of Clarendon; First Commissioner of Land Revenue,
Viscount Duncannon; Home Secretary, Marquess of
Normanby; Foreign Secretary, Viscount Palmerston;
Colonial Secretary, Lord John Russell; President of the
Board of Control, Right Hon. Sir John Cam Hobhouse,
Bart.; President of the Board of Trade and Master of
the Mint, Right Hon. Henry Labouchere; Chancellor
of the Exchequer, Right Hon. Francis Thornhill Baring;
Chief Secretary for Ireland, Viscount Morpeth.

The Queen's Speech.

My Lords and Gentlemen,

I have the satisfaction to receive from foreign
Powers assurances of their friendly disposition, and of
their earnest desire to maintain peace.

The position of affairs in the Levant had long been
a cause of uneasiness and a source of danger to the
general tranquillity. With a view to avert the evils
which a continuance of that state of things was calculated to occasion, I concluded with the Emperor of
Austria, the King of Prussia, the Emperor of Russia,
and the Sultan, a Convention intended to effect a pacification of the Levant; to maintain the integrity of the
Ottoman Empire; and thereby to afford additional
security to the peace of Europe.

I have given instructions that this Convention shall
be laid before you.

I rejoice to be able to inform you that the measures

which have been adopted in execution of these engagements have been attended with signal success, and I trust that the objects which the contracting parties had in view are on the eve of being completely accomplished.

In the course of these transactions my naval forces have co-operated with those of the Emperor of Austria, and with the land and sea forces of the Sultan, and have displayed upon all occasions their accustomed gallantry and skill.

Having deemed it necessary to send to the coast of China a naval and military force, to demand reparation and redress for the injuries inflicted upon some of my subjects by the officers of the Emperor of China, and for indignities offered to an Agent of my Crown, I, at the same time, appointed Plenipotentiaries to treat upon these matters with the Chinese Government.

The Plenipotentiaries were, by the last accounts, in negotiation with the Government of China, and it will be a source of much gratification to me if that Government shall be induced, by its own sense of justice, to bring these matters to a speedy settlement by an amicable arrangement.

Serious differences have arisen between Spain and Portugal, about the execution of a treaty concluded by those Powers in 1835, for regulating the navigation of the Douro. Both parties have accepted my mediation, and I hope to be able to effect a reconciliation between them upon terms honourable to both.

I have concluded with the Argentine Republic, and with the Republic of Hayti, treaties for the suppression of the slave trade, which I have directed to be laid before you.

Gentlemen of the House of Commons,

I have directed the Estimates for the year to be laid before you.

However sensible of the importance of adhering to the principles of economy, I feel it my duty to recommend that adequate provision be made for the exigencies of the public service.

My Lords and Gentlemen,

Measures will be submitted to you, without delay, which have for their object the more speedy and effectual administration of justice. The vital importance of this subject is sufficient to ensure for it your early and most serious consideration.

The powers of the Commissioners appointed under the Act for the Amendment of the Laws relating to the Poor expire at the termination of the present year. I feel assured that you will earnestly direct your attention to enactments which so deeply concern the interests of the community.

It is always with entire confidence that I recur to the advice and assistance of my Parliament. I place my reliance upon your wisdom, loyalty, and patriotism; and I humbly implore of Divine Providence that all your councils may be so directed as to advance the great interests of morality and religion, to preserve peace, and to promote by enlightened legislation the welfare and happiness of all classes of my subjects.

Mover of Address in the Lords, Earl of Ducie.
Seconder   ,,   ,,   Lord Lurgan.
Mover of Address in the Commons, Lord Brabazon.
Seconder   ,,   ,,   Mr. Grantley Berkeley.

Prorogation of Parliament by Her Majesty in Person.

Date.—June 22nd, 1841.

The Queen's Speech.

My Lords and Gentlemen,

On a full consideration of the present state of public affairs, I have come to the determination of proroguing Parliament, with a view to its immediate dissolution.

The paramount importance of the trade and industry of the country, and my anxiety that the exigencies of the public service should be provided for in the manner least burdensome to the community, have induced me to resort to the means which the Constitution has entrusted to me, of ascertaining the sense of my people upon matters which so deeply concern their welfare.

I entertain the hope that the progress of public business may be facilitated, and that divisions, injurious to the course of steady policy and useful legislation, may be removed by the authority of a new Parliament, which I shall direct to be summoned without delay.

Gentlemen of the House of Commons,

I thank you for the readiness with which you have voted the sums necessary for the civil and military establishments.

My Lords and Gentlemen,

In the exercise of my prerogative I can have no other object than that of securing the rights and promoting the interests of my subjects; and I rely on the co-operation of my Parliament, and the loyal zeal of my people, for support in the adoption of such measures as are necessary to maintain that high station among the nations of the world which it has pleased Divine Providence to assign to this country.

PARLIAMENT II.—SESSION I.

OPENING OF PARLIAMENT BY COMMISSION.

Date.—August 24th, 1841.

The Lords Commissioners were:—The Lord Chancellor; the Marquess of Lansdowne; the Marquess of Normanby; the Earl of Clarendon; and Viscount Duncannon.

The Cabinet.—First Lord of the Treasury, Right Hon. Sir Robert Peel, Bart.; Lord Chancellor, Lord Lyndhurst; President of the Council, Lord Wharncliffe; First Lord of the Admiralty, Earl of Haddington; Lord of the Privy Seal, Duke of Buckingham; Home Secretary, Right Hon. Sir James Graham, Bart.; Foreign Secretary, Earl of Aberdeen; Colonial Secretary, Lord Stanley; President of the Board of Control, Lord Ellenborough; Secretary at War, Right Hon. Sir Henry Hardinge; President of the Board of Trade, Earl of Ripon; Chancellor of the Exchequer, Right Hon. Henry Goulburn; Paymaster-General, Right Hon. Sir Edward Knatchbull, Bart.

The Queen's Speech.

My Lords and Gentlemen,

We are commanded by Her Majesty to acquaint you that Her Majesty has availed herself of the earliest opportunity of resorting to your advice and assistance after the dissolution of the last Parliament.

Her Majesty continues to receive from foreign Powers gratifying assurances of their desire to maintain with Her Majesty the most friendly relations.

Her Majesty has the satisfaction of informing you that the objects for which the Treaty of the 15th of July 1840, was concluded between Her Majesty, the Emperor of Austria, the King of Prussia, the Emperor of Russia, and the Sultan, have been fully accomplished, and it is gratifying to Her Majesty to be enabled to state that the temporary separation which the measures taken in the execution of that treaty created between the contracting parties and France has now ceased.

Her Majesty trusts that the union of the principal Powers upon all matters affecting the great interests of Europe, will afford a firm security for the maintenance of peace.

Her Majesty is glad to be able to inform you that, in consequence of the evacuation of Ghorian by the Persian troops, Her Majesty has ordered her Minister to the Court of Persia to return to Teheran.

Her Majesty regrets that the negotiations between her Plenipotentiaries in China and the Chinese Government have not yet been brought to a satisfactory conclusion, and that it has been necessary to call into action the forces which Her Majesty has sent to the China seas; but Her Majesty still trusts that the Emperor of China will see the justice of the demands which Her Majesty's Plenipotentiaries have been instructed to make.

Her Majesty is happy to inform you that the differences which had arisen between Spain and Portugal about the execution of a treaty concluded by those Powers in 1835, for regulating the navigation of the

Douro, have been adjusted amicably and with honour to both parties, by the aid of Her Majesty's mediation

The debt incurred by the Legislature of Upper Canada for the purposes of public works, is a serious obstacle to further improvements which are essential to the prosperity of the United Province. Her Majesty has authorised the Governor-General to make a communication on the subject to the Council and Assembly of Canada. Her Majesty will direct the papers to be laid before you, and trusts that your earnest attention will be directed to matters so materially affecting the welfare of Canada and the strength of the Empire.

Gentlemen of the House of Commons,

We have to assure you that Her Majesty relies with entire confidence on your loyalty and zeal to make adequate provision for the public service, as well as for the further application of sums granted by the last Parliament.

My Lords and Gentlemen,

We are more especially commanded to declare to you that the extraordinary expenses which the events in Canada, China, and the Mediterranean have occasioned, and the necessity of maintaining a force adequate to the protection of our extensive possessions, have made it necessary to consider the means of increasing the public revenue. Her Majesty is anxious that this object should be effected in the manner least burdensome to her people, and it has appeared to Her Majesty, after full deliberation, that you may at this juncture properly direct your attention to the revision of duties affecting the productions of foreign countries.

It will be for you to consider whether some of these duties are not so trifling in amount as to be unproductive to the revenue, while they are vexatious to commerce. You may further examine whether the principle of protection, upon which others of these duties are founded, be not carried to an extent injurious alike to the income of the State and the interests of the people.

Her Majesty is desirous that you should consider the laws which regulate the trade in corn. It will be for you to determine whether these laws do not aggravate the natural fluctuations of supply, whether they do not embarrass trade, derange currency, and, by their operation, diminish the comfort and increase the privations of the great body of the community.

Her Majesty feeling the deepest sympathy with those of her subjects who are now suffering from distress and want of employment, it is her earnest prayer that all your deliberations may be guided by wisdom, and may conduce to the happiness of her beloved people.

Mover of Address in the Lords, Earl Spencer.
Seconder,   „   „   Marquess of Clanricarde.
Mover of Address in the Commons, Mr. Mark Phillips.
Seconder „   „   Mr. J. C. Dundas.

PROROGATION OF PARLIAMENT BY COMMISSION.

Date.—October 7th, 1841.

The Lords Commissioners were:—The Lord Chancellor; the Duke of Wellington; the Duke of Buckingham; the Earl of Shaftesbury; and Lord Wharncliffe.

The Queen's Speech.

My Lords and Gentlemen,

We are commanded by Her Majesty to acquaint you that it appears advisable to Her Majesty to bring to a close the present Session of Parliament.

In conformity with the advice of her Parliament, and in pursuance of the declared intentions of Her Majesty, Her Majesty has taken the requisite measures for the formation of a new Administration, and the arrangements for that purpose have been completed by Her Majesty.

Gentlemen of the House of Commons,

We have it in command from Her Majesty to thank you for the supplies which you have granted to Her Majesty for those branches of the public service for which complete provision had not been made by the late Parliament.

My Lords and Gentlemen,

The measures which it will be expedient to adopt for the purpose of equalising the public income and the annual expenditure, and other important objects connected with the trade and commerce of the country, will necessarily occupy your attention at an early period after the recess.

Her Majesty has commanded us to repeat the expression of her deep concern at the distress which has prevailed for a considerable period in some of the principal manufacturing districts, and to assure you that you may rely upon the cordial concurrence of Her Majesty in all such measures as shall appear, after mature consideration, best calculated to prevent the recurrence of that distress, and to promote the great object of all Her Majesty's wishes—the happiness and contentment of her people.

PARLIAMENT II.—SESSION II.

OPENING OF PARLIAMENT BY HER MAJESTY IN PERSON.

Date.—February 3rd, 1842.

The Cabinet.—First Lord of the Treasury, Right Hon. Sir Robert Peel, Bart.; Lord Chancellor, Lord Lyndhurst; President of the Council, Lord Wharncliffe; First Lord of the Admiralty, Earl of Haddington; Lord of the Privy Seal, Duke of Buccleuch and Queensberry; Home Secretary, Right Hon. Sir James Graham, Bart.; Foreign Secretary, Earl of Aberdeen; Colonial Secretary, Lord Stanley; President of the Board of Control, Lord Fitzgerald; Secretary at War, Right Hon. Sir Henry Hardinge; President of the Board of Trade, Earl of Ripon; Chancellor of the Exchequer, Right Hon. Henry Goulburn; Paymaster-General, Right Hon. Sir Edward Knatchbull, Bart.; Without Office, Duke of Wellington.

The Queen's Speech.

My Lords and Gentlemen,

I cannot meet you in Parliament assembled without making a public acknowledgment of my gratitude to Almighty God, on account of the birth of the Prince, my son; an event which has completed the measure of my domestic happiness, and has been hailed with every demonstration of affectionate attachment to my person and government by my faithful and loyal people.

I am confident that you will participate in the satisfaction which I have derived from the presence in this country of my good brother and ally, the King of Prussia, who, at my request, undertook in person the office of sponsor at the christening of the Prince of Wales.

I receive from all Princes and States the continued assurance of their earnest desire to maintain the most friendly relations with this country.

It is with great satisfaction that I inform you that I have concluded with the Emperor of Austria, the King of the French, the King of Prussia, and the Emperor of Russia, a treaty for the more effectual suppression of the Slave Trade, which, when the ratifications shall have been exchanged, will be communicated to Parliament.

There shall also be laid before you a treaty which I have concluded with the same Powers, together with the Sultan, having for its object the security of the Turkish Empire, and the maintenance of the general tranquillity.

The restoration of my diplomatic relations and intercourse with the Court of Teheran has been followed by the completion of a commercial treaty with the King of Persia, which I have directed to be laid before you.

I am engaged in negotiations with several Powers, which I trust, by leading to conventions founded on the just principle of mutual advantage, may extend the trade and commerce of the country.

I regret that I am not enabled to announce to you

the re-establishment of peaceful relations with the Government of China.

The uniform success which has attended the hostile operations directed against that Power, and my confidence in the skill and gallantry of my naval and military forces encourage the hope on my part that our differences with the Government of China will be brought to an early termination, and our commercial relations with that country placed on a satisfactory basis.

Gentlemen of the House of Commons,

The estimates for the year have been prepared, and will be laid before you.

I rely with entire confidence on your disposition, while you enforce the principles of a wise economy, to make that provision for the service of the country which the public exigencies require.

My Lords and Gentlemen,

I recommend to your immediate attention the state of the finances and of the expenditure of the country.

You will have seen with regret that for several years past the annual income has been inadequate to bear the public charges; and I feel confident that, fully sensible of the evil which must result from a continued deficiency of this nature during peace, you will carefully consider the best means of averting it.

I recommend also to your consideration the state of the laws which affect the import of corn and of other articles, the produce of foreign countries.

Measures will be submitted for your consideration, for the amendment of the Law of Bankruptcy, and for the improvement of the Jurisdiction exercised by the Courts of England and Wales.

It will also be desirable that you should consider, with a view to their revision, the laws which regulate the Registration of Electors of Members to serve in Parliament.

I have observed with deep regret the continued distress in the manufacturing districts of the country.

The sufferings and privations which have resulted from it have been borne with exemplary patience and fortitude.

I feel assured that your deliberations on the various important matters which will occupy your attention will be directed by a comprehensive regard for the interests and permanent welfare of all classes of my subjects, and I fervently pray that they may tend in their result to improve the national resources, and to encourage the industry and promote the happiness of my people.

Mover of Address in the Lords, Marquess of Abercorn.
Seconder   „   „   Earl of Dalhousie.
Mover of Address in the Commons, Earl of March.
Seconder   „   „   Mr. Beckett.

PROROGATION OF PARLIAMENT BY HER MAJESTY IN PERSON.

Date.—August 12th, 1842.

The Queen's Speech.

My Lords and Gentlemen,

The state of public business enables me to release you from further attendance in Parliament.

I cannot take leave of you without expressing my

3

grateful sense of the assiduity and zeal with which
you have applied yourselves to the discharge of your
public duties during the whole course of a long and
most laborious session.

You have had under your consideration measures of
the greatest importance connected with the financial and
commercial interests of the country, calculated to maintain the public credit, to improve the national resources,
and, by extending trade and stimulating the demand for
labour, to promote the general and permanent welfare of
all classes of my subjects.

Although measures of this description have necessarily occupied much of your attention, you have at the
same time effected great improvements in several
branches of jurisprudence, and in laws connected with
the administration of domestic affairs.

I return you my especial acknowledgments for the
renewed proof which you afforded me of your loyalty
and affectionate attachment, by your ready and unanimous concurrence in an Act for the increased security
and protection of my person.

I continue to receive from all foreign Powers
assurances of their friendly disposition towards this
country.

Although I have deeply to lament the reverses which
have befallen a division of my army to the westward of
the Indus, yet I have the satisfaction of reflecting that
the gallant defence of the city of Jellalabad, crowned
by a decisive victory in the field, has eminently proved
the courage and discipline of the European and native
troops, and the skill and fortitude of their distinguished
commander.

Gentlemen of the House of Commons,

The liberality with which you have granted the supplies, to meet the exigencies of the public service, demands my warm acknowledgments.

My Lords and Gentlemen,

You will concur in the expression of humble gratitude to Almighty God for the favourable season which His bounty has vouchsafed to us, and for the prospect of a harvest more abundant than those of recent years.

There are, I trust, indications of gradual recovery from that depression which has affected many branches of manufacturing industry, and has exposed large classes of my people to privations and sufferings which have caused me the deepest concern.

You will, I am confident, be actuated, on your return to your several counties, by the same enlightened zeal for the public interests which you have manifested during the discharge of your Parliamentary duties, and will do your utmost to encourage, by your example and active exertions, that spirit of order and submission to the law which is essential to the public happiness, and without which there can be no enjoyment of the fruits of peaceful industry, and no advance in the career of social improvement.

PARLIAMENT II.—SESSION III.

Opening of Parliament by Commission.

Date.—February 2nd, 1843.

The Lords Commissioners were:—The Lord Chancellor; the Lord President of the Council; the Archbishop of Canterbury; the Lord of the Privy Seal;

the Duke of Buccleuch; the Earl of Shaftesbury; and Lord Wharncliffe.

The Cabinet.—First Lord of the Treasury, Right Hon. Sir Robert Peel, Bart.; Lord Chancellor, Lord Lyndhurst; President of the Council, Lord Wharncliffe; First Lord of the Admiralty, Earl of Haddington; Commander in Chief, Duke of Wellington; Lord of the Privy Seal, Duke of Buccleuch and Queensberry; Home Secretary, Right Hon. Sir James Graham, Bart.; Foreign Secretary, Earl of Aberdeen; Colonial Secretary, Lord Stanley; President of the Board of Control, Lord Fitzgerald; Secretary at War, Right Hon. Sir Henry Hardinge; President of the Board of Trade, Earl of Ripon; Chancellor of the Exchequer, Right Hon. Sir Henry Goulburn; Paymaster-General, Right Hon. Sir Edward Knatchbull, Bart.

The Queen's Speech.

My Lords and Gentlemen,

We are commanded by Her Majesty to acquaint you that Her Majesty receives from all Princes and States assurances of a friendly disposition towards this country, and of an earnest desire to co-operate with Her Majesty in the maintenance of general peace.

By the treaty which Her Majesty has concluded with the United States of America, and by the adjustment of those differences which, from their long continuance, had endangered the preservation of peace, Her Majesty trusts that the amicable relations of the two countries have been confirmed.

The increased exertions which, by the liberality of Parliament, Her Majesty was enabled to make for the termination of hostilities with China, have been eminently successful.

The skill, valour, and discipline of the naval and military forces employed upon this service have been most conspicuous, and have led to the conclusion of peace upon the terms proposed by Her Majesty.

Her Majesty rejoices in the prospect that, by the free access which will be opened to the principal marts of that prosperous and extensive Empire, encouragement will be given to the commercial enterprise of her people.

As soon as the ratification of the treaty shall have been exchanged, it will be laid before you.

In concert with her Allies, Her Majesty has succeeded in obtaining for the Christian population of Syria the establishment of a system of administration which they were entitled to expect from the engagements of the Sultan, and from the good faith of this country.

The differences for some time existing between the Turkish and Persian Governments had recently led to acts of hostility; but as each of these States had accepted the joint mediation of England and Russia, Her Majesty entertains a confident hope that their mutual relations will be speedily amicably adjusted.

Her Majesty has concluded with the Emperor of Russia a treaty of commerce and navigation, which will be laid before you. Her Majesty regards this treaty with great satisfaction, as the foundation for increased intercourse between Her Majesty's subjects and those of the Emperor.

Her Majesty is happy to inform you that complete success has attended the recent military operations in Afghanistan.

Her Majesty has the greatest satisfaction in recording her high sense of the ability with which these operations have been directed, and of the constancy and valour which have been manifested by the European and Native forces.

The superiority of Her Majesty's arms has been established by decisive victories on the scenes of former disaster, and the complete liberation of Her Majesty's subjects who were held in captivity, and for whom Her Majesty felt the deepest interest, has been effected.

We are commanded by Her Majesty to inform you that it has not been deemed advisable to continue the occupation by a military force of the countries to the westward of the Indus.

Gentlemen of the House of Commons,

Her Majesty has directed the Estimates for the ensuing year to be laid before you.

Such reductions have been made in the account of the naval and military force as have been deemed compatible, under present circumstances, with the efficient performance of the public service throughout the extended Empire of Her Majesty.

My Lords and Gentlemen,

Her Majesty regrets the diminished receipt from some of the ordinary sources of revenue.

Her Majesty fears that it must be in part attributed to the reduced consumption of many articles caused by that depression of the manufacturing industry of the country which has so long prevailed, and which Her Majesty has so deeply lamented.

In considering, however, the present state of the revenue, Her Majesty is assured that you will bear in mind that it has been materially affected by the extensive reductions in the import duties, which received your sanction during the last session of Parliament, and that little progress has been hitherto made in the collection of those taxes which were imposed for the purpose of supplying the deficiency from that and other causes.

Her Majesty feels confident that the future produce of the revenue will be sufficient to meet every exigency of the public service.

Her Majesty commands us to acquaint you that Her Majesty derived the utmost gratification from the loyalty and affectionate attachment to Her Majesty which were manifested on the occasion of her visit to Scotland.

Her Majesty regrets that in the course of last year the public peace in some of the manufacturing districts was seriously disturbed, and the lives and properties of Her Majesty's subjects were endangered by tumultous assemblages and acts of open violence.

The ordinary law, promptly enforced, was sufficient for the effectual repression of these disorders. Her Majesty relies upon its efficacy, and upon the zealous support of her loyal and peaceable subjects, for the maintenance of tranquillity.

We are commanded by Her Majesty to acquaint you that measures connected with the improvement of the law, and with various questions of domestic policy, will be submitted for your consideration.

Her Majesty confidently relies on your zealous endeavours to promote the public welfare, and fervently prays that the favour of Divine Providence may direct and prosper your counsels, and make them conducive to the happiness and contentment of her people.

Mover of Address in the Lords, Earl of Powis.
Seconder „ „ Earl of Eglintoun.
Mover of Address in the Commons, Viscount Courtenay.
Seconder „ „ Mr. W. P. S. Miles.

PROROGATION OF PARLIAMENT BY HER MAJESTY IN PERSON.

Date.—August 24th, 1843.

The Queen's Speech.

My Lords and Gentlemen,

The state of public business enables me to close this protracted session, and to release you from further attendance on your Parliamentary duties.

I thank you for the measures you have adopted for enabling me to give full effect to the treaties I have concluded with foreign Powers.

I have given my cordial assent to the Bill which you presented to me for increasing the means of spiritual instruction in populous parishes, by making a portion of the revenues of the Church available for the endowment of additional ministers.

I confidently trust that the wise and benevolent intentions of the Legislature will be aided by the zeal and liberality of my subjects, and that better provision will thus be made for public worship and for pastoral superintendence in many districts of the country.

I view with satisfaction the passing of the Act for removing doubts respecting the Jurisdiction of the Church of Scotland in the Admission of Ministers, and for securing to the people, and to the Courts of the Church, the full exercise of their respective rights.

It is my earnest hope that this measure will tend to restore religious peace in Scotland, and to avert the dangers which have threatened a sacred institution of the utmost importance to the happiness and welfare of that part of my dominions.

I continue to receive from all foreign Powers assurances of their friendly disposition, and of their earnest desire for the maintenance of peace.

Gentlemen of the House of Commons,

I thank you for the readiness and liberality with which you have voted the supplies for the current year. It will be my constant object to combine a strict regard to economy with the consideration which is due to the exigencies of the public service.

My Lords and Gentlemen,

In some districts of Wales the public peace has been interrupted by lawless combination and disturbances unconnected with political causes. I have adopted the measures which I deemed best calculated for the repression of outrage, and for the detection and punishment of the offenders.

I have at the same time directed an inquiry to be made into the circumstances which have led to insubordination and violence in a part of the country usually distinguished for good order and willing obedience to the law.

I have observed with the deepest concern the persevering efforts which are made to stir up discontent and disaffection among my subjects in Ireland, and to excite them to demand a repeal of the Legislative Union.

It has been, and ever will be, my earnest desire to administer the government of that country in a spirit of strict justice and impartiality, and to co-operate with Parliament in effecting such amendments in the existing laws as may tend to improve the social condition, and to develop the natural resources of Ireland.

From a deep conviction that the Legislative Union is not less essential to the attainment of these objects than to the strength and stability of the Empire, it is my firm determination, with your support, and under the blessing of Divine Providence, to maintain inviolate that great bond of connection between the two countries.

I have forborne from requiring any additional powers for the counteraction of designs hostile to the concord and welfare of my dominions, as well from my unwillingness to distrust the efficacy of the ordinary law, as from my reliance on the good sense and patriotism of my people, and on the solemn declarations of Parliament in support of the Legislative Union.

I feel assured that those of my faithful subjects who have influence and authority in Ireland will discourage, to the utmost of their power, a system of pernicious agitation, which disturbs the industry and retards the improvement of that country, and excites feelings of mutual distrust and animosity between different classes of my people.

PARLIAMENT II.—SESSION IV.

OPENING OF PARLIAMENT BY HER MAJESTY IN PERSON.

Date.—February 1st, 1844.

The Cabinet.—First Lord of the Treasury, Right Hon. Sir Robert Peel, Bart; Lord Chancellor, Lord Lyndhurst; President of the Council, Lord Wharncliffe; First Lord of the Admiralty, Earl of Haddington ; Commander-in-Chief, Duke of Wellington; Lord of the Privy Seal, Duke of Buccleuch and Queensberry; Home Secretary, Right Hon. Sir James Graham, Bart.; Foreign Secretary, Earl of Aberdeen ; Colonial Secretary, Lord Stanley ; President of the Board of Control, Earl of Ripon; Sectretary at War, Right Hon. Sir Henry Hardinge ; President of the Board of Trade and Master of the Mint, Right Hon. W. E. Gladstone ; Chancellor of the Exchequer, Right Hon. Henry Goulburn ; Paymaster-General, Right Hon. Sir Edward Knatchbull, Bart.

The Queen's Speech.

My Lords and Gentlemen,

It affords me great satisfaction again to meet you in Parliament, and to have the opportunity of profiting by your assistance and advice.

I entertain a confident hope that the general peace, so necessary for the happiness and prosperity of all nations, will continue uninterrupted.

My friendly relations with the King of the French, and the good understanding happily established between my Government and that of His Majesty, with the continued assurances of the peaceful and amicable dispositions of all Princes and States, confirm me in this expectation.

I have directed that the treaty which I have concluded with the Emperor of China shall be laid before you, and I rejoice to think that it will in its results prove highly advantageous to the trade of this country.

Throughout the whole course of my negotiations with the Government of China I have uniformly disclaimed the wish for any exclusive advantages.

It has been my desire that equal favour should be shown to the industry and commercial enterprise of all nations.

The hostilities which took place during the past year in Scinde have led to the annexation of a considerable portion of that country to the British possessions in the East.

In all the military operations, and especially in the battles of Meeanee and Hyderabad, the constancy and valour of the troops, native and European, and the skill and gallantry of their distinguished commander have been most conspicuous.

I have directed that additional information, explanatory of the transactions in Scinde, shall be forthwith communicated to you.

Gentlemen of the House of Commons,

The estimates for the ensuing year will be immediately laid before you.

They have been prepared with strict regard to economy, and at the same time with a due consideration of those exigencies of the public service which are connected with the maintenance of our maritime strength, and the multiplied demands on the naval and military establishments from the various parts of a widely-extended Empire.

My Lords and Gentlemen,

I congratulate you on the improved condition of several important branches of the trade and manufactures of the country.

I trust that the increased demand for labour has relieved, in a corresponding degree, many classes of my faithful subjects from sufferings and privations which at former periods I have had occasion to deplore.

For several successive years the annual produce of the revenue fell short of the Public Expenditure.

I confidently trust that in the present year the public income will be amply sufficient to defray the charges upon it.

I feel assured that in considering all matters connected with the financial concerns of the country, you will bear in mind the evil consequences of accumulating debt during the time of peace, and that you will firmly resolve to uphold that public credit, the maintenance of which concerns equally the permanent interests and the honour and reputation of a great country.

In the course of the present year the opportunity will occur of giving notice to the Bank of England on the subject of the Revision of the Charter.

It may be advisable that during this session of Parliament, and previously to the arrival of the period assigned for the giving of such notice, the state of the law with regard to the privileges of the Bank of England, and to other banking establishments, should be brought under your consideration.

At the close of the last session of Parliament I declared to you my firm determination to maintain inviolate the Legislative Union between Great Britain and Ireland.

I expressed at the same time my earnest desire to co-operate with Parliament in the adoption of all such measures as might tend to improve the social condition of Ireland, and to develop the natural resources of that part of the United Kingdom.

I am resolved to act in strict conformity with this declaration.

I forbear from observation on events in Ireland in respect to which proceedings are pending before the proper legal tribunal.

My attention has been directed to the state of the law and practice with regard to the occupation of land in Ireland.

I have deemed it advisable to institute extensive local inquiries into a subject of so much importance, and have appointed a Commission, with ample authority to conduct the requisite investigation.

I recommend to your early consideration the enactments at present in force in Ireland concerning the Registration of Voters for Members of Parliament.

You will probably find that a revision of the Law of Registration, taken in conjunction with other causes at present in operation, would produce a material diminution of the number of county voters, and that it may be advisable on that account to consider the state of the law with a view to an extension of the County Franchise in Ireland.

I commit to your deliberate consideration the various

important questions of public policy which will necessarily come under your review, with full confidence in
your loyalty and wisdom, and with an earnest prayer to
Almighty God to direct and favour your efforts to promote the welfare of all classes of my people.

Mover of Address in the Lords, Earl of Eldon.
Seconder   „   „   Lord Hill.
Mover of Address in the Commons, Lord Clive.
Seconder   „   „   Mr. Cardwell.

PROROGATION OF PARLIAMENT BY COMMISSION.

Date.—September 5th, 1844.

The Lords Commissioners were :—The Lord Chancellor; the Lord President of the Council; the Lord
of the Privy Seal; the Duke of Wellington; Earl
Delawarr; Earl Dalhousie.

The Queen's Speech.

My Lords and Gentlemen,

        We are commanded by Her Majesty, in relieving
you from further attendance in Parliament, to express
to you the warm acknowledgments of Her Majesty for
the zeal and assiduity with which you have applied
yourselves to the discharge of your public duties during
a laborious and protracted session.

The result has been the completion of many legislative measures, calculated to improve the administration
of the law, and to promote the public welfare.

Her Majesty has given her cordial assent to the Bill
which you presented to Her Majesty, for regulating the
Issue of Bank Notes, and for conferring certain privileges upon the Bank of England for a limited period.

Her Majesty trusts that these measures will tend to place the pecuniary transactions of the country upon a sounder basis without imposing any inconvenient restrictions on commercial credit or enterprise.

We are directed to inform you that Her Majesty continues to receive from her Allies, and from all foreign Powers, assurances of their friendly disposition.

Her Majesty has recently been engaged in discussions with the Government of the King of the French, on events calculated to interrupt the good understanding and friendly relations between this country and France; you will rejoice to learn that, by the spirit of justice and moderation which has animated the two Governments, this danger has been happily averted.

Gentlemen of the House of Commons,

We are commanded by Her Majesty to thank you for the readiness with which you voted the supplies for the service of the year.

Her Majesty has observed with the utmost satisfaction that by the course to which you have steadily adhered in maintaining inviolate the public faith, and inspiring a just confidence in the stability of the national resources, you have been enabled to make a considerable reduction in the annual charge on account of the Interest of the Public Debt.

My Lords and Gentlemen,

Her Majesty desires us to congratulate you on the improvement which has taken place in the condition of our manufactures and commerce, and on the prospect that through the bounty of Divine Providence we shall enjoy the blessing of an abundant harvest.

Her Majesty rejoices in the belief that on your return to your several districts you will find generally prevailing throughout the country a spirit of loyalty and cheerful obedience to the law.

Her Majesty is confident that these dispositions, so important to the peaceful development of our resources and to our national strength, will be confirmed and encouraged by your presence and example.

We are commanded by Her Majesty to assure you that, when you shall be called upon to resume the discharge of your Parliamentary functions, you may place entire reliance on the cordial co-operation of Her Majesty in your endeavours to improve the social condition, and to promote the happiness and contentment of her people.

PARLIAMENT II.—SESSION V.

OPENING OF PARLIAMENT BY HER MAJESTY IN PERSON.

Date.—February 4th, 1845.

The Cabinet.—First Lord of the Treasury, Right Hon. Sir Robert Peel, Bart.; Lord Chancellor, Lord Lyndhurst; President of the Council, Lord Wharncliffe; First Lord of the Admiralty, Earl of Haddington; Commander-in-Chief, Duke of Wellington; Lord of the Privy Seal, Duke of Buccleugh and Queensberry; Home Secretary, Right Hon. Sir James Robert George Graham, Bart.; Foreign Secretary, Earl of Aberdeen; Colonial Secretary, Lord Stanley; President of the Board of Control, Earl of Ripon; Secretary at War, Right Hon. Sidney Herbert; Chancellor of the Duchy

4

of Lancaster, Lord Granville Charles Henry Somerset ;
First Commissioner of Land Revenue, Earl of Lincoln :
Chancellor of the Exchequer, Right Hon. Henry
Goulburn ; Paymaster-General, Right Hon. Sir Edward
Knatchbull, Bart.

The Queen's Speech.

My Lords and Gentlemen,

I rejoice that I am enabled, on again meeting
you in Parliament, to congratulate you on the improved
condition of the country.

Increased (activity pervades almost every branch of
manufacture. Trade and commerce have been extended
at home and abroad ; and among all classes of my
people there is generally prevalent a spirit of loyalty
and cheerful obedience to the law.

I continue to receive from all foreign Powers and
States assurances of their friendly disposition.

I have had much satisfaction in receiving at my
Court the Sovereigns who in the course of last year
visited the country.

The journey of the Emperor of Russia, undertaken
at a great sacrifice of private convenience, was a proof
of the friendship of His Imperial Majesty, and most
acceptable to my feelings.

The opportunity of personal intercourse thus afforded
to me may, I hope, be the means of still further improving those amicable relations which have long existed
between Great Britain and Russia.

The visit of the King of the French was rendered
especially welcome to me, inasmuch as it had been
preceded by discussions which might have impaired the

good understanding happily established between the two countries.

I regard the maintenance of this good understanding as essential to the best interests of both, and I rejoice to witness that the sentiments so cordially expressed by all classes of my subjects on the occasion of His Majesty's visit were entirely in unison with my own.

Gentlemen of the House of Commons,

The estimates for the ensuing year have been prepared, and will forthwith be laid before you.

The progress of steam navigation, and the demands for protection to the extended commerce of the country, will occasion an increase in the estimates connected with the naval service.

My Lords and Gentlemen,

I have observed, with sincere satisfaction, that the improvement which is manifest in other parts of the country has extended to Ireland.

The political agitation and excitement which I have had heretofore occasion to lament, appear to have gradually abated, and, as a natural result, private capital has been more freely applied to useful public enterprises, undertaken through the friendly co-operation of individuals interested in the welfare of Ireland.

I have carried into effect, in the spirit in which it was conceived, the Act for the more effectual application of charitable donations and bequests.

I recommend to your favourable consideration the policy of improving and extending the opportunities for Academical Education in Ireland.

The Report of the Commission appointed to inquire

into the law and practice in respect to the occupation of land is nearly prepared, and shall be communicated to you immediately after its presentation.

The state of the law in regard to the privileges of the Bank of Ireland and to other banking establishments in that country, and in Scotland, will, no doubt, occupy your attention.

The health of the inhabitants of large towns and populous districts in this part of the United Kingdom has been the subject of recent inquiry before a Commission, the report of which shall be immediately laid before you.

It will be highly gratifying to me if the information and suggestions contained in that report shall enable you to devise the means of promoting the health and comfort of the poorer classes of my subjects.

I congratulate you on the success of the measures which, three years since, were adopted by Parliament for the purpose of supplying the deficiency in the public revenue, and arresting the accumulation of debt in the time of peace.

The Act which was passed at that time for imposing a tax upon income will shortly expire.

It will be for you, in your wisdom, to determine whether it may not be expedient to continue its operation for a further period, and thus to obtain the means of adequately providing for the public service, and at the same time of making a reduction in other taxation.

Whatever may be the result of your deliberations in this respect, I feel assured that it will be your determination to maintain an amount of revenue amply sufficient to meet the necessary expenditure of the country, and firmly to uphold that public credit which is indispensable to the national welfare.

The prospect of continued peace, and the general state of domestic prosperity and tranquillity, afford a favourable opportunity for the consideration of the important matters to which I have directed your attention ; and I commit them to your deliberation, with the earnest prayer that you may be enabled, under the superintending care and protection of Divine Providence, to strengthen the feeling of mutual confidence and good-will between different classes of my subjects, and to improve the condition of my people.

Mover of Address in the Lords, Marquess of Camden.
Seconder   „   „   Lord Glenlyon.
Mover of Address in the Commons, Mr. Charteris.
Seconder   „   „   Mr. T. Baring.

Prorogation of Parliament by Her Majesty in Person.

Date.—August 9th, 1845.

The Queen's Speech.

My Lords and Gentlemen,

I rejoice that the state of public business enables me to release you from further attendance in Parliament.

In closing this laborious session, I must express to you my warm acknowledgments for the zeal and assiduity with which you have applied yourselves to the consideration of many subjects deeply affecting the public welfare.

I have given my cordial assent to the Bills which

you presented to me for remitting the duties on many articles of import, and for removing restrictions on the free application of capital and skill to certain branches of our manufactures.

The reduction of taxation will necessarily cause an immediate loss of revenue, but I trust that its effect in stimulating commercial enterprise and enlarging the means of consumption, will ultimately provide an ample compensation for any temporary sacrifice.

I have witnessed with peculiar satisfaction the unremitting attention which you have bestowed on the measures recommended by me to your consideration at the commencement of the session, for improving and extending the means of academical education in Ireland.

You may rely upon my determination to carry those measures into execution in the manner best calculated to inspire confidence in the institutions which have received your sanction, and to give effect to your earnest desire to promote the welfare of that part of my dominions.

From all foreign Powers I continue to receive assurances of their friendly disposition towards this country.

The convention which I have recently concluded with the King of the French, for the more effectual suppression of the Slave Trade, will, I trust, by establishing a cordial and active co-operation between the two Powers, afford a better prospect than has hitherto existed of complete success in the attainment of an object for which this country has made so many sacrifices.

Gentlemen of the House of Commons,

I thank you for the liberality with which you have voted the supplies for the services of the current year.

My Lords and Gentlemen,

On your return to your several counties, duties will devolve upon you scarcely less important than those from the performance of which I now relieve you.

I feel assured that you will promote and confirm, by your influence and example, that spirit of loyalty and contentment which you will find generally prevalent throughout the country.

In the discharge of all the functions intrusted to you for the public welfare, you may confidently rely on my cordial support ; and I implore the blessing of Divine Providence on our united efforts to encourage the industry and increase the comforts of my people, and to inculcate those religious and moral principles which are the surest foundation for our security and happiness.

PARLIAMENT II.—SESSION VI.

OPENING OF PARLIAMENT BY HER MAJESTY IN PERSON.

Date.—January 22nd, 1846.

The Cabinet.—First Lord of the Treasury, Right Hon. Sir Robert Peel, Bart. ; Lord Chancellor, Lord Lyndhurst; President of the Council, Duke of Buccleuch and Queensberry; Lord Privy Seal, Earl of Haddington; First Lord of the Admiralty, Earl of Ellenborough ; Commander-in-Chief, Duke of Wellington ; Home Secretary, Right Hon. Sir James Robert George Graham, Bart. ; Foreign Secretary, Earl of Aberdeen ; Colonial Secretary, Right Hon. W. E. Gladstone ; President of the Board of Control, Earl of Ripon ; Secretary at War, Right Hon. Sidney Herbert ; Chan-

cellor of the Duchy of Lancaster, Lord G. C. H.
Somerset; First Commissioner of Land Revenue, Earl
of Lincoln; Chancellor of the Exchequer, Right Hon.
Henry Goulburn.

The Queen's Speech

My Lords and Gentlemen,

It gives me great satisfaction again to meet you
in Parliament, and to have the opportunity of recurring to your assistance and advice.

I continue to receive from my allies, and from other
foreign Powers, the strongest assurances of their desire
to cultivate the most friendly relations with the country.

I rejoice that in concert with the Emperor of Russia,
and through the success of our joint mediation, I have
been enabled to adjust the differences which had long
prevailed between the Ottoman Porte and the King of
Persia, and had seriously endangered the tranquillity of
the East.

For several years a desolating and sanguinary warfare
has afflicted the States of the Rio de la Plata. The
commerce of all nations has been interrupted, and acts
of barbarity have been committed unknown to the practice of a civilised people. With the King of the French
I am endeavouring to effect the pacification of those
States.

The convention concluded with France in the course
of last year, for the more effectual suppression of the
Slave Trade, is about to be carried into immediate execution by the active co-operation of the two Powers on
the coast of Africa.

It is my desire that our present union, and the good

understanding which so happily exists between us, may always be employed to promote the interests of humanity, and to secure the peace of the world.

I regret that the conflicting claims of Great Britain and the United States in respect of the territory on the north-western coast of America, although they have been made the subject of repeated negotiations, still remain unsettled. You may be assured that no effort, consistent with national honour, shall be wanting on my part to bring this question to an early and peaceful termination.

Gentlemen of the House of Commons,

The estimates for the year will be laid before you at an early period.

Although I am deeply sensible of the importance of enforcing economy in all branches of the expenditure, yet I have been compelled, by a due regard to the exigencies of the public service, and to the state of our naval and military establishments, to propose some increase in the estimates which provide for their efficiency.

My Lords and Gentlemen,

I have observed with deep regret the very frequent instances in which the crime of deliberate assassination has been of late committed in Ireland.

It will be your duty to consider whether any measures can be devised calculated to give increased protection to life, and to bring to justice the perpetrators of so dreadful a crime.

I have to lament that, in consequence of the failure of the potato crop in several parts of the United Kingdom, there will be a deficient supply of an article of food which forms the chief subsistence of great numbers of my people.

The disease by which the plant has been affected has prevailed to the greatest extent in Ireland.

I have adopted all such precautions as it was in my power to adopt, for the purpose of alleviating the sufferings which may be caused by this calamity; and I shall confidently rely on your co-operation in devising such other means for effecting the same benevolent purpose as may require the sanction of the Legislature.

I have had great satisfaction in giving my assent to the measures which you have presented to me from time to time, calculated to extend commerce, and to stimulate domestic skill and industry by the repeal of prohibitory and the relaxation of protective duties.

The prosperous state of the revenue, the increased demand for labour, and the general improvement which has taken place in the internal condition of the country, are strong testimonials in favour of the course you have pursued.

I recommend you to take into your early consideration, whether the principles on which you have acted may not with advantage be yet more extensively applied; and whether it may not be in your power, after a careful review of the existing duties upon many articles, the produce or manufactures of other countries, to make such further reductions and remissions as may tend to ensure the continuance of the great benefits to which I have adverted, and, by enlarging our commercial intercourse, to strengthen the bonds of amity with foreign Powers.

Any measures which you adopt for effecting these great objects will, I am convinced, be accompanied by such precautions as shall prevent permanent loss to the revenue, or injurious results to any of the great interests of the country.

I have full reliance on your just and dispassionate consideration of matters so deeply affecting the public welfare.

It is my earnest prayer that, with the blessing of Divine Providence on your counsels, you may be enabled to promote friendly feelings between different classes of my subjects, to provide additional security for the continuance of peace, and to maintain contentment and happiness at home, by increasing the comforts and bettering the condition of the great body of my people.

Mover of Address in the Lords, Earl of Home.
*Seconder   „   „   Lord De Ros.
Mover of Address in the Commons, Lord F. Egerton.
*Seconder   „   „   Mr. E. Beckett
                                                    Denison.

PROROGATION OF PARLIAMENT BY COMMISSION.

Date.—August 28th, 1846.

The Lords Commissioners were :—The Lord Chancellor; the Lord President of the Council ; the Lord of the Privy Seal; the Lord Chamberlain of the Household ; and the Chancellor of the Duchy of Lancaster.

The Queen's Speech.

My Lords and Gentlemen,

Her Majesty has to lament that the recurrence of a failure in the potato crop, in an aggravated degree, will cause a serious deficiency in the quantity of a material article of food.

Her Majesty has given her cordial assent to measures by which this calamity may be mitigated in that part of the United Kingdom where the cultivation of the potato has hitherto afforded the chief supply for the sustenance of the people.

Her Majesty has seen with pleasure that a considerable diminution of crime and outrage has taken place in the counties of Ireland which had been most disturbed.

Her Majesty is confident that on your return to your several counties you will find a spirit of loyalty generally prevalent. The extension of works of improvement has increased the demand for labour, and the tranquillity of the country has favoured the pursuit of industry in all its branches.

Her Majesty trusts that by a combination of prudence with enterprise, and of a willing obedience to law with a desire for social progress, her people will, through the Divine blessing, enjoy the full advantages of peace.

PARLIAMENT II.—SESSION VII.

OPENING OF PARLIAMENT BY HER MAJESTY IN PERSON.

Date.—January 19th, 1847.

The Cabinet.—First Lord of the Treasury, Right. Hon. Lord John Russell; Lord Chancellor, Right Hon. Lord Cottenham; President of the Council, Most Hon. Marquess of Lansdowne; Lord of the Privy Seal, Right Hon Earl of Minto; Home Secretary, Right Hon. Sir George Grey; Foreign Secretary, Right Hon.

Viscount Palmerston; Colonial Secretary, Right Hon.
Earl Grey; Chancellor of the Exchequer, Right
Hon. Sir Charles Wood; First Lord of the Admiralty,
Right. Hon Earl of Auckland; President of the Board
of Control, Right Hon. Sir John Cam Hobhouse ; President of the Board of Trade, Earl of Clarendon ; Paymaster of the Forces, Right Hon. Thomas Babington
Macaulay ; Chief Secretary for Ireland; Right Hon.
Henry Labouchere; Postmaster-General, Most Hon.
the Marquess of Clanricarde ; Chancellor of the Duchy
of Lancaster, Right Hon. Lord Campbell; Chief Commissioner of Woods and Forests, Right Hon. Viscount
Morpeth.

The Queen's Speech.

My Lords and Gentlemen,

It is with the deepest concern that upon your again
assembling I have to call your attention to the dearth
of provisions which prevails in Ireland and in parts of
Scotland.

In Ireland especially, the loss of the usual food of
the people has been the cause of severe sufferings, of
disease, and of greatly increased mortality among the
poorer classes. Outrages have become more frequent,
chiefly directed against property ; and the transit of
provisions has been rendered unsafe in some parts of
the country.

With a view to mitigate these evils, very large
numbers of men have been employed, and received
wages, in pursuance of an Act passed in the last session of Parliament. Some deviations from that Act,
which have been authorised by the Lord Lieutenant in

order to promote more useful employment, will, I trust,
receive your sanction. Means have been taken to lessen
the pressure of want in districts which are most remote
from the ordinary sources of supply. Outrages have
been repressed, as far as it was possible, by the military
and police.

It is satisfactory to me to observe, that in many of
the most distressed districts the patience and resignation
of the people have been most exemplary.

The deficiency of the harvest in France and Germany,
and other parts of Europe, has added to the difficulty of
obtaining adequate supplies of provisions.

It will be your duty to consider what further measures
are required to alleviate the existing distress. I recommend to you to take into your serious consideration
whether, by increasing for a limited period the facilities
for importing corn from foreign countries, and by the
admission of sugar more freely into breweries and
distilleries, the supply of food may be beneficially
augmented.

I have likewise to direct your earnest consideration
to the permanent condition of Ireland. You will perceive, in the absence of political excitement, an opportunity for taking a dispassionate survey of the social
evils which afflict that part of the United Kingdom.
Various measures will be laid before you, which, if
adopted by Parliament, may tend to raise the great mass
of the people in comfort, to promote agriculture, and to
lessen the pressure of that competition for land which
has been the fruitful source of crime and misery.

The marriage of the Infanta Luisa Fernandez of
Spain to the Duke of Montpensier has given rise to a

correspondence between my Government and those of France and Spain.

The extinction of the free state of Cracow has appeared to me to be so manifest a violation of the Treaty of Vienna, that I have commanded that a protest against that act should be delivered to the Courts of Vienna, St. Petersburg, and Berlin, which were parties to it. Copies of these several papers will be laid before you.

I entertain confident hopes that the hostilities in the River Plate, which have so long interrupted commerce, may soon be terminated; and my efforts, in conjunction with those of the King of the French, will be earnestly directed to that end.

My relations generally with foreign Powers inspire me with the fullest confidence in the maintenance of peace.

Gentlemen of the House of Commons,

I have directed the estimates to be prepared with a view to provide for the efficiency of the public service with a due regard for economy.

My Lord and Gentlemen,

I have ordered every requisite preparation to be made for putting into operation the Act of last session of Parliament, for the Establishment of Local Courts for the Recovery of Small Debts. It is my hope that the enforcement of civil rights in all parts of the country to which the Act relates, may by this measure be materially facilitated.

I recommend to your attention measures which will be laid before you for improving the health of towns, an object the importance of which you will not fail to appreciate.

Deeply sensible of the blessings which, after a season of calamity, have been so often vouchsafed to this nation by a superintending Providence, I confide these important matters to your care, in a full conviction that your discussions will be guided by an impartial spirit, and in the hope that the present sufferings of my people may be lightened, and that their future condition may be improved, by your deliberative wisdom.

Mover of Address in the Lords, Lord Hatherton.
Seconder ,, ,, Lord Carew.
Mover of Address in the Commons, Mr. C. Howard.
Seconder ,, ,, Mr. Ricardo.

PROROGATION OF PARLIAMENT BY HER MAJESTY IN PERSON.

Date.—July 23rd, 1847.

The Queen's Speech.

My Lords and Gentlemen,

I have much satisfaction in being able to release you from the duties of a laborious and anxious session. I cannot take leave of you without expressing my grateful sense of the assiduity and zeal with which you have applied yourselves to the consideration of the public interests.

Your attention has been principally directed to the measures of immediate relief which a great and unprecedented calamity rendered necessary.

I have given my cheerful assent to those laws which, by allowing the free admission of grain, and by affording facilities for the use of sugar in breweries and distilleries, tend to increase the quantity of human food, and to promote commercial intercourse.

I rejoice to find that you have in no instance proposed new restrictions, or interfered with the liberty of foreign· or internal trade, as a mode of relieving distress. I feel assured that such measures are generally ineffectual, and in some cases aggravate the evils for the alleviation of which they are adopted.

I cordially approve of the acts of large and liberal bounty by which you have assuaged the sufferings of my Irish subjects.

I have also readily given my sanction to a law to make better provision for the permanent relief of the destitute in Ireland. I have likewise given my assent to various Bills calculated to promote the agriculture and develop the industry of that portion of the United Kingdom. My attention shall be directed to such further measures as may be conducive to those salutary purposes

My relations with foreign Powers continue to inspire me with confidence in the maintenance of peace.

It has afforded me great satisfaction to find that the measures which, in concert with the King of the French, the Queen of Spain, and the Queen of Portugal, I have taken for the pacification of Portugal, have been attended with success, and that the civil war which, for many months, had afflicted that country, has at last been brought to a bloodless termination.

I indulge the hope that future differences between political parties in that country may be settled without an appeal to arms.

Gentlemen of the House of Commons,

I thank you for your willingness in granting me the necessary supplies; they shall be applied with due care and economy to the public service.

I am happy to inform you, that, notwithstanding the high price of food, the revenue has, up to the present time, been more productive than I had reason to anticipate. The increased use of articles of general consumption has chiefly contributed to this result. The revenue derived from sugar, especially, has been greatly augmented by the removal of the duties on foreign sugar.

The various grants which you have made for education in the United Kingdom, will, I trust, be conducive to the religious and moral improvement of my people.

My Lords and Gentlemen,

I think proper to inform you, that it is my intention immediately to dissolve the present Parliament.

I rely with confidence on the loyalty to the Throne and attachment to the free institutions of this country which animate the great body of my people. I join with them in supplication to Almighty God, that the dearth by which we have been afflicted may, by the Divine blessing, be converted into cheapness and plenty.

PARLIAMENT III.—SESSION I.

OPENING OF PARLIAMENT BY COMMISSION.

Date.—November 23rd, 1847.

The Lords Commissioners were:—The Lord President; the Marquess of Clanricarde; Earl Spencer; the Earl of Auckland.

The Cabinet.—First Lord of the Treasury, Right Hon. Lord John Russell; Lord Chancellor, Right Hon. Lord Cottenham; President of the Council, Most Hon. the Marquess of Lansdowne; Lord of the Privy Seal, Right Hon. the Earl of Minto; Home Secretary, Right Hon. Sir George Grey; Foreign Secretary, Right Hon. Viscount Palmerston; Colonial Secretary, Right Hon. Earl Grey; Chancellor of the Exchequer, Right Hon. Sir Charles Wood; First Lord of the Admiralty, Right Hon. Earl of Auckland; President of the Board of Control, Right Hon. Sir John Cam Hobhouse, Bart.; President of the Board of Trade, Right Hon. Henry Labouchere; Paymaster of the Forces, Right Hon. Thomas Babington Macaulay; Postmaster-General, Most Hon. Marquess of Clanricarde; Chancellor of the Duchy of Lancaster, Right Hon. Lord Campbell; Chief Commissioner of Woods and Forests, Right Hon. Viscount Morpeth.

The Queen's Speech.

My Lords and Gentlemen,

Her Majesty has ordered us to declare to you the causes which have induced her to call Parliament together at the present time.

Her Majesty has seen with great concern the distress which has for some time prevailed among the commercial classes. The embarrassments of trade were at one period aggravated by so general a feeling of distrust and of alarm, that Her Majesty, for the purpose of restoring confidence, authorised her Ministers to recommend to the Directors of the Bank of England a course of pro-

5 *

ceeding suited to such an emergency. This course
might have led to an infringement of the law.

Her Majesty has great satisfaction in being enabled
to inform you that the law has not been infringed, that
the alarm has subsided, and that the pressure on the
banking and commercial interests has been mitigated.

The abundant harvest with which this country has
been blessed has alleviated the evils which always accompany a want of employment in the manufacturing
districts.   Her Majesty has, however, to lament the
recurrence of severe distress in some parts of Ireland,
owing to the scarcity of the usual food of the people.
Her Majesty trusts that this distress will be materially
relieved by the exertions which have been made to carry
into effect the law of the last session of Parliament for
the support of the destitute poor.   Her Majesty has
learned with satisfaction that landed proprietors have
taken advantage of the means placed at their disposal
for the improvement of the land.

Her Majesty laments that in some counties of Ireland
atrocious crimes have been committed, and a spirit of
insubordination has manifested itself, leading to an
organised resistance to legal rights.

The Lord Lieutenant has employed with vigour and
energy the means which the law places at his disposal to
detect offenders, and to prevent the repetition of offences.
Her Majesty feels it, however, to be her duty to her
peaceable and well-disposed subjects to ask the assistance of Parliament in taking further precautions against
the perpetration of crime in certain counties and districts
in Ireland.

Her Majesty views with the deepest anxiety and interest the present condition of Ireland, and she recommends to the consideration of Parliament measures which, with due regard to the rights of property, may advance the social condition of the people, and tend to the permanent improvement of that part of the United Kingdom.

Her Majesty has seen with great concern the breaking out of civil war in Switzerland.

Her Majesty is in communication with her allies on the subject, and has expressed her readiness to use, in concert with them, her friendly influence for the purpose of restoring to the Swiss Confederation the blessings of peace.

Her Majesty looks with confidence to the maintenance of the general peace of Europe.

Her Majesty has concluded with the Republic of the Equator a treaty for the suppression of the Slave Trade.

Her Majesty has given directions that this treaty should be laid before you.

Gentlemen of the House of Commons,

Her Majesty has given directions that the esti· mates for the next year should be prepared, for the purpose of being laid before you. They will be framed with a careful regard to the exigencies of the public service.

My Lords and Gentlemen,

Her Majesty recommends to the consideration of Parliament the laws which regulate the navigation of the United Kingdom, with a view to ascertain whether any changes can be adopted which, without danger to our maritime strength, may promote the commercial and colonial interests of the Empire.

Her Majesty has thought fit to appoint a Commission to report on the best means of improving the health of the metropolis; and Her Majesty recommends to your earnest attention such measures as will be laid before you relating to the public health.

Her Majesty has deeply sympathised with the sufferings which afflict the labouring classes in the manufacturing districts in Great Britain and in many parts of Ireland, and has observed with admiration the patience with which these sufferings have been generally borne.

The distress which has lately prevailed among the commercial classes has affected many important branches of the revenue ; but Her Majesty trusts that the time is not distant when, under the blessing of Divine Providence, the commerce and industry of the United Kingdom will have resumed their wonted activity.

Mover of Address in the Lords, Earl of Yarborough.
Seconder   ,,   ,,   Lord Elphinstone.
Mover of Address in the Commons, Mr. Heywood.
Seconder   ,,   ,,   Mr. Shafto Adair.

PROROGATION OF PARLIAMENT BY HER MAJESTY IN PERSON.

Date.—September 5th, 1848.

The Queen's Speech.

My Lords and Gentlemen,

I am happy to be able to release you from the duties of a laborious and protracted session.

The Act for the Prevention of Crime and Outrage in Ireland, which received my assent at the commencement of the session, was attended by the most beneficial effects. The open display of arms intended for criminal purposes, was checked; the course of justice was no longer interrupted; and several atrocious murderers, who had spreadterror through the country, were apprehended, tried, and convicted.

The distress in Ireland consequent upon successive failures in the production of food, has been mitigated by the application of the law for the relief of the poor, and by the amount of charitable contributions raised in other parts of the United Kingdom.

· On the other hand, organised confederacies took advantage of the existing pressure to excite my suffering subjects to rebellion. Hopes of plunder and confiscation were held out to tempt the distressed, while the most visionary prospects were exhibited to the ambitious. In this conjuncture I applied to your loyalty and wisdom for increased powers; and strengthened by your prompt concurrence, my Government was enabled to defeat, in a few days, machinations which had been prepared during many months. The energy and decision shown by the Lord Lieutenant of Ireland in this emergency deserve my warmest approbation.

In the midst of these difficulties you have continued your labours for the improvement of the laws; the Act for Facilitating the Sale of Encumbered Estates will, I trust, gradually remove an evil of great magnitude in the social state of Ireland.

The system of perpetual entails of land established in Scotland, produced very serious evils, both to heirs of entail and to the community, and I have had great satisfaction in seeing it amended upon principles which have long been found to operate beneficially in this part of the United Kingdom.

I have given my cordial assent to the measures which have in view the improvement of the public health, and I entertain an earnest hope that a foundation has been laid for continual advances in this beneficial work.

Gentlemen of the House of Commons,

I have to thank you for the readiness with which you have granted the supplies necessary for the public service.

I shall avail myself of every opportunity which the exigencies of State may allow for enforcing economy.

My Lords and Gentlemen,

I have renewed in a formal manner my diplomatic relations with the Government of France. The good understanding between the two countries has continued without the slightest interruption.

Events of deep importance have disturbed the internal tranquillity of many of the states of Europe, both in the north and in the south. These events have led to hostilities between neighbouring countries.

I am employing my good offices, in concert with other friendly Powers, to bring to an amicable settlement these differences, and I trust that our efforts may be successful.

I am rejoiced to think that an increasing sense of the value of peace encourages the hope that the nations of Europe may continue in the enjoyment of its blessings. Amidst these convulsions I have had the satisfaction of being able to preserve peace for my own dominions, and to maintain domestic tranquillity. The strength of our institutions has been tried, and has not been found wanting. I have studied to preserve the people committed to my charge in the enjoyment of that temperate freedom which they so justly value. My people, on their side, feel too sensibly the advantages of order and security to allow the promoters of pillage and confusion any chance of success in their wicked designs.

I acknowledge with grateful feelings the many marks of loyalty and attachment which I have received from all classes of my people. It is my earnest hope that by cultivating respect to the law and obedience to the precepts of religion, the liberties of this nation may, by the blessing of Almighty God, be perpetuated.

PARLIAMENT III.—SESSION II.

OPENING OF PARLIAMENT BY HER MAJESTY IN PERSON.

Date.—February 1st, 1849.

The Cabinet.—First Lord of the Treasury, Right Hon. Lord John Russell; Lord Chancellor, Right Hon. Lord Cottenham; Chancellor of the Exchequer, Right Hon. Sir Charles Wood, Bart.; President of the Council, Most Hon. Marquess of Lansdowne; Lord of the Privy Seal, Right. Hon. Earl of Minto; Home Secretary, Right Hon. Sir George Grey, Bart.; Foreign Secretary, Right Hon. Viscount Palmerston; Colonial Secretary, Right. Hon. Earl Grey; First Lord of the Admiralty, Right Hon. Sir Francis Thornhill Baring, Bart.; Chancellor of the Duchy of Lancaster, Right Hon. Lord Campbell; President of the Board of Control, Right Hon. Sir John Cam Hobhouse, Bart.; Chief Commissioner of Woods and Forests, Right Hon.

Earl of Carlisle ; Postmaster-General, Most Hon. Marquess of Clanricarde ; President of the Board of Trade, Right Hon. Henry Labouchere.   .

The Queen's Speech.

My Lords and Gentlemen,

The period being arrived at which the business of Parliament is usually resumed, I have called you together for the discharge of your important duties.

It is satisfactory to me to be enabled to state that both in the north and in the south of Europe the contending parties have consented to a suspension of arms for the purpose of negotiating terms of peace.

The hostilities carried on in the Island of Sicily were attended with circumstances so revolting, that the British and French admirals were impelled by motives of humanity to interpose, and to stop further effusion of blood.

I have availed myself of the interval thus obtained to propose, in conjunction with France, to the King of Naples, an arrangement calculated to produce a permanent settlement of affairs in Sicily. The negotiation on these matters is still pending.

It has been my anxious endeavour, in offering my good offices to the various contending Powers, to prevent the extension of the calamity of war, and to lay the foundations for lasting and honourable peace. It is my constant desire to maintain with all foreign States the most friendly relations.

As soon as the interest of the public service will permit, I shall direct the papers connected with these transactions to be laid before you.

A rebellion of a formidable character has broken out in the Punjaub, and the Governor-General of India has been compelled, for the preservation of the peace of the country, to assemble a considerable force, which is now engaged in military operations against the insurgents, but the tranquillity of British India has not been affected by these unprovoked disasters.

I again commend to your attention the restrictions imposed on commerce by the Navigation Laws

If you shall find that these laws are in whole or in part unnecessary for the maintenance of our maritime power, while they fetter trade and industry, you will no doubt deem it right to repeal or modify their provisions.

Gentlemen of the House of Commons,

I have directed the estimates for the service of the year to be laid before you. They will be framed with a most anxious attention to a wise economy.

The present aspect of affairs has enabled me to make large reductions on the estimates of last year.

My Lords and Gentlemen,

I observe with satisfaction that this portion of the United Kingdom has remained tranquil amidst the convulsions which have disturbed so many parts of Europe.

The insurrection in Ireland has not been renewed, but a spirit of disaffection still exists; and I am compelled, to my great regret, to ask for a continuance, for a limited time, of those powers which in the last session you deemed necessary for the public tranquillity.

I have great satisfaction in stating that commerce is reviving from those shocks which at the commencement of last session 1 had to deplore.

The condition of the manufacturing districts is likewise more encouraging than it has been for a considerable period.

It is also gratifying to me to observe that the state of the revenue is one of progressive improvement.

I have to lament, however, that another failure in the potato crop has caused very severe distress in some parts of Ireland.

The operation of the laws for the relief of the poor in Ireland will properly be a subject of your inquiry, and any measures by which those laws may be beneficially amended, and the condition of the people may be improved, will receive my cordial assent.

It is with pride and thankfulness that I advert to the loyal spirit of my people, and that attachment to our institutions which has animated them during a period of commercial difficulty, deficient production of food, and political revolution.

I look to the protection of Almighty God for favour in our continued progress, and I trust that you will assist me in upholding the fabric of the Constitution, founded as it is upon the principles of freedom and justice.

Mover of Address in the Lords, Earl Bruce.
Seconder ,, ,, Lord Bateman.
Mover of Address in the Commons, Lord Harry Vane.
Seconder ,, ,, Mr. E. H. Bunbury.

PROROGATION OF PARLIAMENT BY COMMISSION.

Date.—August 1st, 1849.

The Lord Commissioners were :—The Lord President of the Council; the Lord of the Privy Seal; the Post-master-General; the Earl of St. Germains; and the Chancellor of the Duchy of Lancaster.

The Queen's Speech.

My Lords and Gentlemen,

We have it in command from Her Majesty to inform you that the state of public business enables her to dispense with your attendance in Parliament, and to close the present session.

Her Majesty has directed us to express her satisfaction with the zeal and assiduity with which you have discharged the laborious and anxious duties, in the performance of which you have been occupied.

Her Majesty has given her assent to the important measure you have passed to amend the Navigation Laws, in full confidence that the enterprise, skill, and hardihood of her people will assure to them a full share of the commerce of the world, and maintain upon the seas the ancient renown of this nation.

Her Majesty has commanded us to acquaint you that the friendly character of her relations with foreign Powers affords her a just confidence in the continuance of peace.

The preliminaries of peace between Prussia and Denmark have been signed, under the mediation of Her Majesty, and Her Majesty trusts that this convention may prove the forerunner of a definite and permanent treaty.

Her Majesty's efforts will continue to be directed to promote the restoration of peace in those parts of Europe in which it has been interrupted.

Gentlemen of the House of Commons,

We are commanded by Her Majesty to return you her thanks for the provision which you have made for the public service.

The public expenditure has undergone considerable reductions within the present year, and Her Majesty will continue to apply a watchful economy in every branch of the public service.

My Lords and Gentlemen,

We are commanded by Her Majesty to congratulate you on the happy termination of the War in the Punjaub. The exertions made by the Government of India, and the valour displayed by the army in the field, demand Her Majesty's warmest acknowledgments.

Her Majesty has observed with gratification the spirit of obedience to the laws which has been manifested by her subjects during the period which has elapsed since Her Majesty last addressed her Parliament.

It is the characteristic of our Constitution that it renders the maintenance of order compatible with the fullest enjoyment of political and civil liberty.

The satisfaction with which Her Majesty has viewed the peaceful progress of her people in arts and industry, has been greatly alloyed by the continuance of severe distress in one part of the United Kingdom.

Her Majesty has observed with pleasure your liberal exertions to mitigate the pressure of this calamity, and Her Majesty commands us to thank you for your

unremitting attention to measures calculated to improve
the general condition of Ireland. It is Her Majesty's
fervent hope that it may please the Almighty Disposer
of Events to favour the operation of those laws which
have been sanctioned by Parliament, and to grant to
her Irish people, as the reward of that patience and
resignation with which they have borne their protracted
sufferings, the blessings of an abundant harvest, and of
internal peace.

PARLIAMENT III.—SESSION III.

OPENING OF PARLIAMENT BY COMMISSION.

Date.—January 31st, 1850.

The Lords Commissioners were :—The Lord Chancellor ; the Lord President of the Council ; the Lord
of the Privy Seal ; the Lord Chamberlain of the Household ; and the Lord Bishop of London.

The Cabinet.—First Lord of the Treasury, Right
Hon. Lord John Russell ; Lord Chancellor, Right Hon.
Lord Cottenham ; Chancellor of the Exchequer, Right
Hon. Sir Charles Wood, Bart. ; President of the
Council, Most Hon. Marquess of Lansdowne ; Lord of
the Privy Seal, Right Hon. Earl of Minto ; Home
Secretary, Right Hon. Sir George Grey, Bart. ; Foreign
Secretary, Right Hon. Viscount Palmerston ; Colonial
Secretary, Right Hon. Earl Grey ; First Lord of the
Admiralty, Right Hon. Sir Francis Thornhill Baring,
Bart. ; Chancellor of the Duchy of Lancaster, Right
Hon. Lord Campbell ; President of the Board of
Control, Right Hon. Sir John Cam Hobhouse, Bart. ;

Chief Commissioner of Woods and Forests, Right
Hon. Earl of Carlisle; Postmaster-General, Most Hon.
Marquess of Clanricarde; President of the Board of
Trade, Right Hon. Henry Labouchere.

The Queen's Speech.

My Lords and Gentlemen,

We are commanded by Her Majesty to assure
you that Her Majesty has great satisfaction in again
having recourse to the advice and assistance of her
Parliament.

The decease of Her Majesty Queen Adelaide has
caused Her Majesty deep affliction. The extensive
charity and exemplary virtues of Her late Majesty will
always render her memory dear to the nation.

Her Majesty happily continues in peace and amity
with foreign Powers.

In the course of the autumn, differences of a serious
character arose between the Governments of Austria
and Russia on the one hand, and the Sublime Porte on
the other, in regard to the treatment of a considerable
number of persons who, after the termination of the
civil war in Hungary, had taken refuge in Turkish
territory.

Explanations which took place between the Turkish
and Imperial Governments have, fortunately, removed
any danger to the peace of Europe which might have
arisen out of the differences.

Her Majesty, having been appealed to on this occasion by the Sultan, united her efforts with those of the
Government of France, to which a similar appeal had
been made, in order to assist, by the employment of her

good offices, in effecting an amicable settlement of those differences in a manner consistent with the dignity and independence of the Porte.

Her Majesty has been engaged in communications with foreign States upon the measures which might be rendered necessary by the relaxation of the restrictions formerly imposed by the navigation laws of this country.

The Governments of the United States of America and of Sweden have promptly taken steps to secure to British ships in the ports of their respective countries advantages similar to those which their own ships now enjoy in British ports.

With regard to those foreign States whose navigation laws have hitherto been of a restrictive character, Her Majesty has received from nearly all of them assurances which induce her to hope that our example will speedily lead to a great and general diminution of those obstacles which previously existed to a free intercourse by sea between the nations of the world.

In the summer and autumn of the past year, the United Kingdom was again visited by the ravages of the cholera; but Almighty God, in His mercy, was pleased to arrest the progress of mortality, and to stay this fearful pestilence. Her Majesty is persuaded that we shall best evince our gratitude by vigilant precautions against the more obvious causes of sickness, and an enlightened consideration for those who are most exposed to its attacks.

Her Majesty, in her late visit to Ireland, derived the highest gratification from the loyalty and attachment

6

.

manifested by all classes of her subjects. Although the effects of former years of scarcity are painfully felt in that part of the United Kingdom, they are mitigated by the present abundance of food and the tranquillity which prevails.

Her Majesty has great satisfaction in congratulating you on the improved condition of commerce and manu-factures. It is with regret that Her Majesty has observed the complaints which in many parts of the kingdom have proceeded from the owners and occupiers of land. Her Majesty greatly laments that any portion of her subjects should be suffering from distress; but it is a source of sincere gratification to Her Majesty to witness the increased enjoyment of the necessaries and comforts of life which cheapness and plenty have bestowed upon the great body of her people.

Gentlemen of the House of Commons,

     Her Majesty has directed the estimates for the year to be laid before you. They have been framed with a strict regard to economy, while the efficiency of the various branches of the public service has not been neglected.

     Her Majesty has seen with satisfaction the present state of the revenue.

My Lords and Gentlemen,

     Some of the measures which were postponed at the end of the last session for want of time for their consideration, will be again laid before you. Among the most important of these is one for the better government of the Australian Colonies.

Her Majesty has directed various measures to be prepared for the improvement of the condition of Ireland. The mischiefs arising from party processions, the defects of the laws regulating the relations of landlord and tenant, the imperfect state of the Grand Jury Acts, and the diminished number of electors for members to serve in Parliament, will, together with other matters of serious consequence, form the subjects of measures to be submitted to your consideration.

Her Majesty has learned with satisfaction that the measures which have been already passed for the promotion of the public health are in a course of gradual adoption ; and Her Majesty trusts that, both in the metropolis and in various parts of the United Kingdom, you will be enabled to make further progress in the removal of evils which affect the health and well-being of her subjects.

The favour of Divine Providence has hitherto preserved this kingdom from the wars and convulsions which during the last two years have shaken so many of the states of the continent of Europe.

It is Her Majesty's hope and belief that by continuing liberty with order, by preserving what is valuable, and amending what is defective, you will sustain the fabric of our institutions as the abode and the shelter of a free and happy people.

Mover of Address in the Lords, Earl of Essex.
Seconder ,, ,, Lord Methuen.
Mover of Address in the Commons, Mr. C. P. Villiers.
Seconder ,, ,, Sir James Duke.

6 *

PROROGATION OF PARLIAMENT BY HER MAJESTY IN
PERSON.

Date.—August 15th, 1850.

The Queen's Speech.

My Lords and Gentlemen,

I have the satisfaction of being able to release
you from the duties of a laborious session.

The assiduity and care with which you have applied
yourselves to the business which required your attention
merit my cordial approbation.

The Act for the better government of my Australian Colonies will, I trust, improve the condition of
those rising communities. It will always be gratifying
to me to be able to extend the advantages of representative institutions, which form the glory and happiness
of my people, to colonies inhabited by men who are
capable of exercising with benefit to themselves the
privileges of freedom.

It has afforded me great satisfaction to give my
assent to the Act which you have passed for the
improvement of the merchant naval service of this
country; it is, I trust, calculated to promote the
welfare of every class connected with this essential
branch of the national interest.

The Act for the gradual discontinuance of interments
within the limits of the metropolis is in conformity with
those enlightened views which have for their object the
improvement of the public health. I shall watch with
interest the progress of measures relating to this
important subject.

I have given my cordial assent to the Act for the

extension of the elective franchise in Ireland. I look to the most beneficial consequences from a measure which has been framed with a view to give my people in Ireland a fair participation in the benefits of our representative system.

I have observed with the greatest interest and satisfaction the measures which have been adopted with a view to the improvement of the administration of justice in various departments, and I confidently anticipate they will be productive of much public convenience and advantage.

Gentlemen of the House of Commons,

The improvement of the revenue, and the large reductions which have been made in various branches of expenditure, have tended to give to our financial condition stability and security.

I am happy to find that you have been enabled to relieve my subjects from some of the burthens of taxation, without impairing the sufficiency of our resources to meet the charges imposed upon them.

My Lords and Gentlemen,

I am encouraged to hope that the treaty between Germany and Denmark, which has been concluded at Berlin under my mediation, may lead at no distant period to the restoration of peace in the north of Europe. No endeavour shall be wanting on my part to secure the attainment of this great blessing.

I continue to maintain the most friendly relations with foreign Powers, and I trust that nothing may occur to disturb the general peace.

I have every reason to be thankful for the loyalty

and attachment of my people; and, while I am studious to preserve and to improve our institutions, I rely upon the goodness of Almighty God to favour my efforts, and to guide the destinies of this nation.

PARLIAMENT III.—SESSION IV.

OPENING OF PARLIAMENT BY HER MAJESTY IN PERSON

Date.—February 4th, 1851.

The Cabinet.—First Lord of the Treasury, Right Hon. Lord John Russell; Lord Chancellor, Right Hon. Lord Truro; Chancellor of the Exchequer, Right Hon. Sir Charles Wood, Bart.; President of the Council, Most Hon. Marquess of Lansdowne; Lord of the Privy Seal, Right Hon. Earl of Minto; Home Secretary, Right Hon. Sir George Grey, Bart.; Foreign Secretary, Right Hon. Viscount Palmerston; Colonial Secretary, Right Hon. Earl Grey; First Lord of the Admiralty, Right Hon. Sir F. T. Baring, Bart.; Chancellor of the Duchy of Lancaster, Right Hon. Earl of Carlisle; President of the Board of Control, Right Hon. Sir John Cam Hobhouse, Bart.; Postmaster-General, Most Hon. Marquess of Clanricarde; President of the Board of Trade, Right Hon. Henry Labouchere; Secretary at War, Right Hon. Fox Maule.

The Queen's Speech.

My Lords and Gentlemen,

It is with great satisfaction that I again meet my Parliament, and resort to your advice and assistance in the consideration of measures which affect the welfare of our country.

I continue to maintain the relations of peace and amity with foreign Powers. It has been my endeavour to induce the States of Germany to carry into full effect the provisions of the treaty with Denmark, which was concluded at Berlin in the month of July last year. I am much gratified in being able to inform you that the German Confederation and the Government of Denmark are now engaged in fulfilling the stipulations of that treaty, and thereby putting an end to hostilities which at one time appeared full of danger to the peace of Europe.

I trust that the affairs of Germany may be arranged by mutual agreement in such a manner as to preserve the strength of the Confederation and to maintain the freedom of its separate States.

I have concluded with the King of Sardinia articles additional to the Treaty of September 1841, and I have directed that those articles shall be laid before you.

The Government of Brazil has taken new, and, I hope, efficient, measures for the suppression of the atrocious traffic in slaves.

Gentlemen of the House of Commons,

I have directed the estimates of the year to be prepared and laid before you without delay. They have been framed with a due regard to economy and to the necessities of the public service.

My Lords and Gentlemen,

Notwithstanding the large reductions of taxation which have been effected in late years, the receipts of the revenue have been satisfactory.

The state of the commerce and manufactures of the

United Kingdom has been such as to afford general employment to the labouring classes.

I have to lament, however, the difficulties which are still felt by that important body among my people who are owners and occupiers of land.

But it is my confident hope that the prosperous condition of other classes of my subjects will have a fovourable effect in diminishing those difficulties, and promoting the interests of agriculture.

The recent assumption of certain ecclesiastical titles conferred by a foreign Power, has excited strong feelings in this country, and large bodies of my subjects have presented addresses to me, expressing attachment to the Throne, and praying that such assumptions should be resisted. I have assured them of my resolution to maintain the rights of my Crown, and the independence of the nation against all encroachment, from whatever quarter it may proceed. I have, at the same time, expressed my earnest desire and firm determination, under God's blessing, to maintain unimpaired the religious liberty which is so justly prized by the people of this country.

It will be for you to consider the measure which will be laid before you on this subject.

The administration of justice in the several departments of law and equity will, no doubt, receive the serious attention of Parliament; and I feel confident that the measures which may be submitted to you with a view of improving the administration, will be discussed with that mature deliberation which important changes in the highest courts of judicature in the kingdom imperatively demand.

A measure will be laid before you providing for the establishment of a system of registration of deeds and instruments relating to the transfer of property. This measure is the result of inquiries which I have caused to be made into the practicability of adopting a system of registration calculated to give security to titles, to diminish the causes of litigation to which they have hitherto been liable, and to reduce the cost of transfers.

To combine the progress of improvement with the stability of our institutions will, I am confident, be your constant care. We may esteem ourselves fortunate that we can pursue without disturbance the course of calm and peaceable amelioration; and we have every cause to be thankful to Almighty God for the measure of tranquillity and happiness which has been vouchsafed to us.

Mover of Address in the Lords, Earl of Effingham.
Seconder   „   „   Lord Cremorne.
Mover of Address in the Commons, Marquess of Kildare.
Seconder   „   „   Mr. Peto.

PROROGATION OF PARLIAMENT BY HER MAJESTY IN PERSON.

Date.—August 8th, 1851.

The Queen's Speech.

My Lords and Gentlemen,

I am glad to be able to release you from your attendance in Parliament, and I thank you for the diligence with which you have performed your laborious duties.

I continue to maintain the most friendly relations with foreign Powers.

I am happy to be able to congratulate you on the very considerable diminution which has taken place in the African and Brazilian Slave Trade. The exertions of my squadrons on the coasts of Africa and Brazil, assisted by the vigilance of the cruisers of France and of the United States, and aided by the co-operation of the Brazilian Government, have mainly contributed to this result.

Gentlemen of the House of Commons,

I thank you for the readiness with which you have granted the supplies necessary for the service of the year.

My Lords and Gentlemen,

It is satisfactory to observe that, notwithstanding very large reductions of taxes the revenue for the past year considerably exceeded the public expenditure for the same period.

I am rejoiced to find that you have thereby been enabled to relieve my people from an impost which restricted the enjoyment of light and air in their dwellings. I trust that this enactment, with others to which your attention has been and will be directed, will contribute to the health and comfort of my subjects.

I thank you for the assiduity with which you have applied yourselves to the consideration of a measure framed for the purpose of checking the undue assumption of ecclesiastical titles conferred by a foreign Power.

It gives me the highest satisfaction to find that, while repelling unfounded claims, you have maintained inviolate the great principles of religious liberty so happily established among us.

The attention you have bestowed on the administration of justice in the courts of law and equity will, I trust, prove beneficial, and lead to further improvements.

I have willingly given my consent to a Bill relating to the administration of the land revenues of the Crown, which will, I hope, conduce to the better management of that department, and at the same time tend to the promotion of works of public utility.

It has been very gratifying to me, on an occasion which has brought many foreigners to this country, to observe the spirit of kindness and good-will which so generally prevailed.

It is my anxious desire to promote among nations the cultivation of all those arts which are fostered by peace, and which, in their turn, contribute to maintain the peace of the world.

In closing the present session, it is with feelings of gratitude to Almighty God that I acknowledge the general spirit of loyalty and willing obedience to the law which animates my people. Such a spirit is the best security at once for the progress and the stability of our free and happy institutions.

PARLIAMENT III.—SESSION V.

OPENING OF PARLIAMENT BY HER MAJESTY IN PERSON.

Date.—February 3rd, 1852.

The Cabinet.—First Lord of the Treasury, Right Hon. Lord John Russell ; Lord Chancellor, Right Hon. Lord Truro ; Chancellor of the Exchequer, Right Hon. Sir C. Wood, Bart.; President of the Council, Most Hon. Marquess of Lansdowne ; Lord of the Privy Seal,

Right Hon. Earl of Minto; Home Secretary, Right
Hon. Sir George Grey, Bart.; Foreign Secretary, Right
Hon. Earl Granville; Colonial Secretary, Right Hon.
Earl Grey; First Lord of the Admiralty, Right Hon.
Sir Francis Thornhill Baring, Bart.; Chancellor of the
Duchy of Lancaster, Right Hon. Earl of Carlisle;
President of the Board of Control, Right Hon. Fox
Maule; Postmaster-General, Most Hon. Marquess of
Clanricarde; President of the Board of Trade, Right
Hon. Henry Labouchere; First Commissioner of Works
and Public Buildings, Right Hon. Lord Seymour.

The Queen's Speech.

My Lords and Gentlemen,

The period has arrived when, according to usage,
I can again avail myself of your advice and assistance
in the preparation and adoption of measures which the
welfare of the country may require.

I continue to maintain the most friendly relations
with foreign Powers.

The complicated affairs of the Duchies of Holstein
and Sleswig have continued to engage my attention.
I have every reason to expect that the treaty between
Germany and Denmark, which was concluded at Berlin
in the year before last, will in a short time be fully and
completely executed.

I regret that the war which unfortunately broke out
on the eastern frontier of the Cape of Good Hope more
than a year ago still continues. Papers will be laid
before you containing full information as to the progress
of the war, and the measures which have been taken
for bringing it to a termination.

While I have observed with sincere satisfaction the tranquillity which has prevailed throughout the greater portion of Ireland, it is with much regret that I have to inform you, that certain parts of the counties of Armagh, Monaghan, and Louth have been marked by the commission of outrages of the most serious description. The powers of the existing law have been promptly exerted for the detection of the offenders, and for the repression of a system of crime and violence fatal to the best interests of the country. My attention will continue to be directed to this important object.

Gentlemen of the House of Commons,

I have ordered estimates of the expenses of the current year to be laid before you.

I rely with confidence on your loyalty and zeal to make adequate provision for the public service.

Where any increase has been made in the estimates of the present over the past year, such explanations will be given as will, I trust, satisfy you that such increase is consistent with a steady adherence to a pacific policy, and with the dictates of a wise economy.

My Lords and Gentlemen,

The improvement of the administration of justice in its various departments has continued to receive my anxious attention ; and in furtherance of that object I have directed Bills to be prepared, founded upon the reports made to me by the respective Commissions appointed to inquire into the practice and proceedings of the Superior Courts of Law and Equity, as nothing tends more to the peace, prosperity, and contentment of a country than the speedy and impartial administration

of justice. I earnestly recommend these measures to
your deliberate attention.

The Act of 1848 for suspending the operation of a
previous Act conferring Representative Institutions in
New Zealand will expire early in the next year. I am
happy to believe that there is no necessity for its
renewal, and that no obstacle any longer exists to the
enjoyment of Representative Institutions by New Zealand. The form of these institutions will, however,
require your consideration ; and the additional information which has been obtained since the passing of the
Acts in question will, I trust, enable you to arrive at a
decision beneficial to that important colony.

It gives me great satisfaction to be able to state to
you that the large reductions of taxes which have taken
place of late years have not been attended with a pro-
portionate diminution of the national income. The
revenue of the past year has been fully adequate to the
demands of the public service, while the reduction of
taxation has tended greatly to the relief and comfort of
my subjects.

I acknowledge with thankfulness to Almighty God that
tranquillity, good order, and willing obedience to the laws
continue to prevail generally throughout the country.

It appears to me that this is a fitting time for calmly
considering whether it may not be advisable to make
such amendments in the Act of the late reign, relating
to the Representation of the Commons in Parliament, as
may be deemed calculated to carry into more complete
effect the principles upon which that law is founded.

I have the fullest confidence that in any such consideration you will firmly adhere to the acknowledged

principles of the Constitution, by which the prerogatives of the Crown, the authority of both Houses of Parliament, and the rights and liberties of the people are equally secured.

Mover of Address in the Lords, Earl of Albemarle.
Seconder   ,,   ,,   Lord Leigh.
Mover of Address in the Commons, Sir R. W. Bulkeley.
Seconder   ,,   ,,   Mr. Bonham Carter.

DISSOLUTION OF PARLIAMENT BY HER MAJESTY IN PERSON.

Date —July 1st, 1852.
The Queen's Speech.

My Lords and Gentlemen,

I am induced, by considerations of public policy, to release you at an earlier period than usual from your legislative duties.

The zeal and diligence, however, with which you have applied yourselves to your Parliamentary labours have enabled me in this comparatively short session to give my assent to many measures of high importance, and, I trust, of great and permanent advantage.

I receive from all foreign Powers assurances that they are animated by the most friendly dispositions towards this country ; and I entertain a confident hope that the amicable relations happily subsisting between the principal European States may be so firmly established as, under Divine Providence, to secure to the world a long continuance of the blessings of peace. To this great end my attention will be unremittingly directed.

I rejoice that the final settlement of the affairs of
Holstein and Sleswig, by the general concurrence of
the Powers chiefly interested, has removed one cause
of recent difference and of future anxiety.

The amicable termination of the discussions which
have taken place between the Sublime Porte and the
Pacha of Egypt afford a guarantee for the tranquillity
of the East, and an encouragement to the extension of
commercial enterprise.

The refusal on the part of the King of Ava of redress
justly demanded for insults and injuries offered to my
subjects at Rangoon, has necessarily led to an interruption of friendly relations with that Sovereign. The
promptitude and vigour with which the Governor-
General of India has taken the measures thus rendered
unavoidable, have merited my entire approbation ; and I
am confident that you will participate in the satisfaction
with which I have observed the conduct of all the naval
and military forces, European and Indian, by whose
valour and discipline the important captures of Rangoon
and Martaban have been accomplished, and in the hope
which I entertain that these signal successes may lead
to an early and honourable peace.

Treaties have been concluded by my naval commanders with the King of Dahomey and all the African
Chiefs whose rule extends along the Bight of Benin,
for the total abolition of the slave trade, which is at
present wholly suppressed upon that coast.

I have had great satisfaction in giving my assent to
the measure which you have wisely adopted for the
better organisation of the Militia: a Constitutional force
which, being limited to purposes of internal defence,

can afford no just ground of jealousy to neighbouring Powers, but which, in the event of any sudden and unforeseen disturbance of my foreign relations, would at all times contribute essentially to the protection and security of my dominions.

Gentlemen of the House of Commons,

I thank you for the liberal provision which you have made for the exigencies of the public service. The expenditure which you have authorised shall be applied with a due regard to economy and efficiency.

The recent discoveries of extensive gold-fields have produced in the Australian Colonies a temporary disturbance of society requiring prompt attention. I have taken such steps as appeared to me most urgently necessary for the mitigation of this serious evil. I shall continue anxiously to watch the important results which must follow from these discoveries. I have willingly concurred with you in an Act, which, by rendering available to those Colonies the portion arising within them of the hereditary revenue placed at the disposal of Parliament on my accession to the throne, may enable them to meet their necessarily increased expenditure.

My Lords and Gentlemen,

I have gladly assented to the important Bills which you have passed for effecting reforms, long and anxiously desired, in the practice and proceedings of the Superior Courts of Law and Equity, and generally for improving the administration of justice. Every measure which simplifies the forms and diminishes the

delay and expense of legal proceedings, without intro-
ducing uncertainty of decision, impairing the authority
of the courts, or lowering the high standard of the
judicial bench, is a valuable boon conferred on the community at large.

I hope that the measures which you have adopted
for promoting extramural interment of the dead, and
for improving the supply of water, may be found
effectual for the remedy of evils, the existence of which
has long been a reproach to this great metropolis, and
may conduce to the health and comfort of its inhabitants.

The extension of popular rights and legislative
powers to my subjects resident in the Colonies is always
to me an object of deep interest; and I trust that the
representative institutions which, in concert with you, I
have sanctioned for New Zealand, may promote the
welfare and contentment of the population of that
distant but most interesting colony, and confirm their
loyalty and attachment to my Crown.

It is my intention, without delay, to dissolve this
present Parliament; and it is my earnest prayer that, in
the exercise of the high functions which, according to
our free Constitution, will devolve upon the several
constituencies, they may be directed by an All-wise
Providence to the selection of representatives whose
wisdom and patriotism may aid me in my unceasing
endeavours to sustain the honour and dignity of my
Crown, to uphold the Protestant institutions of the
country, and the civil and religious liberty which is their
natural result, to extend and improve the national
education, to develop and encourage Industry, Art, and

Science, and to elevate the moral and social condition, and thereby promote the welfare and happiness of my people.

PARLIAMENT IV.—SESSION I.

OPENING OF PARLIAMENT BY HER MAJESTY IN PERSON.

Date.—November 11th, 1852.

The Cabinet.—First Lord of the Treasury, Right Hon. Earl of Derby; Lord Chancellor, Right Hon. Lord St. Leonards; Chancellor of the Exchequer, Right Hon Benjamin Disraeli; President of the Council, Right Hon. Earl of Lonsdale; Lord of the Privy Seal, Most Hon. Marquess of Salisbury; Home Secretary, Right Hon. Spencer Horatio Walpole; Foreign Secretary, Right Hon. Earl of Malmesbury; Colonial Secretary, Right Hon. Sir John Somerset Pakington, Bart.; First Lord of the Admiralty, Most Noble Duke of Northumberland; President of the Board of Control, Right Hon. John Charles Herries; Postmaster-General, Right Hon. Earl of Hardwicke; President of the Board of Trade, Right Hon. Joseph Warner Henley; First Commissioner of Works and Public Buildings, Right Hon. Lord John James Robert Manners.

The Queen's Speech.

My Lords and Gentlemen,

I cannot meet you for the first time after the Dissolution of Parliament, without expressing my deep sorrow, in which I am sure you will participate, that your deliberations can no longer be aided by the counsels

7 *

of that illustrious man whose great achievements have exalted the name of England, and in whose loyalty and patriotism the interests of my throne and of my people ever found an unfailing support. I rely with confidence on your desire to join with me in taking such steps as may mark your sense of the irreparable loss which the country has sustained by the death of Arthur Duke of Wellington.

I am happy to acknowledge the readiness with which my subjects in general have come forward, in pursuance of the Act of last session, to join the ranks of the Militia; and I confidently trust that the force thus raised by voluntary enlistment will be calculated to give effective aid to my regular army for the protection and security of the country.

I continue to receive from all foreign Powers assurances of their anxious desire to maintain the friendly relations now happily subsisting with my Government.

Frequent and well-founded complaints on the part of my North American Colonies, of infractions, by citizens of the United States, of the Fishery Convention of 1818, induced me to despatch, for the protection of their interests, a class of vessels better adapted to the service than those which had been previously employed. This step has led to discussions with the Government of the United States; and while the rights of my subjects have been firmly maintained, the friendly spirit in which the question has been treated induces me to hope that the ultimate result may be a mutually beneficial extension and improvement of our commercial intercourse with that great Republic.

The special mission which, in concert with the Prince

President of the French Republic, I deemed it right to
send to the Argentine Confederation, has been received
with the utmost cordiality; and the wise and enlightened
policy of the Provisional Director has already opened
to the commerce of the world the great rivers, hitherto
closed, which afford an access to the interior of the vast
continent of South America.

I have the satisfaction of announcing to you that the
sincere and zealous efforts of the Government of Brazil
for the suppression of the slave trade, now nearly
extinguished on that coast, have enabled me to suspend the stringent measures which I had been compelled
reluctantly to adopt; a recurrence to which, I anxiously
hope, may be proved to be unnecessary.

The Government of Her Most Faithful Majesty have
fully recognised the justice of the claim which my
Government have long urged for the abolition of the
discriminating duties on the export of wine, and have
passed a decree for giving complete effect to the stipulations of the treaty on this subject.

You will probably deem it advisable to resume the
inquiries which were commenced by the late Parliament
with a view to legislation on the subject of the future
government of my East Indian Possessions.

Gentlemen of the House of Commons,

The estimates for the ensuing year will in due
time be laid before you.

The advancement of the fine arts and of practical
science will be readily recognised by you as worthy the
attention of a great and enlightened nation. I have
directed that a comprehensive scheme shall be laid

before you, having in view the promotion of these objects, towards which I invite your aid and co-operation.

My Lords and Gentlemen,

It gives me pleasure to be enabled, by the blessing of Providence, to congratulate you on the generally improved condition of the country, and especially of the industrious classes. If you should be of opinion that recent legislation, in contributing, with other causes, to this happy result, has at the same time inflicted unavoidable injury on certain important interests, I recommend you dispassionately to consider how far it may be practicable equitably to mitigate that injury, and to enable the industry of the country to meet successfully that unrestricted competition to which Parliament, in its wisdom, has decided that it should be subjected.

I trust that the general improvement, notwithstanding many obstacles, has extended to Ireland; and while I rely with confidence on your aid, should it be required, to restrain that unhappy spirit of insubordination and turbulence which produces many and aggravates all of the evils which afflict that portion of my dominions, I recommend to you the adoption of such a generous and liberal policy towards Ireland as may encourage and assist her to rally from the depression in which she has been sunk by the sufferings of late years.

Anxious to promote the efficiency of every branch of our National Church, I have thought fit to issue a Commission to inquire and report to me how far, in their opinion, the capitular institutions of the country are capable of being made more effective for the great objects of religious worship, religious education, and ecclesiastical discipline.

I have directed that the reports of the Commissioners for inquiring into the system of education pursued at Oxford and Cambridge should be communicated to the Governing Bodies of those Universities, for their consideration ; and I rely upon your readiness to remove any legal difficulties which may impede the desire of the Universities at large, or of the several colleges, to introduce such amendments into their existing system as they may deem to be more in accordance with the requirements of the present time.

The system of secondary punishments has usefully occupied the labours of successive Parliaments ; and I shall rejoice if you shall find it possible to devise means by which, without giving encouragement to crime, transportation to Van Diemen's Land may at no distant period be altogether discontinued.

The subject of legal reform continues to engage my anxious attention. The Acts passed in the last session of Parliament have been followed up by the orders necessary for putting them in operation. Inquiries are in progress, by my direction, with a view of bringing into harmony the testamentary jurisdiction of my several courts ; and Bills will be submitted to you for effecting further improvements in the administration of the law.

To these and other measures affecting the social condition of the country, I am persuaded that you will give your earnest and zealous attention, and I pray that by the blessing of Almighty God your deliberations may

be guided to the well-being and happiness of my
people.

> *Mover of Address in the Lords,* Earl of Donough-
> more.
> *Seconder* „   „   Marquess of Bath.
> *Mover of Address in the Commons,* Lord Lovaine.
> *Seconder,* „   „   Mr. E. C. Eger-
> ton.

PROROGATION OF PARLIAMENT BY COMMISSION.

Date.—August 20th, 1853.

The Lords Commissioners were :—The Lord Chancellor ; the Lord President of the Council ; the Lord of
the Privy Seal ; the Lord Chamberlain ; and the Secretary of State for the Colonies.

The Queen's Speech.

My Lords and Gentlemen,

We are commanded by Her Majesty to release
you from your attendance in Parliament, and at the
same time to express Her Majesty's cordial approbation
of the zeal and assiduity with which, during a protracted and laborious session, you have applied yourselves to the consideration of many subjects of great
importance to the public welfare.

Her Majesty has seen with much satisfaction that,
by the remission and reduction of taxes which tended
to cramp the operations of trade and industry, you have
given fresh extension to a system of beneficent legislation, and have largely increased the means of obtaining
the necessaries of life.

The provision which you have made for meeting the demands of the public service, not only in the present but also in future years, is of a nature to give permanent stability to our finances, and thereby to aid in consolidating the strength and resources of the Empire.

The buoyant state of the revenue and the steady progress of our foreign trade, are proofs of the wisdom of the commercial policy now firmly established; while the prosperity which pervades the great trading and producing classes, happily without even a partial exception, affords continued and increasing evidence of the enlarged comforts of the people.

The measure which you have passed for the future Government of India, has been readily sanctioned by Her Majesty, in the persuasion that it will prove to have been wisely framed, and that it is well calculated to promote the improvement and welfare of Her Majesty's Eastern dominions.

Her Majesty regards with peculiar satisfaction the provision you have made for the better administration of charitable trusts.　The obstacles which existed to the just and beneficial use of property set apart for purposes of charity and of education, have been a serious public evil, to which Her Majesty is persuaded that in your wisdom you have now applied an efficient remedy.

Gentlemen of the House of Commons,

We are commanded by Her Majesty to thank you for the supplies which you have granted for the service of the present year, and for the provision which you have made for the defence of the country both by sea and land. Her Majesty will apply them with a due regard to economy, and consistently with that spirit which has at all times made our national security the chief object of her care.

My Lords and Gentlemen,

Her Majesty commands us to inform you, that she continues to receive from her allies the assurance of their unabated desire to cultivate the most friendly relations with this country.

It is with deep interest and concern that Her Majesty has viewed the serious misunderstanding which has recently arisen between Russia and the Ottoman Porte.

The Emperor of the French has united with Her Majesty in earnest endeavours to reconcile differences, the continuance of which might involve Europe in war.

Acting in concert with her allies, and relying on the exertions of the Conference now assembled at Vienna, Her Majesty has good reason to hope that an honourable arrangement will speedily be accomplished.

Her Majesty rejoices to be able to announce to you the termination of the war on the frontiers of the settlement of the Cape of Good Hope; and she trusts that the establishment of representative government in that Colony may lead to the development of its resources, and enable it to make efficient provision for its future defence.

We are also commanded to congratulate you that, by the united exertions of the naval and military forces of Her Majesty and of the East India Company, the war in Burmah has been brought to an honourable and successful issue; the objects of the war having been fully obtained, and due submission made by the Burmese Government, peace has been proclaimed.

Her Majesty contemplates, with grateful satisfaction and thankfulness to Almighty God, the tranquillity which prevails throughout Her dominions, together with that peaceful industry and obedience to the laws which ensure the welfare of all classes of her subjects. It is the first desire of Her Majesty to promote the advance of every social improvement, and, with the aid of your wisdom, still further to extend the prosperity and happiness of her people.

PARLIAMENT IV.—SESSION II.

OPENING OF PARLIAMENT BY HER MAJESTY IN PERSON.

Date.—January 31st, 1854.

The Cabinet.—First Lord of the Treasury, Right Hon. Earl of Aberdeen; Lord Chancellor, Right Hon. Lord Cranworth; Chancellor of the Exchequer, Right Hon. William Ewart Gladstone; President of the Council, Right Hon. Earl Granville; Lord of the Privy Seal, His Grace the Duke of Argyll; Home Secretary, Right Hon. Viscount Palmerston; Foreign Secretary, Right Hon. Earl of Clarendon; Colonial Secretary, His Grace the Duke of Newcastle; First Lord of the Admiralty, Right Hon. Sir James Robert George Graham, Bart.; President of the Board of Control, Right Hon. Sir C. Wood, Bart.; Secretary at War, Right Hon. Sidney Herbert; First Commissioner of Public Works and Buildings, Right Hon. Sir William

Molesworth, Bart. ; Most Hon. Marquess of Lansdowne;
Right Hon. Lord John Russell.

The Queen's Speech.

My Lords and Gentlemen,

I am always happy to meet you in Parliament,
and on the present occasion it is with peculiar satisfaction that I recur to your assistance and advice.

The hopes which I expressed at the close of the last
session, that a speedy settlement would be effected of
the differences existing between Russia and the Ottoman
Porte, have not been realised ; and I regret to say that a
state of warfare has ensued. I have continued to act in
cordial co-operation with the Emperor of the French; and
my endeavours, in conjunction with my allies, to preserve and restore peace between the contending parties,
although hitherto unsuccessful, have been unremitting.
I will not fail to persevere in these endeavours ; but as
the continuance of the war may deeply affect the
interests of this country and of Europe, I think it
requisite to make a further augmentation of my naval
and military forces, with the view of supporting my
representations, and of more effectually contributing to
the restoration of peace.

I have directed that the papers explanatory of the
negotiations which have taken place upon this subject
shall be communicated to you without delay.

Gentlemen of the House of Commons,

The estimates for the year will be laid before
you, and I trust you will find that, consistently with the
exigencies of the public service at this juncture, they
have been framed with a due regard to economy.

My Lords and Gentlemen,

In the year which has just terminated, the blessing of an abundant harvest has not been vouchsafed to us. By this dispensation of Providence the price of provisions has been enhanced, and •the privations of the poor have been increased; but their patience has been exemplary, and the care of the Legislature, evinced by the reduction of taxes affecting the necessaries of life, has greatly tended to preserve a spirit of contentment.

I have the satisfaction of announcing to you that the commerce of the country is still prosperous; that trade, both of export and import, has been largely on the increase; and that the revenue of the past year has been more than adequate to the demands of the public service.

I recommend to your consideration a Bill which I have ordered to be framed, for opening the coasting trade of the United Kingdom to the ships of all friendly nations; and I look forward with satisfaction to the removal of the last legislative restriction upon the use of foreign shipping for the benefit of my people.

Communications have been addressed, by my command, to the Universities of Oxford and Cambridge, with reference to the improvement which it may be desirable to effect in their institutions. These communications will be laid before you, and measures will be proposed for your consideration, with the view of giving effect to such improvements.

The establishments requisite for the conduct of the Civil Service, and the arrangements bearing upon its condition, have recently been under review; and I shall direct a plan to be laid before you, which will have for its object to improve the system of admission, and thereby to increase the efficiency of the service.

The recent measures of legal reform have proved highly beneficial, and the success which has attended them may well encourage you to proceed with further amendments. Bills will be submitted to you for transferring from the Ecclesiastical to the Civil Courts the cognisance of testamentary and of matrimonial causes, and for giving increased efficiency to the Superior Courts of Common Law.

The laws relating to the relief of the poor have of late undergone much salutary amendment; but there is one branch to which I earnestly direct your attention. The Law of Settlement impedes the freedom of labour; and if this restraint can with safety be relaxed, the workman may be enabled to increase the fruits of his industry, and the interests of capital and of labour will be more firmly united.

Measures will be submitted to you for the amendment of the laws relating to the Representation of the Commons in Parliament.

Recent experience has shown that it is necessary to take more effectual precautions against the evils of bribery and corrupt practices at elections. It will also be your duty to consider whether more complete effect may not be given to the principles of the Act of the last reign, whereby reforms were made in the representation of the people in Parliament. In recommending this subject to your consideration, my desire is to remove every cause of just complaint, to increase general confidence in the Legislature, and to give additional stability to the settled institutions of the State.

I submit to your wisdom the consideration of these important subjects; and I pray to God to prosper your counsels and to guide your decisions.

Mover of Address in the Lords, Earl of Carnarvon.
*Seconder   ,,   ,,   * Earl of Ducie.
Mover of Address in the Commons, Viscount Castle-
                                                    rosse.
*Seconder   ,,   ,,   * Mr. Thomson
                                      Hankey.

PROROGATION OF PARLIAMENT BY HER MAJESTY IN PERSON.

Date.—August 12th, 1854.

The Queen's Speech.

My Lords and Gentlemen,

I am enabled by the state of public business to release you from a longer attendance in Parliament.

Gentlemen of the House of Commons,

In closing the session, it affords me great pleasure to express my sense of the zeal and energy you have shown, in providing means for the vigorous prosecution of the war, in which, notwithstanding my efforts to avert it, we are now engaged. This liberality in granting the supplies for the public service demands my warmest thanks; and although I lament the increased burthens of my people, I fully recognise your wisdom in sacrificing considerations of present convenience, and in providing for the immediate exigencies of the war without an addition being made to the permanent debt of the country.

My Lords and Gentlemen,

In cordial co-operation with the Emperor of the French, my efforts will be directed to the effectual repression of that ambitious and aggressive spirit on the part of Russia, which has compelled us to take up arms in defence of an ally, and to secure the future tranquillity of Europe.

You will join with me in admiration of the courage and perseverance manifested by the troops of the Sultan in their defence of Silistria, and in the various military operations on the Danube.

The engrossing interest of matters connected with the progress of the war has prevented the due consideration of some of those subjects which, at the opening of the session, I had recommended to your attention; but I am happy to acknowledge the labour and diligence with which you have perfected various important measures well calculated to prove of great public utility.

You have not only passed an Act for opening the coasting trade of the United Kingdom, and for removing the last legislative restriction upon the use of foreign vessels, but you have also revised and consolidated the whole Statute Law relating to Merchant Shipping.

The Act for establishing the direct control of the House of Commons over the charges incurred in the collection of the revenue will give more complete effect to an important principle of the Constitution, and will promote simplicity and regularity in our system of public accounts.

I rejoice to perceive that amendments in the administration of the law have continued to occupy your attention, and I anticipate great benefit from the improvements you have made in the forms of procedure in the Superior Courts of Common Law.

The means you have adopted for the better government of the University of Oxford, and the improvement in its constitution, I trust, will tend greatly to increase the usefulness and to extend the renown of this great seminary of learning.

I have willingly given my assent to the measure you have passed for the Prevention of Bribery and of Corrupt Practices at Elections, and I hope that it may prove effectual in the correction of an evil which, if unchecked, threatens to fix a deep stain upon our representative system.

It is my earnest desire that on returning to your respective counties you may preserve a spirit of union and concord. Deprived of the blessings of peace abroad, it is more than ever necessary that we should endeavour to confirm and increase the advantages of our internal situation; and it is with the greatest satisfaction that I regard the progress of active industry and the general prosperity which happily prevails throughout the country.

Deeply sensible of these advantages, it is my humble prayer that we may continue to enjoy the favour of the Almighty, and that, under His gracious protection, we may be enabled to bring the present contest to a just and honourable termination.

PARLIAMENT IV.—SESSION III.

OPENING OF PARLIAMENT BY HER MAJESTY IN PERSON.

Date.—December 12th, 1854.

The Cabinet.—First Lord of the Treasury, Right
Hon. Viscount Palmerston; Lord Chancellor, Right
Hon. Lord Cranworth; President of the Council,
Right Hon. Earl Granville; Lord of the Privy Seal,
His Grace the Duke of Argyll; Home Secretary, Right
Hon. Sir George Grey, Bart.; Foreign Secretary, Right
Hon. Earl of Clarendon; Colonial Secretary, Right Hon.
Lord John Russell; Secretary at War, Right Hon. Lord
Panmure; Chancellor of the Exchequer, Right Hon.
Sir George Cornewall Lewis, Bart.; First Lord of the
Admiralty, Right Hon. Sir Charles Wood, Bart.; Presi-
dent of the Board of Control, Right Hon. Robert
Vernon Smith; Chancellor of the Duchy of Lancaster,
Right Hon. Earl of Harrowby; Postmaster-General,
Right Hon. Viscount Canning; First Commissioner of
Works and Public Buildings, Right Hon. Sir William
Molesworth, Bart.; Most Hon. Marquess of Lansdowne.

The Queen's Speech.

My Lords and Gentlemen,

I have called you together at this unusual period
of the year, in order that by your assistance I may take
such measures as will enable me to prosecute the war in
which we are engaged with the utmost vigour and
effect.

This assistance I know will be readily given, for I
cannot doubt that you share my conviction of the necessity of sparing no effort to augment my forces now
engaged in the Crimea; the exertions they have made,

and the victories they have obtained, are not exceeded in the brightest pages of our history, and have filled me with admiration and gratitude.

The hearty and efficient co-operation of the brave troops of my Ally, the Emperor of the French, and the glory acquired in common, cannot fail to cement still more closely the union which happily subsists between the two nations.

It is with satisfaction I inform you, that, together with the Emperor of the French, I have concluded a treaty of alliance with the Emperor of Austria, from which I anticipate important advantages to the common cause.

I have also concluded a treaty with the United States of America, by which subjects of long and difficult discussion have been equitably adjusted.

These treaties will be laid before you.

Although the prosecution of the war will naturally engage your chief attention, I trust that other matters of great interest and importance to the general welfare will not be neglected.

I rejoice to observe that the general prosperity of my subjects remains uninterrupted.

The state of the revenue affords me entire satisfaction, and I trust that by your wisdom and prudence you will continue to promote the progress of agriculture, commerce, and manufactures.

Gentlemen of the House of Commons,

In the estimates which will be presented to you, I trust you will find that ample provision has been made for the exigencies of the public service.

8 *

My Lords and Gentlemen,

I rely with confidence on your patriotism and public spirit. I feel assured that in the momentous contest in which we are engaged you will exhibit to the world the example of a united people. Thus shall we obtain the respect of other nations, and may trust that, by the blessing of God, we shall bring the war to a successful termination.

Mover of Address in the Lords, The Duke of Leeds.
Seconder ,, ,, Lord Ashburton.
Mover of Address in the Commons, Mr. H. Herbert.
Seconder ,, ,, Mr. Leveson-
Gower.

PROROGATION OF PARLIAMENT BY COMMISSION.

Date.—August 14th, 1855.

The Lords Commissioners were :—The Lord Chancellor ; the Lord President of the Council ; the Lord Privy Seal ; Lord Stanley of Alderley ; and the Earl of Harrowby.

The Queen's Speech.

My Lords and Gentlemen,

We are commanded by Her Majesty to release you from further attendance in Parliament, and at the same time to express the warm acknowledgments of Her Majesty for the zeal and assiduity with which you have applied yourselves to the discharge of your public duties during a long and laborious session.

Her Majesty has seen with great satisfaction, that, while you have occupied yourselves in providing means for the vigorous prosecution of the war, you have given your attention to many measures of great public utility. Her Majesty is convinced that you will share her satisfaction at finding that the progress of events has tended to cement more firmly that union which has so happily been established between her Government and that of her Ally the Emperor of the French ; and Her Majesty trusts that an alliance founded on a sense of the general interests of Europe, and consolidated by good faith, will long survive the events which have given rise to it, and will contribute to the permanent well-being and prosperity of the two great nations whom it has linked in the bonds of honourable friendship.

The accession of the King of Sardinia to the Treaty between Her Majesty, the Emperor of the French, and the Sultan, has given additional importance and strength to that alliance; and the efficient force which his Sardinian Majesty has sent to the seat of war to co-operate with the allied armies, will not fail to maintain the high reputation by which the army of Sardinia has ever been distinguished.

Her Majesty has commanded us to thank you for having enabled her to avail herself, as far as has been found to be required, of those patriotic offers of extended service which she has received from the militia of the United Kingdom, and for the means of reinforcing her brave army in the Crimea by an enlistment of volunteers from abroad.

Her Majesty acknowledges with satisfaction the measure which you have adopted for giving effect to the convention by which, in conjunction with her Ally the Emperor of the French, she has made arrangements for assisting the Sultan to provide the means which are necessary to enable him to maintain in efficiency the Turkish army, which has so gallantly withstood the assaults of its enemies.

Her Majesty, in giving her assent to the Bill which you presented to her for the Local Management of the Metropolis, trusts that the arrangements provided by that measure will lead to many improvements conducive to the convenience and health of this great city. The abolition of the duty on newspapers will tend to diffuse useful information among the poorer classes of Her Majesty's subjects. The principle of limited liability which you have judiciously applied to joint stock associations will afford additional facilities for the employment of capital, and the improvements which you have made in the laws which regulate Friendly Societies will encourage habits of industry and thrift among the labouring classes of the community.

Her Majesty trusts that the measures to which she has given her assent for improving the constitutions of New South Wales, Victoria, and Tasmania, and for bestowing on the important and flourishing colonies of Australia extended powers of self-government, will assist the development of their great natural resources, and will promote the contentment and happiness of their inhabitants.

Her Majesty commands us to say that she has been deeply gratified by the zeal for the success of Her Majesty's arms, and by the sympathy for her soldiers and sailors manifested throughout her Indian and Colonial empire, and Her Majesty acknowledges with great satisfaction the generous contributions which her subjects in India, and the legislatures and inhabitants of

the colonies, have sent for the relief of the sufferers by
the casualties of war.

Gentlemen of the House of Commons,

Her Majesty commands us to convey to you her
cordial thanks for the readiness and zeal with which you
have provided the necessary supplies for carrying on the
war in which Her Majesty is engaged.

Her Majesty laments the burthens and sacrifices which
it has become necessary to impose upon her faithful
people, but she acknowledges the wisdom with which
you have alleviated the weight of those burthens by the
mixed arrangements which you have made for providing
those supplies.

My Lords and Gentlemen,

Her Majesty has commanded us to say that she
has seen with sincere regret that the endeavours which,
in conjunction with her Ally the Emperor of the French,
she made at the recent conference at Vienna to bring
the war to a conclusion on conditions consistent with
the honour of the Allies, and with the future security of Europe, have proved ineffectual. But, those
endeavours having failed, no other course is left to Her
Majesty but to prosecute the war with all possible
vigour ; and Her Majesty, relying upon the support of
her Parliament, upon the manly spirit and patriotism of
her people, upon the never-failing courage of her army
and her navy, whose patience under suffering, and whose
power of endurance Her Majesty has witnessed with
admiration, upon the steadfast fidelity of her Allies, and,
above all, upon the justice of her cause, humbly puts
her trust in the Almighty Dispenser of Events for such

an issue of the great contest in which she is engaged as may secure to Europe the blessings of a firm and lasting peace.

On your return to your several counties you will have duties to perform little less important than those which belong to your attendance in Parliament. Her Majesty trusts that your powerful influence will be exerted for the welfare and happiness of her people, the promotion of which is the object of Her Majesty's constant care and the anxious desire of her heart.

PARLIAMENT IV.—SESSION IV.

OPENING OF PARLIAMENT BY HER MAJESTY IN PERSON.

Date.—January 31st, 1856.

The Cabinet.—First Lord of the Treasury, Right Hon. Viscount Palmerston ; Lord Chancellor, Right Hon. Lord Cranworth ; President of the Council, Right Hon. Earl Granville ; Lord of the Privy Seal, Right Hon. Earl of Harrowby ; Home Secretary, Right Hon. Sir George Grey, Bart. ; Foreign Secretary, Right Hon. Earl of Clarendon ; Colonial Secretary, Right Hon. Henry Labouchere ; Secretary at War, Right Hon. Lord Panmure ; Chancellor of the Exchequer, Right Hon. Sir G. Cornewall Lewis, Bart ; First Lord of the Admiralty, Right Hon. Sir Charles Wood, Bart. ; President of the Board of Control, Right Hon. Robert Vernon Smith ; President of the Board of Trade, Right Hon. Lord Stanley of Alderley ; Chancellor of the Duchy of Lancaster, Right Hon. Matthew Talbot Baines ; Postmaster-General, His Grace the Duke of Argyll ; Most Hon. Marquis of Lansdowne.

The Queen's Speech.

My Lords and Gentlemen,

Since the close of the last Session of Parliament the armies of the Allies have achieved a signal and important success. Sebastopol, the great stronghold of Russia in the Black Sea, has yielded to the persevering constancy and to the daring bravery of the allied forces.

The naval and military preparations for the ensuing year have necessarily occupied my serious attention; but while determined to omit no effort which could give vigour to the operations of the war, I have deemed it my duty not to decline any overtures which might reasonably afford a prospect of a safe and honourable peace. Accordingly, when the Emperor of Austria lately offered to myself and to my august Ally the Emperor of the French to employ his good offices with the Emperor of Russia with a view to endeavour to bring about an amicable adjustment of the matters at issue between the contending Powers, I consented, in concert with my Allies, to accept the offer thus made; and I have the satisfaction to inform you that certain conditions have been agreed upon, which I hope may prove the foundation of a general Treaty of Peace.

Negotiations for such a treaty will shortly be opened at Paris.

In conducting those negotiations I shall be careful not to lose sight of the object for which the war was undertaken, and I shall deem it right in no degree to relax my naval and military preparations until a satisfactory treaty of peace shall have been concluded.

Although the war in which I am engaged was brought on by events in the south of Europe, my attention has not been withdrawn from the state of things in the north ; and in conjunction with the Emperor of the French, I have concluded with the King of Sweden and Norway a treaty containing defensive engagements applicable to his dominions, and tending to the preservation of the balance of power in that part of Europe.

I have also concluded a treaty of friendship, commerce, and navigation with the Republic of Chili. I have given directions that these treaties shall be laid before you.

Gentlemen of the House of Commons,

The estimates for the ensuing year will be laid before you. You will find them framed in such a manner as to provide for the exigencies of war, if peace should unfortunately not be concluded.

My Lords and Gentlemen,

It is gratifying to me to observe that, notwithstanding the pressure of the war, and the burthens and sacrifices which it has unavoidably imposed upon my people, the resources of my empire remain unimpaired. I rely with confidence on the manly spirit and enlightened patriotism of my loyal subjects for a continuance of that support which they have so nobly afforded me ; and they may be assured that I shall not call upon them for exertions beyond what may be required by a due regard for the great interests, the honour, and the dignity of the Empire.

There are many subjects concerned with internal

improvement, which I recommend to your attentive consideration.

The difference which exists, in several important particulars, between the commercial laws of Scotland and those of the other parts of the United Kingdom, has occasioned inconvenience to a large portion of my subjects engaged in trade. Measures will be proposed to you for remedying this evil.

Measures will also be proposed to you for improving the laws relating to partnership, by simplifying those laws, and thus rendering more easy the employment of capital in commerce.

The system under which merchant shipping is liable to pay local dues and passing tolls has been the subject of much complaint. Measures will be proposed to you for affording relief in regard to these matters.

Other important measures for improving the law in Great Britain and in Ireland will be proposed to you, which will, I doubt not, receive your attentive consideration.

Upon these and all other matters upon which you may deliberate I fervently pray that the blessing of Divine Providence may favour your counsels, and guide them to the promotion of the great object of my unvarying solicitude, the welfare and the happiness of my people. ;

Mover of Address in the Lords, Earl of Gosford.
Seconder   „   „   Earl of Abingdon.
Mover of Address in the Commons, Mr. Byng.
Seconder   „   „   Mr. Baxter.

PROROGATION OF PARLIAMENT BY COMMISSION.

Date.—July 29th, 1856.

The Lords Commissioners were :—The Lord Chan-cellor; the Lord of the Privy Seal; the President of the Board of Trade; the Lord Willoughby D'Eresby; and the Lord Monteagle.

The Queen's Speech.

My Lords and Gentlemen,

We are commanded by Her Majesty to release you from further attendance in Parliament, and at the same time to express to you her warm acknowledgments for the zeal and assiduity with which you have applied yourselves to the discharge of your public duties during the session.

When Her Majesty met you in Parliament at the opening of the session, Her Majesty was engaged, in co-operation with her Allies, the Emperor of the French, the King of Sardinia, and the Sultan, in an arduous war, having for its objects matters of high European importance; and Her Majesty appealed to your loyalty and patriotism for the necessary means to carry on that war with the energy and vigour essential to success. .

You answered nobly the appeal thus made to you; and Her Majesty was enabled to prepare for the opera-tions of the expected campaign naval and military forces worthy of the power and reputation of this country.

Happily it became unnecessary to apply those forces to the purposes for which they had been destined. A treaty was concluded by which the objects for which the war had been undertaken were fully attained, and an honourable peace has saved Europe from the calamities of continued warfare.

Her Majesty trusts that the benefits resulting from that peace will be extensive and permanent ; and that while the friendships and alliances which were cemented by common exertions during the contest will gain strength by mutual interests in peace, those asperities which inherently belong to conflict will give place to the confidence and good-will with which a faithful execution of engagements will inspire those who have learnt to respect each other as antagonists.

Her Majesty commands us to thank you for your support in the hour of trial, and to express to you her fervent hope that the prosperity of her faithful people, which was not materially checked by the pressure of war, may continue and be increased by the genial influences of peace.

Her Majesty is engaged in negotiations on the subject of questions in connection with the affairs of Central America, and Her Majesty hopes that the differences which have arisen on those matters between Her Majesty's Government and that of the United States may be satisfactorily adjusted.

We are commanded by Her Majesty to inform you that Her Majesty desires to avail herself of this occasion to express the pleasure which it afforded her to receive, during the war in which she has been engaged, numerous and honourable proofs of loyalty and public spirit from Her Majesty's Indian territories, and from other colonial possessions, which constitute so valuable and important a part of the dominions of Her Majesty's Crown.

Her Majesty has given her cordial assent to the Act for rendering more effectual the Police in Counties and Boroughs in England and Wales. This Act will mate-rially add to the security of persons and property, and will thus afford increased encouragement to the exertions of honest industry. Her Majesty rejoices to think that the Act for the Improvement of the Internal Arrange-ments of the University of Cambridge, will give fresh powers of usefulness to that ancient and renowned seat of learning.

The Act for Regulating Joint Stock Companies will afford additional facilities for the advantageous employ-ment of capital, and they will tend to promote the development of the resources of the country; while the Acts passed relating to the mercantile laws of England and Scotland will diminish the inconvenience which the differences of those laws occasion to Her Majesty's subjects engaged in trade.

Her Majesty has seen with satisfaction that you have given your attention to the arrangements connected with county courts. It is Her Majesty's anxious wish that justice should be attainable by all classes of her sub-jects with as much speed and with as little expense as may be consistent with the due investigation of the merits and causes to be tried.

Her Majesty trusts that the Act for placing the coast-guard under the direction of the Board of Admiralty will afford the groundwork for arrangements for providing, in time of peace, means applicable to national defence on the occurrence of any future emergency.

Gentlemen of the House of Commons,

We are commanded by Her Majesty to thank you for the readiness with which you have granted the supplies for the present year.

My Lords and Gentlemen,

Her Majesty commands us to congratulate you on the favourable state of the revenue, and upon the thriving condition of all branches of the national industry, and she acknowledges with gratitude the loyalty of her faithful subjects, and that spirit of order and that respect for the law which prevail in every part of her dominions. Her Majesty commands us to express her confidence, that on your return to your homes you will promote, by your influence and example, in your several districts, that continued and progressive improvement which is the vital principle of well-being of nations ; and Her Majesty fervently prays that the blessing of Almighty God may attend your steps, and prosper your doings for the welfare and happiness of her people.

PARLIAMENT IV.—SESSION V.

OPENING OF PARLIAMENT BY COMMISSION.

Date.—February 3rd, 1857.

The Lords Commissioners were :—The Lord Chancellor ; the Lord of the Privy Seal ; the Lord Steward of the Household ; the President of the Board of Trade ; and the Postmaster-General.

The Cabinet.—First Lord of the Treasury, Right Hon. Viscount Palmerston ; Lord Chancellor, Right

Hon. Lord Cranworth; President of the Council, Right Hon. Earl Granville; Lord of the Privy Seal, Right Hon. Earl of Harrowby; Home Secretary, Right Hon. Sir George Grey, Bart.; Foreign Secretary, Right Hon. Earl of Clarendon; Colonial Secretary, Right Hon. Henry Labouchere; Secretary at War, Right Hon. Lord Panmure; Chancellor of the Exchequer, Right Hon. Sir G. C. Lewis, Bart.; First Lord of the Admiralty, Right Hon. Sir Charles Wood, Bart.; President of the Board of Control, Right Hon. Robert Vernon Smith; President of the Board of Trade, Right Hon. Lord Stanley of Alderley, Chancellor of the Duchy of Lancaster, Right Hon. M. Talbot Baines; Postmaster-General, His Grace the Duke of Argyll; Most Hon. the Marquis of Lansdowne.

The Queen's Speech.

My Lords and Gentlemen,

We are commanded to assure you that Her Majesty has great satisfaction in recurring again to the advice and assistance of Her Parliament.

We are commanded by Her Majesty to inform you that difficulties which arose in regard to some of the provisions of the Treaty of Paris delayed the complete execution of the stipulations of that treaty.

Those difficulties have been overcome in a satisfactory manner, and the intentions of the treaty have been fully maintained.

An insurrectionary movement which took place in September last in the Swiss canton of Neufchâtel, for the purpose of re-establishing in that canton the authority of the King of Prussia, as Prince of Neufchâtel, led to serious difference between his Prussian Majesty and the

Swiss Confederation, threatening at one time to disturb the general peace of Europe. But Her Majesty commands us to inform you, that, in concert with her august Ally the Emperor of the French, she is endeavouring to bring about an amicable settlement of the matter in dispute, and Her Majesty entertains a confident expectation that an honourable and satisfactory arrangement will be concluded.

In consequence of certain discussions which took place during the conferences at Paris, and which are recorded in the protocols that were laid before you, Her Majesty and the Emperor of the French caused communications to be made to the Government of the King of the Two Sicilies for the purpose of inducing him to adopt a course of policy calculated to avert dangers which might disturb that peace which has so recently been restored to Europe.

Her Majesty commands us to inform you, that the manner in which those friendly communications were received by His Sicilian Majesty was such as to lead Her Majesty and the Emperor of the French to discontinue their diplomatic relations with His Sicilian Majesty; and they have accordingly withdrawn their missions from the Court of Naples.

Her Majesty has directed that papers relating to this subject shall be laid before you.

Her Majesty commands us to inform you that she has been engaged in negotiations with the Government of the United States, and also with the Government of Honduras, which she trusts will be successful in removing all cause of misunderstanding with respect to Central America.

• Her Majesty has concluded a treaty of friendship and commerce with Siam, which will be laid before you.

Her Majesty commands us to express to you her regret that the conduct of the Persian Government has led to hostilities between Her Majesty and the Shah of Persia.

The Persian Government, in defiance of repeated warnings, and in violation of its engagements, has besieged and captured the important city of Herat.

We are commanded by Her Majesty to inform you, that a British naval and military force, despatched from Bombay, has taken possession of the Island of Karrack and of the town of Bushire, with a view to induce the Shah to accede to the just demands of Her Majesty's Government.

Her Majesty has seen with satisfaction that the naval and military forces employed on this occasion have displayed their accustomed gallantry and spirit.

Her Majesty commands us to inform you that acts of violence, insults to the British flag, and infractions of treaty rights committed by the local Chinese authorities at Canton, and a pernicious refusal of redress, have rendered it necessary for Her Majesty's officers in China to have recourse to measures of force to obtain satisfaction.

Those measures had, up to the date of the last accounts, been taken with great forbearance, but with signal success as regards the conflicts to which they had led.

We are commanded to inform you that Her Majesty trusts that the Government of Pekin will see the propriety of affording the satisfaction demanded, and of faithfully fulfilling its treaty engagements.

Gentlemen of the House of Commons,

Her Majesty has directed the estimates for the ensuing year to be laid before you. They have been prepared with every attention to economy, and with a due regard to the efficient performance of the public service at home and abroad.

My Lords and Gentlemen,

Her Majesty commands us to inform you that Bills will be submitted to your consideration for the consolidation and the amendment of important portions of the law ; and Her Majesty doubts not that you will give your earnest attention to matters so deeply affecting the interests of all classes of her subjects.

Her Majesty commands us to recommend to your consideration the expediency of renewing for a further period the privileges of the Bank of England, the conditions imposed on the issue of bank notes in the United Kingdom, and the state of the law relating to joint stock banks.

Her Majesty commands us to express the gratification which it affords her to witness the general well-being and contentment of her people, and to find that, notwithstanding the sacrifices unavoidably attendant upon such a war as that which has lately terminated, the resources of the country remain unimpaired, and its productive industry continues unchecked in its course of progressive development.

Her Majesty commits with confidence the great interests of the country to your wisdom and care, and she fervently prays that the blessing of Almighty God may attend your deliberations, and prosper your counsels for the advancement of the welfare and happiness of her faithful people.

Mover of Address in the Lords, Earl of Cork.
Seconder ,, ,, Earl of Airlie.
Mover of Address in the Commons, Sir John Ramsden.
Seconder ,, ,, Sir Andrew Agnew.

DISSOLUTION OF PARLIAMENT BY COMMISSION.

Date.—March 21st, 1857.

The Lords Commissioners were :—The Lord Chancellor; the Lord President of the Council; the Lord of the Privy Seal; the Lord Chamberlain of the Household; and Lord Stanley of Alderley (President of the Board of Trade).

The Queen's Speech.

My Lords and Gentlemen,

We are commanded by Her Majesty to inform you, that in releasing you at this early period from your attendance in Parliament, it is Her Majesty's intention immediately to dissolve the present Parliament, in order to ascertain in the most constitutional manner the sense of her people upon the present state of public affairs.

Gentlemen of the House of Commons,

We are commanded by Her Majesty to thank you for the liberal provision which you have made for the exigencies of the public service during the period that will elapse before the new Parliament, which Her Majesty will direct immediately to be called, shall have been able to give its deliberate attention to these matters.

My Lords and Gentlemen,

We are commanded by Her Majesty to express the satisfaction which she feels at your having been able during the present session materially to reduce the burthens of her people.

Her Majesty commands us to assure you, that it is her fervent prayer that the several constituencies of the United Kingdom, upon whom will devolve the exercise of those high functions which by the Constitution belong to them, may be guided by an all-wise Providence to the selection of representatives whose wisdom and patriotism may aid Her Majesty in her constant endeavours to maintain the honour and dignity of her Crown, and to promote the welfare and happiness of her people.

PARLIAMENT V.—SESSION I.

OPENING OF PARLIAMENT BY COMMISSION.

Date.—May 7th, 1857.

The Lords Commissioners were :—The Lord Chancellor ; the Lord President of the Council ; the Lord Steward ; Lord Stanley, of Alderley; and the Duke of Argyll.

The Cabinet.—First Lord of the Treasury, Right Hon. Viscount Palmerston ; Lord Chancellor, Right Hon. Lord Cranworth ; President of the Council, Right Hon. Earl Granville ; Lord of the Privy Seal, Right Hon. Earl of Harrowby ; Home Secretary, Right Hon. Sir George Grey, Bart. ; Foreign Secretary, Right

Hon. Earl of Clarendon ; Colonial Secretary, Right Hon.
Henry Labouchere ; Secretary at War, Right Hon. Lord
Panmure ; Chancellor of the Exchequer, Right Hon.
Sir G. C. Lewis, Bart. ; First Lord of the Admiralty,
Right Hon. Sir Charles Wood, Bart. ; President of the
Board of Control, Right Hon. Robert Vernon Smith ;
President of the Board of Trade, Right Hon. Lord
Stanley of Alderley ; Chancellor of the Duchy of Lan-
caster, Right Hon. Matthew Talbot Baines ; Postmaster-
General, His Grace the Duke of Argyll ; Most Hon.
Marquess of Lansdowne.

The Queen's Speech.

My Lords and Gentlemen,

We are commanded to inform you that Her
Majesty has availed herself of the earliest opportunity
of having recourse to your advice and assistance after
the dissolution of the last Parliament ; and Her Majesty
trusts that there will be found sufficient time during
the present session to enable you satisfactorily to deal
with various important matters, some of which had
occupied the attention of Parliament in the beginning
of this year.

We are commanded by Her Majesty to inform you
that the general aspect of affairs in Europe affords a
well-grounded confidence in the continuance of peace.

All the main stipulations of the Treaty of Paris have
been carried into execution, and it is to be hoped that
what remains to be done in regard to these matters will
be speedily accomplished.

The negotiations upon the subject of the differences
which had arisen between the King of Prussia and the

Swiss Confederation, in regard to the affairs of Neufchâtel, are drawing to a close, and will, Her Majesty trusts, be terminated by an arrangement honourable and satisfactory to all parties.

The negotiations in which Her Majesty has been engaged with the Government of the United States, and with the Government of Honduras, in regard to the affairs of Central America, have not yet been brought to a close.

We are commanded by Her Majesty to inform you that a treaty of peace between Her Majesty and the Shah of Persia was signed at Paris on the 4th of March by Her Majesty's Ambassador at Paris and by the Ambassador of the Shah ; and Her Majesty will give directions that this treaty shall be laid before you as soon as the ratifications thereof shall have been duly exchanged.

Her Majesty commands us to express to you her regret that, at the date of the latest advices from China, the differences which had arisen between the High Commissioner at Canton and Her Majesty's civil and naval officers in China, still remain unadjusted.   But Her Majesty has sent to China a Plenipotentiary fully instructed to deal with all matters of difference, and that Plenipotentiary will be supported by an adequate naval and military force, in the event of such assistance becoming necessary.

We are commanded to inform you that Her Majesty, in conjunction with several other European Powers, has concluded a treaty with the King of Denmark for the redemption of the Sound dues.   This treaty, together with a separate convention between Her Majesty and the King

of Denmark, completing the arrangement, will be laid
before you, and Her Majesty will cause the measures
necessary for fulfilling the engagements thereby contracted to be submitted for your consideration.

Gentlemen of the House of Commons,

Her Majesty has directed the estimates for the
present year to be laid before you.

They have been prepared with a careful attention to
economy, and with a due regard to the efficiency of the
departments of the public service to which they severally
relate.

My Lords and Gentlemen,

Her Majesty commands us to recommend to your
earnest consideration measures which will be proposed
to you for the consolidation and improvement of the
law.

Bills will be submitted to you for improving the laws
relating to the testamentary and matrimonial jurisdiction now exercised by the Ecclesiastical Courts, and
also for checking fraudulent breaches of trust.

Her Majesty commands us to express to you Her
heartfelt gratification at witnessing the continued well-
being and contentment of her people, and the progressive development of productive industry throughout her
dominions.

Her Majesty confidently commits to your wisdom and
care the great interests of her Empire, and fervently
prays that the blessing of Almighty God may be vouchsafed to your deliberations, and may lead you to con-
clusions conducive to the objects of Her Majesty's

constant solicitude, the welfare and happiness of her loyal and faithful people.

Mover of Address in the Lords, Marquess of Towns-
hend.
Seconder „ „ Earl of Portsmouth.
Mover of Address in the Commons, Mr. Dodson.
Seconder „ „ Mr. Buchanan.

PROROGATION OF PARLIAMENT BY COMMISSION.

Date.—August 28th, 1857.

The Lords Commissioners were :—The Archbishop of Canterbury; the Lord Chancellor ; the Lord President of the Council ; the Lord of the Privy Seal; and Lord Panmure.

The Queen's Speech.

My Lords and Gentlemen,

We are commanded by Her Majesty to release you from further attendance in Parliament; and at the same time to express to you Her Majesty's cordial acknowledgments for the zeal and assiduity with which you have performed your important duties during a session which, though shorter than usual, has never-theless been unusually laborious.

Her Majesty commands us to express to you her satisfaction that the present state of affairs in Europe inspires a well-grounded confidence in the continuance of peace.

The arrangements connected with the full execution of the stipulations of the Treaty of Paris have, from various causes, not yet been completed ; but Her Majesty trusts that, by the earnest efforts of the contracting parties to that treaty, all that remains to be done with reference to its stipulations may ere long be satisfactorily settled.

Her Majesty commands us to inform you that the extensive mutinies which have broken out among the native troops of the Army of Bengal, followed by serious disturbances in many parts of that Presidency, have occasioned to Her Majesty extreme concern ; and the barbarities which have been inflicted upon many of Her Majesty's subjects in India, and the sufferings which have been endured, have filled Her Majesty's heart with the deepest grief; while the conduct of many civil and military officers, who have been placed in circumstances of much difficulty, and have been exposed to great danger, has excited Her Majesty's warmest admiration.

Her Majesty commands us to inform you that she will omit no measure calculated to quell these grave disorders ; and Her Majesty is confident that, with the blessing of Providence, the powerful means at her disposal will enable her to accomplish that end.

Gentlemen of the House of Commons,

Her Majesty commands us to thank you for the liberal supplies which you have voted for the service of the present year, and for the assurances which you have given her of your readiness to afford Her Majesty whatever support may be necessary for the restoration of tranquillity in India.

Her Majesty has been gratified to find that you have been enabled to provide the amount required to be paid to Denmark for the redemption of the Sound dues, without on that account adding to the National Debt.

My Lords and Gentlemen,

Her Majesty commands us to convey to you her heartfelt acknowledgments for the provision which you have made for her beloved daughter, the Princess Royal, on her approaching marriage with His Royal Highness Prince Frederick William of Prussia.

Her Majesty commands us to inform you that she has seen with satisfaction that, although the present session has been short, you have been able to pass many Acts of great importance, and to which Her Majesty has given her cordial assent.

The Acts for establishing a more efficient Jurisdiction for the Proving of Wills in England and Ireland, correct defects which have for many years been complained of.

The Act for amending the Law relating to Divorce and to Matrimonial Causes will remedy evils which have long been felt.

The several Acts for the Punishment of Fraudulent Breaches of Trust;

For amending the Law relating to Secondary Punishments;

For amending the Law concerning Joint Stock Banks;

For consolidating and amending the Law relating to Bankruptcy and Insolvency in Ireland;

For the Better Care and Treatment of Pauper Lunatics in Scotland;

For improving the Organization of the County Police in Scotland;

Together with other Acts of less importance, but likewise tending to the progressive improvement of the law, have met with Her Majesty's ready assent.

We are commanded by Her Majesty to express to you

her confidence that, on your return to your several
counties, you will employ that influence which so justly
belongs to you to promote the welfare and happiness of
her loyal and faithful people; and she prays that the
blessing of Almighty God may attend and prosper your
endeavours.

PARLIAMENT V.—SESSION II.

OPENING OF PARLIAMENT BY HER MAJESTY IN PERSON.

Date.—December 3rd, 1857.

The Cabinet.—First Lord of the Treasury, Right
Hon Viscount Palmerston; Lord Chancellor, Right
Hon. Viscount Cranworth; President of the Council,
Right Hon. Earl Granville; Lord of the Privy Seal,
Most Hon. Marquess of Clanricarde; Home Secretary,
Right Hon. Sir George Grey, Bart.; Foreign Secre-
tary, Right Hon. Earl of Clarendon; Colonial Secretary,
Right Hon. Henry Labouchere; Secretary at War, Right
Hon Lord Panmure; Chancellor of the Exchequer,
Right Hon. Sir George C. Lewis, Bart.; First Lord of
the Admiralty, Right. Hon. Sir Charles Wood, Bart.;
President of the Board of Control, Right Hon. Robert
Vernon Smith; President of the Board of Trade, Right
Hon. Lord Stanley of Alderley; Chancellor of the
Duchy of Lancaster, Right Hon. Matthew Talbot
Baines; Postmaster-General, His Grace the Duke of
Argyll; Most Hon. Marquess of Lansdowne.

The Queen's Speech.

My Lords and Gentlemen,

Circumstances have recently arisen, connected
with the commercial interests of the country, which have

induced me to call Parliament together before the usual
time.

The failure of certain joint-stock banks and of some
mercantile firms produced such an extent of distrust as
led me to authorise my Ministers to recommend to the
Directors of the Bank of England the adoption of a
course of proceeding which appeared necessary for
allaying the prevalent alarm. As that course has involved a departure from the existing law, a Bill for
indemnifying those who advised and those who adopted
it will be submitted for your consideration.

I have observed with great regret that the disturbed
state of commercial transactions in general has occasioned a diminution of employment in the manufacturing
districts, which, I fear, cannot fail to be attended with
much local distress. I trust, however, that this evil
may not be of long duration; and the abundant harvest
with which it has graciously pleased Divine Providence
to bless this land will, I hope, in some degree mitigate
the sufferings which this state of things must unavoidably produce.

While I deeply deplore the severe suffering to which
many of my subjects in India have been exposed, and
while I grieve for the extensive bereavements and sorrow
which it has caused, I have derived the greatest satisfaction from the distinguished successes which have
attended the heroic exertions of the comparatively
small forces which have been opposed to greatly superior
numbers, without the aid of the powerful reinforcements
despatched from this country to their assistance. The
arrival of those reinforcements will, I trust, speedily
complete the suppression of this widely-spread revolt.

The gallantry of the troops employed against the mutineers, their courage in action, their endurance under privation, fatigue, and the effects of climate—the high spirit and self-devotion of the officers—the ability, skill, and persevering energy of the commanders — have excited my warmest admiration ; and I have observed with equal gratification that many civilians placed in extreme difficulty and danger have displayed the highest qualities, including, in some instances, those that would do honour to veteran soldiers.

It is satisfactory to know that the general mass of the population of India has taken no part in the rebellion, while the most considerable of the Native Princes have acted in the most friendly manner, and have rendered important services.

I have given directions that papers relating to these matters shall be laid before you.

The affairs of my East Indian dominions will require your serious consideration ; and I recommend them to your earnest attention.

The nations of Europe are in the enjoyment of the blessings of peace, which nothing seems likely to disturb.

The stipulations of the treaty which I concluded with the Shah of Persia have been faithfully carried into execution, and the Persian forces have evacuated the territory of Herat.

Gentlemen of the House of Commons,

I have given directions that the estimates for the next year shall be prepared for the purpose of being laid before you.

They will be framed with a careful regard to the exigencies of the public service.

My Lords and Gentlemen,

Your attention will be called to the laws which regulate the representation of the people in Parliament, with a view to consider what amendments may be safely and beneficially made therein.

Measures will be submitted for your consideration for simplifying and amending the laws relating to real property, and also for consolidating and amending several important branches of the criminal law.

I confidently commit to your wisdom the great interests of my Empire, and I fervently pray that the blessing of Almighty God may attend your counsels, and may guide your deliberations to those ends which are dearest to my heart—the happiness and prosperity of my loyal and faithful people.

Mover of Address in the Lords, Lord Portman.
Seconder „ „ Lord Carew.
Mover of Address in the Commons, Mr. C. W. Martyn.
Seconder „ „ Mr. Akroyd.

PROROGATION OF PARLIAMENT BY COMMISSION.

Date.—August 2nd, 1858.

The Lords Commissioners were :—The Lord Chancellor; the Lord President of the Council ; the Lord of the Privy Seal; the Lord Chamberlain of the Household ; and the Duke of Beaufort.

The Queen's Speech.

My Lords and Gentlemen,

We are commanded by Her Majesty to express her satisfaction at being enabled to release you from the duties of a session which, though interrupted, has by your unremitting assiduity been productive of many important measures.

Her Majesty is happy to believe that her relations with foreign Powers are such as to enable Her Majesty to look with confidence to the preservation of general peace.

Her Majesty trusts that the labours of the Plenipotentiaries, now sitting in conference at Paris, may lead to a satisfactory solution of the various questions which have been referred to them.

The efforts, the gallantry and devotedness displayed in India by Her Majesty's forces and those of the East India Company, have been above all praise; and Her Majesty hopes that those efforts have already been so far crowned with success that the formidable revolt which has raged throughout a large portion of her Indian possessions may now, under the blessing of Almighty God, be speedily suppressed, and peace be restored to those important provinces.

In this hope Her Majesty has given her willing assent to the Act which you have passed for transferring to her direct authority the government of her Indian dominions; and Her Majesty hopes to be enabled so to discharge the high functions which she has assumed as, by a just and impartial administration of the law, to secure its advantages alike to her subjects of every race and creed, and, by promoting their welfare, to establish and strengthen her Empire in India.

Gentlemen of the House of Commons,

Her Majesty commands us to thank you for the judicious liberality with which you have made provision for the exigencies of the public service.

The present state of the revenue authorises Her Majesty to entertain a confident hope that the supplies which you have granted will be found fully adequate to the demands upon them.

My Lords and Gentlemen,

The sanitary condition of the metropolis must always be a subject of deep interest to Her Majesty, and Her Majesty has readily sanctioned the Act which you have passed for the purification of that noble river, the present state of which is little creditable to a great country, and seriously prejudicial to the health and comfort of the inhabitants of the metropolis.

Her Majesty has willingly assented to an Act whereby greater facilities are given for the acquisition by towns and districts of such powers as may be requisite for promoting works of local improvement, and thus extending more widely the advantages of municipal· self-government.

Her Majesty trusts that the Act which you have passed for the future Government of the Scotch Universities will be found highly advantageous to those venerable institutions, and will greatly promote and extend a system of sound moral and religious education in Scotland.

The Transfer of Land Bill, which extends the powers

10

hitherto exercised by the Encumbered Estates Commissioners, and facilitates the acquisition of an indefensible title by purchasers of land in Ireland, cannot fail to be highly beneficial to the landed proprietors, and to advance the prosperity of that part of Her Majesty's dominions.

The Act to which Her Majesty has assented, for the establishment of the Colony of British Columbia, was urgently required in consequence of the recent discoveries of gold in that district; but Her Majesty hopes that this new Colony in the Pacific may be but one step in the career of steady progress, by which Her Majesty's dominions in North America may ultimately be peopled by an unbroken chain, from the Atlantic to the Pacific, by a loyal and industrious population of subjects of the British Crown.

Her Majesty thankfully acknowledges the diligence and perseverance which has enabled you in a comparatively short time to pass these and other measures of inferior but not insignificant importance.

Many of you, in returning to your respective counties, have extensive influence to exercise, and duties to perform of hardly less value to the community than those from the labours of which you are about to be released; and Her Majesty entertains a confident assurance that, under the guidance of Providence, that influence will be so employed, and those duties so performed as to redound to your own honour, and to promote the general welfare and the happiness of a loyal and contented people.

PARLIAMENT V.—SESSION III.

OPENING OF PARLIAMENT BY HER MAJESTY IN PERSON.

Date.—February 3rd, 1859.

The Cabinet.—First Lord of the Treasury, Right Hon. Earl of Derby; Lord Chancellor, Right Hon. Lord Chelmsford; President of the Council, Most Hon. Marquess of Salisbury; Lord of the Privy Seal, Right Hon. Earl of Hardwicke; Home Secretary, Right Hon. Spencer Horatio Walpole; Foreign Secretary, Right Hon. Earl of Malmesbury; Colonial Secretary, Right Hon Sir Edward George Bulwer-Lytton, Bart.; Secretary at War, Right Hon. Jonathan Peel; Secretary for India, Right Hon. Lord Stanley; Chancellor of the Exchequer, Right Hon. Benjamin Disraeli; First Lord of the Admiralty, Right Hon. Sir J. Somerset Pakington; President of the Board of Trade, Right Hon. Joseph Warner Henley; First Commissioner of Works and Public Buildings, Right Hon. Lord John James Robert Manners.

The Queen's Speech.

My Lords and Gentlemen,

In recurring at the usual season to the advice of my Parliament, I am happy to think that, in the internal state of the country, there is nothing to excite disquietude, and much to call for satisfaction and thankfulness. Pauperism and crime have considerably diminished during the past year, and a spirit of general contentment prevails.

The blessing of the Almighty on the valour of my troops in India and on the skill of their commanders,

10 *

has enabled me to inflict signal chastisement upon those who are still in arms against my authority, whenever they have ventured to encounter my forces ; and I trust that, at no distant period, I may be able to announce to you the complete pacification of that great empire, and to devote my attention to the improvement of its condition, and to the obliteration of all traces of the present unhappy conflict.

On assuming, by your advice, the direct government of that portion of my dominions, I deemed it proper to make known by Proclamation the principles by which it was my intention to be guided, and the clemency which I was disposed to show towards those who might have been seduced into revolt, but who might be willing to return to their allegiance. I have directed that a copy of that Proclamation should be laid before you.

I receive from all Powers assurances of their friendly feelings. To cultivate and confirm those feelings, to maintain inviolate the faith of public treaties, and to contribute, as far as my influence can extend, to the preservation of the general peace, are the objects of my unceasing solicitude.

I have concluded, with the Sovereigns who were parties to the Treaty of Paris of 1856, a Convention relative to the organisation of the principalities of Moldavia and Wallachia. Those Rouman provinces are now proceeding to establish, under its provisions, their new form of government.

A treaty of commerce which I have concluded with the Emperor of Russia, and which will be laid before you, is a satisfactory indication of the complete re-establishment of those amicable relations which, until their late unfortunate interruption, had long subsisted between us, to the mutual advantage of our respective dominions.

The measures which, in concert with my Ally the Emperor of the French, I thought necessary to take upon the coast of China, have resulted in a treaty, by which further effusion of blood has been prevented, and which holds out the prospect of greatly increased intercourse with that extensive and densely-peopled empire.

Another treaty into which I have entered with the Emperor of Japan, opens a fresh field for commercial enterprise in a populous and highly civilised country, which has hitherto been jealously guarded against the intrusion of foreigners. As soon as the ratification of these treaties shall have been exchanged, they will be laid before you.

I have great satisfaction in announcing to you that the Emperor of the French has abolished a system of negro emigration from the east coast of Africa, against which, as unavoidably tending, however guarded, to the encouragement of the slave trade, my Government has never ceased to address to His Imperial Majesty its most earnest but friendly representations.

This wise act on the part of His Imperial Majesty induces me to hope that negotiations, now in progress at Paris, may tend to the total abandonment of the system, and to the substitution of a duly regulated supply of substantially free labour.

The state of the Republic of Mexico, distracted by civil war, has induced me to carry forbearance to its utmost limits, in regard to the wrongs and indignities to which British residents have been subjected at the hands of the two contending parties.

They have at length been carried to such an extent that I have been compelled to give instructions to the commander of my naval forces in those seas to demand and, if necessary, to enforce due reparation.

Gentlemen of the House of Commons,

I have directed that the estimates of the ensuing year shall be submitted to you. They have been framed with a due regard to economy, and to the efficiency of the public service.

The universal introduction of steam power into naval warfare will render necessary a temporary increase of expenditure in providing for the reconstruction of the British navy; but I am persuaded that you will cheerfully vote whatever sums you may find to be requisite for an object of such vital importance as the maintenance of the maritime power of the country.

My Lords and Gentlemen,

Your labours have, in recent sessions, been usefully directed to various measures of legal and social improvement. In the belief that further measures of a similar character may be wisely and beneficially introduced, I have desired that Bills may be submitted to you without delay, for assimilating and amending the laws relating to bankruptcy and insolvency; for bringing together into one set of statutes, in a classified form, and with such modifications as experience will suggest to you, the laws relating to crimes and offences in England and Ireland; for enabling the owners of land in England to obtain for themselves an indefeasible title to their estate and interests, and for registering such titles with simplicity and security.

Your attention will be called to the state of the laws which regulate the representation of the people in Parliament, and I cannot doubt that you will give to this great subject a degree of calm and impartial consideration proportioned to the magnitude of the interests involved in the result of your discussions.

These and other propositions for the amendment of the laws, which will be brought under your notice as the progress of public business may permit, I commend to the exercise of your deliberate judgment: and I earnestly pray that your counsels may be so guided as to ensure the stability of the throne, the maintenance and improvement of our institutions, and the general welfare and happiness of my people.

Mover of Address in the Lords, Earl of Winchelsea.
Seconder   „   „   Lord Ravensworth.
Mover of Address in the Commons, Mr. Trefusis.
Seconder   „   „   Mr. Beecroft.

DISSOLUTION OF PARLIAMENT BY COMMISSION.

Date.—August 19th, 1859.

The Lords Commissioners were:—The Lord Chancellor; the Lord President of the Council; the Lord of the Privy Seal; the Lord Steward of the Household; and the Lord Chamberlain of the Household.

The Queen's Speech

My Lords and Gentlemen,

We are commanded by Her Majesty to inform you that it is Her Majesty's intention forthwith to dissolve the present Parliament, with a view to enable the people to express, in the mode prescribed by the Constitution, their opinion upon the state of public affairs.

Gentlemen of the House of Commons,

We are commanded by Her Majesty to thank you for the wise liberality with which you have granted the necessary supplies for the military and naval defences of the country, and for the provision which you have made for the exigencies of the other branches of the public service, during the interval which must elapse before the estimates for the year can be considered by the new Parliament, which Her Majesty will direct immediately to be called.

My Lords and Gentlemen,

Her Majesty commands us to inform you that the appeal which she is about to make to her people has been rendered necessary by the difficulties experienced in carrying on the public business of the country, as indicated by the fact that within little more than a year two successive administrations have failed to retain the confidence of the House of Commons; and Her Majesty prays that, under the blessing of Divine Providence, the steps which she is about to take may have the effect of facilitating the discharge of her high functions, and of enabling her to conduct the Government of the country under the advice of a Ministry possessed of the confidence of her Parliament and her people.

PARLIAMENT VI.—SESSION I.

OPENING OF PARLIAMENT BY HER MAJESTY IN PERSON.

Date.—June 7th, 1859.

The Cabinet.—First Lord of the Treasury, Right. Hon. Viscount Palmerston; Lord Chancellor, Right Hon. Lord Campbell; President of the Council, Right Hon. Earl Granville; Lord of the Privy Seal, His Grace the Duke of Argyll; Home Secretary, Right. Hon. Sir George Cornewall Lewis, Bart.; Foreign Secretary, Right Hon. Lord John Russell; Colonial Secretary, His Grace the Duke of Newcastle; Secretary at War, Right Hon. Sidney Herbert; Secretary for India, Right Hon. Sir Charles Wood, Bart.; Chancellor of the Exchequer, Right Hon. W. E. Gladstone; First Lord of the Admiralty, His Grace the Duke of Somerset; President of the Board of Trade, Right Hon. Thomas Milner Gibson; Postmaster-General, Right Hon. Earl of Elgin; Chancellor of the Duchy of Lancaster, Right Hon. Sir George Grey; Chief Commissioner of the Poor Law Board, Right Hon. Charles Pelham Villiers; Chief Secretary for Ireland, Right Hon. Edward Cardwell.

The Queen's Speech.

My Lords and Gentlemen,

I avail myself with satisfaction, in the present state of public affairs, of the advice of my Parliament, which I have summoned to meet with the least possible delay.

I have directed that papers shall be laid before you, from which you will learn how earnest and unceasing have been my endeavours to preserve the peace of Europe.

Those endeavours have unhappily failed, and war has been declared between France and Sardinia on the one side and Austria on the other. Receiving assurances of friendship from both the contending parties, I intend to maintain between them a strict and impartial neutrality; and I hope, with God's assistance, to preserve to my people the blessings of continued peace.

Considering, however, the present state of Europe, I have deemed it necessary, for the security of my dominions and the honour of my Crown, to increase my naval forces to an amount exceeding that which has been sanctioned by Parliament.

I rely with confidence on your cordial concurrence in this precautionary measure of defensive policy.

The King of the Two Sicilies, having announced to me the death of the King his father, and his own accession, I have thought fit, in concert with the Emperor of the French, to renew my diplomatic intercourse with the Court of Naples, which had been suspended during the late reign.

All my other foreign relations continue on a perfectly satisfactory footing.

Gentlemen of the House of Commons,

The estimates for the year, for which provision has not been made by the late Parliament, will be immediately laid before you, together with such supplementary estimates as present circumstances render indispensably necessary for the public service.

My Lords and Gentlemen,

I have directed a Bill to be prepared for giving effect, so far as the aid of Parliament may be required, to certain suggestions of the Commissioners whom I had appointed to inquire into the best mode of efficiently manning the royal navy, and I recommend this important subject to your immediate attention.

Measures of legal and social improvement, the progress of which in the late Parliament was necessarily interrupted by the dissolution, will again be brought under your consideration.

I should with pleasure give my sanction to any well-considered measure for the amendment of the laws which regulate the representation of my people in Parliament; and should you be of opinion that the necessity of giving your immediate attention to measures of urgency relating to the defence and financial condition of the country will not leave you sufficient time for legislating with due deliberation during the present session on a subject at once so difficult and so extensive, I trust that at the commencement of the next session your earnest attention will be given to a question of which an early and satisfactory settlement would be greatly to the public advantage.

I feel assured that you will enter with zeal and diligence on the discharge of your Parliamentary duties; and I pray that the result of your deliberations may tend to secure to the country the continuance of peace abroad and progressive improvement at home.

Mover of Address in the Lords, Earl of Powis.
Seconder ,, ,, Viscount Lifford.
Mover of Address in the Commons, Mr. A. F. Egerton.
Seconder ,, ,, Sir James Elphinstone.

PROROGATION OF PARLIAMENT BY COMMISSION.

Date.—August 13th, 1859.

The Lords Commissioners were :—The Lord Chancellor ; the Lord President of the Council; the First Lord of the Admiralty ; the Lord Steward of the Household ; the Lord Chamberlain of the Household.

The Queen's Speech.

My Lords and Gentlemen,

We are commanded by Her Majesty to release you from further attendance in Parliament, and at the same time to convey to you Her Majesty's acknowledgments for the zeal and assiduity with which you have applied yourselves to the performance of your important duties during the session of Parliament now about to close.

Various circumstances which occasioned interruptions in the usual course of business, prevented the completion of important measures which Her Majesty pointed out to the attention of her Parliament in the beginning of the present year ; but Her Majesty trusts that those matters will be taken into your earnest consideration at an early period of your next session.

The war which had broken out in Northern Italy having been brought to a close by the Peace of Villafranca, overtures have been made to Her Majesty with a view to ascertain whether, if conferences should be held by the Great Powers of Europe, for the purpose of settling arrangements connected with the present state and future condition of Italy, a Plenipotentiary would be sent by Her Majesty to assist at such conferences ;

but Her Majesty has not yet received the information necessary to enable her to decide whether Her Majesty may think fit to take part in any such negotiations.

Her Majesty would rejoice to find herself able to contribute to the establishment of arrangements calculated to place the general peace on satisfactory and lasting foundations.

Her Majesty, in accordance with the stipulations of the Treaty of Tientsing, has instructed her Plenipotentiary in China to repair to the Imperial Court at Pekin, and Her Majesty trusts that such direct communication with the Imperial Government will have a beneficial effect upon the relations between the two countries.

Her Majesty commands us to inform you that she looks forward with confidence to the continued maintenance of those friendly relations which so happily subsist between Her Majesty and all Foreign Powers and States.

Her Majesty is glad to be able to congratulate you on the complete restoration of tranquillity in her Indian dominions.

It will be her earnest endeavour to promote their internal improvement, and to obliterate the traces of those conflicts which Her Majesty witnessed with such deep concern.

The financial arrangements of that portion of Her Majesty's Empire will continue to engage Her Majesty's serious attention.

Her Majesty has much satisfaction in giving her assent to the Bills which you presented to her for the formation of a naval and of a military reserve force.   A complete and permanent system of national defence must at all times be an object of paramount importance.

Gentlemen of the House of Commons,

Her Majesty commands us to convey to you her cordial thanks for the readiness and zeal with which you have provided the necessary supplies for the service of the year.

My Lords and Gentlemen,

Her Majesty commands us to express to you her heart felt gratification at witnessing the general well-being and contentment which prevail throughout her dominions; the happiness of Her Majesty's people is the object dearest to her heart.

In returning to your respective counties, you will have duties to perform intimately connected with the attainment of this end; and Her Majesty fervently prays that the blessing of Almighty God may attend your exertions in the performance of those duties, for the common good of all classes of Her Majesty's subjects.

PARLIAMENT VI.—SESSION II.

OPENING OF PARLIAMENT BY HER MAJESTY IN PERSON.

Date.—January 24th, 1860.

The Cabinet.—First Lord of the Treasury, Right Hon. Viscount Palmerston; Lord Chancellor, Right Hon. Lord Campbell; President of the Council, Right Hon. Earl Granville; Lord of the Privy Seal, His Grace the Duke of Argyll; Home Secretary, Right Hon. Sir George Cornewall Lewis, Bart.; Foreign Secretary,

Right Hon. Lord John Russell; Colonial Secretary, His Grace the Duke of Newcastle; Secretary at War, Right Hon. Sidney Herbert; Secretary for India, Right Hon. Sir Charles Wood, Bart.; Chancellor of the Exchequer, Right Hon. William Ewart Gladstone; First Lord of the Admiralty, His Grace the Duke of Somerset; President of the Board of Trade, Right Hon. Thomas Milner Gibson; Postmaster-General, Right Hon. Earl of Elgin; Chancellor of the Duchy of Lancaster, Right Hon. Sir George Grey, Bart.; Chief Commissioner of the Poor Law Board, Right Hon. Charles Pelham Villiers; Chief Secretary for Ireland, Right Hon. Edward Cardwell.

The Queen's Speech.

My Lords and Gentlemen,

It is with great satisfaction that I again meet you in Parliament, and have recourse to your assistance and advice.

My relations with foreign Powers continue to be on a friendly and satisfactory footing.

At the close of the last session I informed you that overtures had been made to me, to ascertain whether, if a conference should be held by the Great Powers of Europe, for the purpose of settling arrangements connected with the present state and future condition of Italy, a Plenipotentiary would be sent by me to assist at such a conference. I have since received a formal invitation from the Emperor of Austria, and from the Emperor of the French, to send a Plenipotentiary to a Congress to consist of the representatives of the eight Powers who were parties to the Treaties of Vienna of

1815; the objects of such Congress being stated to be, to receive communication of the Treaties concluded at Zurich; and to deliberate, associating with the above-mentioned Powers the Courts of Rome, of Sardinia, and of the Two Sicilies, on the means best adapted for the pacification of Italy, and for placing its prosperity on a solid and durable basis.

Desirous at all times to concur in proceedings having for their object the maintenance of peace, I accepted the invitation; but, at the same time, I made known that in such a Congress I should steadfastly maintain the principle that no external force should be employed to impose upon the people of Italy any particular govern-ment or constitution.

Circumstances have arisen which have led to a post-ponement of the Congress, without any day having been fixed for its meeting; but whether in Congress or sepa-rate negotiation, I shall endeavour to obtain for the people of Italy freedom from foreign interference by force of arms in their internal concerns; and I trust that the affairs of the Italian peninsula may be peace-fully and satisfactorily settled.

Papers on this subject will soon be laid before you.

I am in communication with the Emperor of the French, with a view to extend the commercial inter-course between the two countries, and thus to draw still closer the bonds of friendly alliance between them.

A dispute having arisen between Spain and Morocco, I endeavoured, by friendly means, to prevent a rupture, but, I regret to say, without success.

I will direct papers on this subject to be laid before you.

My Plenipotentiary and the Plenipotentiary of the Emperor of the French having, in obedience to their instructions, proceeded to the mouth of the Peiho river, in order to repair to Pekin to exchange in that city the ratifications of the Treaty of Tien-tsin, in pursuance of the Fifty-sixth Article of that Treaty, their further progress was opposed by force, and a conflict took place between the Chinese forts at the mouth of the river and the naval forces by which the Plenipotentiaries were escorted.

The allied forces displayed on this occasion their usual bravery ; but, after sustaining a severe loss, were compelled to retire.

I am preparing, in concert and co-operation with the Emperor of the French, an expedition intended to obtain redress and a fulfilment of the stipulations of the Treaty of Tien-tsin.

It will be gratifying to me if the prompt acquiescence of the Emperor of China in the moderate demands which will be made by the Plenipotentiaries shall obviate the necessity for the employment of force.

I have directed that papers on this subject shall be laid before you.

An unauthorised proceeding by an officer of the United States in regard to the Island of San Juan, between Vancouver's Island and the mainland, might have led to a serious collision between my forces and those of the United States. Such collision, however, has been prevented by the judicious forbearance of my naval and civil officers on the spot, and by the equitable and conciliatory provisional arrangement proposed on this matter by the Government of the United States.

I trust that the question of boundary, out of which

11

this affair has arisen, may be amicably settled in a manner conformable with the just rights of the two countries, as defined by the First Article of the Treaty of 1846.

The last embers of disturbance in my East Indian dominions have been extinguished; my Viceroy has made a peaceful progress through the districts which had been the principal scene of disorder; and, by a judicious combination of firmness and generosity, my authority has been everywhere solidly and, I trust, permanently established. I have received from my Viceroy the most gratifying accounts of the loyalty of my Indian subjects, and of the good feeling evinced by the native chiefs and the great landowners of the country. The attention of the Government in India has been directed to the development of the internal resources of the country; and I am glad to inform you that an improvement has taken place in its financial prospects.

I have concluded a treaty with the Tycoon of Japan, and a treaty regarding the boundaries with the Republic of Guatemala. I have directed that these treaties shall be laid before you.

Gentlemen of the House of Commons,

I have directed the estimates for the ensuing year to be laid before you. They have been prepared with a view to place the military and naval services, and the defences of the country, upon an efficient footing.

I am glad to be able to inform you that the public revenue is in a satisfactory condition.

My Lords and Gentlemen,

I have accepted with gratification and pride, the extensive offers of voluntary service which I have received from my subjects. This manifestation of public spirit has added an important element to our system of national defence.

Measures will be laid before you for amending the laws which regulate the representation of the people in Parliament, and for placing that representation upon a broader and firmer basis.

I earnestly recommend you to resume your labours for the improvement of our jurisprudence, and particularly in regard to bankruptcy, the transfer of land, the consolidation of the statutes, and such a further fusion of law and equity as may be necessary to insure that in every suit the rights of the parties may be satisfactorily determined by the court in which the suit is commenced.

I am deeply gratified to observe that the great interests of the country are generally in a sound and thriving condition; that pauperism and crime have diminished; and that, throughout the whole of my Empire, both in the United Kingdom and in my Colonies and Possessions beyond sea, there reigns a spirit of loyalty, of contentment, of order, and of obedience to the law.

With heartfelt gratitude to the Almighty Ruler of Nations for these inestimable blessings, I fervently pray that His beneficent power may guide your deliberations for the advancement and consolidation of the welfare and happiness of my people.

Mover of Address in the Lords, Earl Fitzwilliam.
Seconder ,, ,, Lord Truro.
Mover of Address in the Commons, Mr. St. Aubyn.
Seconder ,, ,, Lord Henley.

11 *

PROROGATION OF PARLIAMENT BY COMMISSION.

Date.—August 28th, 1860.

The Lord Commissioners were:—The Lord Chancellor; the Duke of Somerset; the Lord Chamberlain; the Lord Stanley of Alderley; and the Lord Monteagle of Brandon.

The Queen's Speech.

My Lords and Gentlemen,

We are commanded by Her Majesty to release you from further attendance in Parliament, and at the same time to convey to you Her Majesty's acknowledgments for the zeal and assiduity with which you have applied yourselves to the performance of your important duties during the long and laborious session of Parliament now about to close.

Her Majesty commands us to inform you that her relations with foreign Powers are friendly and satisfactory, and Her Majesty trusts that there is no danger of any interruption of the general peace of Europe. Events of considerable importance are indeed taking place in Italy, but if no foreign Power interfere therein, and if the Italians are left to settle their own affairs, the tranquillity of other States will remain undisturbed.

The proposed conferences on the subject of the cession of Savoy and of Nice to France have not yet been held; but Her Majesty confidently trusts that in any negotiations which may take place, full and adequate arrangements will be made for securing, in accordance with the spirit and letter of the Treaty of Vienna of 1815, the neutrality and independence of the Swiss Confederation.

That neutrality and independence were an object to

which all the Powers who were parties to the Treaties of
Vienna attached great importance ; and they are no less
important now than then, for the general interests of
Europe.

Her Majesty commands us to assure you that the
atrocities which have been committed upon the Christian population in Syria have inspired Her Majesty with
the deepest grief and indignation. Her Majesty has
cheerfully concurred with the Emperor of Austria, the
Emperor of the French, the Prince Regent of Prussia,
and the Emperor of Russia, in entering into an engagement with the Sultan, by which temporary military
assistance has been afforded to the Sultan for the
purpose of re-establishing order in that part of his
dominions.

We are commanded by Her Majesty to inform
you that Her Majesty greatly regrets that the pacific
overtures which, by Her Majesty's directions, her
Envoy in China made to the Imperial Government at
Pekin, did not lead to any satisfactory result ; and it has
therefore been necessary that the combined naval and
military forces which Her Majesty and her Ally, the
Emperor of the French, had sent to the China seas
should advance towards the northern provinces of China,
for the purpose of supporting the just demands of the
allied Powers.

Her Majesty, desirous of giving all possible weight to
her diplomatic action in this matter, has sent to China
as Special Ambassador, the Earl of Elgin, who negotiated the Treaty of Tien-tsin, the full and faithful
execution of which is demanded from the Emperor of
China.

Gentlemen of the House of Commons,

Her Majesty commands us to convey to you her warm acknowledgments for the liberal supplies which you have granted for the service of the present year, and for the provision which you have made for those defences which are essential for the security of her dock-yards and arsenals.

My Lords and Gentlemen,

Her Majesty commands us to express to you the gratification and pride with which she has witnessed the rapid progress in military efficiency which her Volunteer Forces have already made, and which is highly honourable to their spirit and patriotism.

Her Majesty has given her cordial assent to the Act for amalgamating her local European force in India with her force engaged for general service.

Her Majesty trusts that the additional freedom which you have given to commerce will lead to fresh develop-ment of productive industry.

Her Majesty has given her ready assent to several measures of great public usefulness.

The Acts for regulating the relations between landlord and tenant in Ireland will, Her Majesty trusts, remove some fertile causes of disagreement.

The Act for amending the law which regulates the discipline of Her Majesty's navy, has established salu-tary rules for the administration of justice by courts-martial, and for maintaining good order in the naval service.

The Act bearing upon Endowed Charities will give means for a less expensive administration of the pro-

perty of charities, and for the speedy and economical
settlement of disputes affecting such property ; while by
another Act, relief has been afforded to Her Majesty's
Roman Catholic subjects with regard to their charitable
endowments.

Several other Acts have been passed for legal reform,
which must lead to the more satisfactory administration
of justice.

Her Majesty has observed with deep satisfaction the
spirit of loyalty, of order, and of obedience to the law,
which prevails among her subjects, both in the United
Kingdom and in her dominions beyond sea ; and Her
Majesty has witnessed with heartfelt pleasure the warm
and affectionate reception given to His Royal Highness
the Prince of Wales by her North American subjects.

You will, on returning to your several counties, have
duties to perform scarcely less important than those
which occupied you during the session of Parliament ;
and Her Majesty fervently prays that the blessing of
Almighty God may attend your efforts, and guide them
to the attainment of the object of her constant solicitude, the welfare and the happiness of her people.

PARLIAMENT VI.—SESSION III.

OPENING OF PARLIAMENT BY HER MAJESTY IN PERSON.

Date.—February 5th, 1861.

The Cabinet.—First Lord of the Treasury, Right
Hon. Viscount Palmerston ; Lord Chancellor, Right
Hon. Lord Campbell ; President of the Council,
Right Hon. Earl Granville ; Lord of the Privy Seal,

His Grace the Duke of Argyll; Home Secretary, Right
Hon. Sir G. Cornewall Lewis; Foreign Secretary, Right
Hon. Lord John Russell; Colonial Secretary, His Grace
the Duke of Newcastle; Secretary at War, Right Hon.
Lord Herbert; Secretary for India, Right Hon. Sir
Charles Wood, Bart.; Chancellor of the Exchequer,
Right Hon. William Ewart Gladstone; First Lord of
the Admiralty, His Grace the Duke of Somerset; Presi-
dent of the Board of Trade, Right Hon. Thomas
Milner Gibson; Postmaster-General, Right Hon. Lord
Stanley of Alderley; Chancellor of the Duchy of Lan-
caster, Right Hon. Sir George Grey; Chief Commis-
sioner of the Poor Law Board, Right Hon. Charles P.
Villiers; Chief Secretary for Ireland, Right Hon
Edward Cardwell.

The Queen's Speech.

My Lords and Gentlemen,

It is with great satisfaction that I meet you again
in Parliament, and have recourse to your advice.

My relations with foreign Powers continue to be
friendly and satisfactory; and I trust that the moderation of the Powers of Europe will prevent any interruption of the general peace.

Events of great importance are taking place in Italy.
Believing that the Italians ought to be left to settle
their own affairs, I have not thought it right to exercise
any active interference in those matters. Papers on
this subject will be laid before you.

I announced to you, at the close of the last session of
Parliament, that the atrocities which had then recently
been committed in Syria, had induced me to concur with

the Emperor of Austria, the Emperor of the French, the Prince Regent of Prussia, and the Emperor of Russia, in entering into an engagement with the Sultan, by which temporary military assistance was to be afforded to the Sultan for the purpose of establishing order in that part of his dominions.

That assistance has been afforded by a body of French troops, who have been sent to Syria as representing the allied Powers. The Sultan has also placed a considerable military force in Syria, under the direction of an able officer; and I trust that tranquillity will soon be re-established in that Province, and that the objects of the Convention will have been fully attained.

I announced to you also, at the close of the last session of Parliament, that the pacific overtures which my Envoy in China had made to the Imperial Government at Pekin, having led to no satisfactory result, my naval and military forces, and those of my Ally, the Emperor of the French, were to advance towards the northern provinces of China, for the purpose of supporting the just demands of the allied Powers, and that the Earl of Elgin had been sent to China, as Special Ambassador, to treat with the Chinese Government.

I am glad to inform you that the operations of the allied forces have been attended with complete success. After the capture of the forts at the mouth of the Peiho, and several engagements with the Chinese army, the allied forces became masters of the imperial city of Pekin; and the Earl of Elgin, and Baron Gros, the Ambassador of the Emperor of the French, were enabled to obtain an honourable and satisfactory settlement of all the matters in dispute.

Throughout these operations, and the negotiations which followed them, the Commanders and Ambassadors of the allied Powers acted with the most friendly concert. Papers on this subject will be laid before you.

The state of my Indian territories is progressively improving, and I trust that their financial condition will gradually partake of the general amendment.

An insurrection of a portion of the natives of New Zealand has interrupted the peace of a part of that colony ; but I hope that the measures which have been taken will speedily suppress these disturbances, and enable my Government to concert such arrangements as may prevent their recurrence.

Serious differences have arisen among the States of the North American Union. It is impossible for me not to look with great concern upon any events which can affect the happiness and welfare of a people nearly allied to my subjects by descent, and closely connected with them by the most intimate and friendly relations. My heartfelt wish is, that these differences may be susceptible of a satisfactory adjustment.

The interest which I take in the well-being of the people of the United States, cannot but be increased by the kind and cordial reception given by them to the Prince of Wales during his recent visit to the continent of America.

I am glad to take this opportunity of expressing my warm appreciation of the loyalty and attachment to my person and throne manifested by my Canadian and other North American subjects, on the occasion of the residence of the Prince of Wales among them.

I have concluded with the Emperor of the French

conventions supplementary to the Treaty of Commerce of the 23rd of January 1860, and in furtherance of the objects of that treaty.

I have also concluded with the King of Sardinia a convention for the reciprocal protection of copyright.

These conventions will be laid before you.

Gentlemen of the House of Commons,

I have directed the estimates for the ensuing year to be laid before you. They have been framed with a due regard to economy, and to the efficiency of the several branches of the public service.

My Lords and Gentlemen,

Measures will be laid before you for the consolidation of important parts of the criminal law; for the improvement of the law of bankruptcy and insolvency; for rendering more easy the transfer of land; for establishing a uniform system of rating in England and Wales; and for several other purposes of public usefulness.

I confidently commit the great interests of my Empire to your wisdom and care; and I fervently pray that the blessing of the Almighty may attend your counsels, and may guide your deliberations to the attainment of the object of my constant solicitude, the welfare and happiness of my people.

Mover of Address in the Lords, Earl of Sefton.
Seconder „ „ Viscount Lismore.
Mover of Address in the Commons, Sir Edward Cole-
brooke.
Seconder „ „ Mr. Paget.

PROROGATION OF PARLIAMENT BY COMMISSION.

Date.—August 6th, 1861.

The Lords Commissioners were:—The Lord Chancellor; the Lord President of the Council; the Lord Steward ; the Lord Chamberlain; and Lord Monteagle of Brandon.

The Queen's Speech.

My Lords and Gentlemen,

We are commanded by Her Majesty to release you from further attendance in Parliament, and at the same time to convey to you Her Majesty's acknowledgments for the zeal and assiduity with which you have applied yourselves to the performance of your duties during the session of Parliament now brought to a close.

Her Majesty commands us to inform you that her relations with foreign Powers are friendly and satisfactory, and Her Majesty trusts that there is no danger of any disturbance of the peace of Europe.

The progress of events in Italy has led to the union of the greater part of that Peninsula in one monarchy under King Victor Emmanuel. Her Majesty has, throughout, abstained from any active interference in the transactions which have led to this result, and her earnest wish as to these affairs is, that they may be settled in the manner best suited to the welfare and happiness of the Italian people.

The dissensions which arose some months ago in the United States of North America have, unfortunately, assumed the character of open war. Her Majesty, deeply lamenting this calamitous result, has determined, in common with the other Powers of Europe, to preserve a strict neutrality between the contending parties.

Her Majesty commands us to inform you that the measures adopted for the restoration of order and tranquillity in Syria, in virtue of conventions between Her Majesty, the Emperor of Austria, the Emperor of the French, the King of Prussia, the Emperor of Russia, and the Sultan, having accomplished their purpose, the European troops which, in pursuance of those conventions, were for a time stationed in Syria to co-operate with the troops and authorities of the Sultan, have been withdrawn ; and Her Majesty trusts that the arrangements which have been made for the administration of the districts which had been disturbed will henceforth secure their internal tranquillity.

Her Majesty has seen with satisfaction the rapid improvement in the internal condition of her East Indian territories, and the progress which has been made towards equalising the revenue and expenditure of that part of her Empire.

Gentlemen of the House of Commons,

Her Majesty commands us to convey to you her warm acknowledgments for the liberal supplies which you have granted for the service of the present year, and Her Majesty has seen with satisfaction that, after amply providing for the wants of the public service, you have been able to make a sensible diminution in the taxes levied upon her people.

My Lords and Gentlemen,

Her Majesty commands us to express to you the

deep gratification with which she witnessed the spirit of devoted patriotism which continues to animate her Volunteer Forces, and the admiration with which she has observed their rapid progress in discipline and military efficiency.

Her Majesty has given her cordial assent to the Act for completing the number of the members of the House of Commons by allotting the forfeited seats of Sudbury and Saint Albans.

Her Majesty trusts that the Act for improving the laws relating to bankruptcy and insolvency will be productive of important advantage to the trade and commerce of her subjects.

Her Majesty has given her ready assent to Acts for consolidating and assimilating the criminal law of England and Ireland, and for promoting the revision of the Statute Law.

Her Majesty has given her assent to important Acts which she trusts will have the effect of opening more largely employment in the public service to the European and Native inhabitants of India, of improving the means of legislation, of furthering the ends of justice, and of promoting the contentment and well-being of all classes of Her Majesty's Indian subjects.

Her Majesty has assented with pleasure to the Act for the improvement of harbours on the coast of the United Kingdom, and for relieving merchant shipping from passing tolls; and also the Act for improving the administration of the law relating to the relief and the removal of the poor.

Her Majesty trusts that the Act for rendering more easy arrangements connected with the drainage of land, will assist agricultural improvements in many parts of the United Kingdom.

Her Majesty has gladly given her assent to many other measures of public usefulness, the result of your labours during the session now brought to its close.

Her Majesty has observed, with heartfelt satisfaction, the spirit of loyalty, of order, and of obedience to the law, which prevails throughout her dominions; and she trusts that by wise legislation, and a just administration of the law, the continuance of this happy state of things will be secured.

On returning to your respective counties you will still have important public duties to perform; and Her Majesty fervently prays that the blessing of Almighty God may attend your exertions, and may guide them to the attainment of the object of Her Majesty's constant solicitude, the welfare and happiness of her people.

PARLIAMENT VI.—SESSION IV.

OPENING OF PARLIAMENT BY COMMISSION.

Date.—February 6th, 1862.

The Lords Commissioners were:—The Lord Chancellor; the Lord Steward of the Household; the Lord Chamberlain of the Household; and Lord Stanley of Alderley.

The Cabinet.—First Lord of the Treasury, Right Hon. Viscount Palmerston; Lord Chancellor, Right Hon. Lord Westbury; President of the Council, Right Hon. Earl Granville; Lord of the Privy Seal, His Grace the Duke of Argyll; Home Secretary, Right Hon. Sir George Grey, Bart.; Foreign Secretary,

Right Hon. Earl Russell ; Colonial Secretary, His Grace
the Duke of Newcastle; Secretary at War, Right Hon.
Sir George Cornewall Lewis, Bart. ; Secretary for India,
Right Hon. Sir Charles Wood, Bart.; Chancellor of the
Exchequer, Right Hon. William Ewart Gladstone ;
First Lord of the Admiralty, His Grace the Duke of
Somerset; President of the Board of Trade, Right
Hon. Thomas Milner Gibson ; Postmaster-General,
Right Hon. Lord Stanley of Alderley ; Chancellor of the
Duchy of Lancaster, Right Hon. Edward Cardwell ;
Chief Commissioner of the Poor Law Board, Right Hon.
Charles P. Villiers.

The Queen's Speech.

My Lords and Gentlemen,

We are commanded by Her Majesty to assure
you that Her Majesty is persuaded that you will deeply
participate in the affliction by which Her Majesty has
been overwhelmed by the calamitous, untimely, and
irreparable loss of her beloved Consort, who has been
her comfort and support.

It has been, however, soothing to Her Majesty, while
suffering most acutely under this awful dispensation of
Providence, to receive from all classes of her subjects
the most cordial assurances of their sympathy with her
sorrow, as well as of their appreciation of the noble
character of him, the greatness of whose loss to Her
Majesty, and to the nation, is so justly and so univer-
sally felt and lamented.

We are commanded by Her Majesty to assure you
that she recurs with confidence to your assistance and
advice.

Her Majesty's relations with all the European Powers continue to be friendly and satisfactory; and Her Majesty trusts there is no reason to apprehend any disturbance of the peace of Europe.

A question of great importance, and which might have led to very serious consequences, arose between Her Majesty and the Government of the United States of North America, owing to the seizure and forcible removal of four passengers from on board a British mail packet by the commander of a ship of war of the United States; but that question has been satisfactorily settled by the restoration of the passengers to British protection, and by the disavowal by the United States' Government of the act of violence committed by their naval officer.

The friendly relations between Her Majesty and the President of the United States, have therefore remained unimpaired.

Her Majesty warmly appreciates the loyalty and patriotic spirit which have been manifested on this occasion by her North American subjects.

The wrongs committed by various parties, and by successive Governments in Mexico, upon foreigners resident within the Mexican territory, and for which no satisfactory redress could be obtained, have led to the conclusion of a convention between Her Majesty, the Emperor of the French, and the Queen of Spain, for the purpose of regulating a combined operation on the coast of Mexico, with a view to obtain that redress which has hitherto been withheld.

That convention, and papers relating to that subject, will be laid before you.

The improvement which has taken place in the rela-

12

tions between Her Majesty's Government and that of
the Emperor of China, and the good faith with which
the Chinese Government have continued to fulfil the
engagements of the Treaty of Tien-tsin, have enabled
Her Majesty to withdraw her troops from the city of
Canton, and to reduce the amount of her force on the
coast and in the seas of China.

Her Majesty, always anxious to exert her influence
for the preservation of peace, has concluded a convention
with the Sultan of Morocco, by means of which the
Sultan has been enabled to raise the amount necessary
for the fulfilment of certain treaty engagements which
he had contracted towards Spain, and thus to avoid the
risk of a renewal of hostilities with that Power. That
convention, and papers connected with it, will be laid
before you.

Gentlemen of the House of Commons,

Her Majesty commands us to inform you that
she has directed the estimates for the ensuing year to be
laid before you. They have been framed with a due
regard to prudent economy, and to the efficiency of the
public service.

My Lords and Gentlemen,

Her Majesty commands us to inform you that
measures for the improvement of the law will be laid
before you, and among them will be a Bill for rendering
the title to land more simple, and its transfer more
easy.

Other measures of public usefulness relating to Great
Britain and to Ireland will be submitted for your
consideration.

Her Majesty regrets that in some parts of the United Kingdom, and in certain branches of industry, temporary causes have produced considerable pressure and privation ; but Her Majesty has reason to believe that the general condition of the country is sound and satisfactory.

Her Majesty confidently recommends the general interests of the nation to your wisdom and your care ; and she fervently prays that the blessing of Almighty God may attend your deliberations, and may guide them to the promotion of the welfare and happiness of her people.

Mover of Address in the Lords, Lord Dufferin.
Seconder,   „   „   Earl of Shelburne.
Mover of Address in the Commons, Mr. W. Portman.
Seconder   „   „   Mr. Western Wood.

PROROGATION OF PARLIAMENT BY COMMISSION.

Date.—August 7th, 1862.

The Lords Commissioners were:—The Lord Chancellor; the Lord Steward of the Household; Earl Russell ; and Lord Kingsdown.

The Queen's Speech.

My Lords and Gentlemen,

We are commanded by Her Majesty to release you from further attendance in Parliament, and at the same time to convey to you Her Majesty's acknowledgments for the zeal and assiduity with which you have applied yourselves to the performance of your duties during the session now brought to a close.

12 *

Her Majesty commands us to inform you that her relations with foreign Powers are friendly and satisfactory, and that Her Majesty trusts there is no danger of any disturbance of the peace of Europe.

The civil war which has for some time been raging among the States of the North American Union, has, unfortunately, continued in unabated intensity; and the evils with which it has been attended have not been confined to the American Continent; but Her Majesty, having from the outset determined to take no part in that contest, has seen no reason to depart from the neutrality to which she has steadily adhered.

Disturbances have taken place in some of the frontier provinces of the Turkish Empire, and Her Majesty has instructed her Ambassador at Constantinople to attend a Conference to be held in that city by the representatives of the Powers who were parties to the Treaty of Paris of 1856. Her Majesty trusts that the questions to be dealt with in that conference will be settled in a manner consistent wiih the treaty engagements of the Allies, and in accordance with the just rights of the Sultan, and the welfare of the Christian inhabitants of his dominions.

Her Majesty's forces in China, together with those of the Emperor of the French, have lately been employed, in co-operation with those of the Emperor of China, in protecting some of the chief seats of British commerce in China from injury by the civil war which is laying waste portions of that vast empire.

Her Majesty commands us to inform you that she has concluded a commercial treaty with the King of the Belgians, by which the trade of Her Majesty's subjects

in Belgium will be placed, generally, on the footing of
the most favoured nation.

Gentlemen of the House of Commons,

Her Majesty commands us to convey to you her
warm acknowledgments for the liberal supplies which
you have granted for the services of the present year,
and Her Majesty thanks you for having also made provision towards placing Her Majesty's dockyards and
arsenals in a permanent state of defence.

My Lords and Gentlemen,

Her Majesty commands us to express to you the
admiration with which she has witnessed the undiminished zeal and the patriotic spirit which continue
to animate her Volunteer Forces, as well as the military
efficiency which they have attained.

Her Majesty has observed with satisfaction the kindly
intercourse which has subsisted between Her Majesty's
subjects and the numerous foreigners who have been
attracted this year to the United Kingdom, and Her
Majesty trusts that the interchange of mutual courtesies
will strengthen the foundations of international friendship and good-will.

Her Majesty has given her ready assent to an Act for
carrying into effect the treaty which Her Majesty has
concluded with the President of the United States for
the suppression of the Slave Trade, and Her Majesty
trusts that the co-operation of the United States' navy
with her own, may go far to extinguish the desolating
crime against which the treaty is directed.

Her Majesty earnestly hopes that the steps which
have been taken for rendering more effectual the aid

provided by Parliament for the extension of education among the poorer classes of her subjects will tend to promote an object of great national importance.

Her Majesty has given her willing assent to many measures of public utility which you have submitted to her during this session.

The severe distress which prevails in some of the manufacturing districts has inspired Her Majesty with deep concern and warm sympathy, mingled with admiration of the manly bearing and exemplary fortitude with which the pressure has been endured. Her Majesty trusts that the Act for enabling Boards of Guardians to provide Additional Means of Relief will mitigate that distress.

The Act for rendering more easy the Transfer of Land will add to the value of real property, and will make titles more simple and secure, and will diminish the expense attending purchases and sales.

The Act for the better Regulation of Parochial Assessments will tend to a more equal distribution of local taxation; while the Act for the better Administration of the Highways will, Her Majesty trusts, improve the means of communication in many parts of the country.

The Act for establishing Uniformity of Weights and Measures in Ireland will apply a remedy to inconveniences which have been much felt and complained of, as affecting the trading transactions in that part of the United Kingdom; and the Act for amending the Law relating to the Poor will extend to the poorer classes of Her Majesty's subjects in Ireland better means of obtaining relief and medical attendance.

The Act for the better Regulation of Merchant Shipping, Her Majesty trusts, will prove advantageous to the maritime commerce of the country.

In returning to your several counties, you will still have important duties to perform; and Her Majesty fervently prays that the blessing of Almighty God may assist your efforts, and may direct them to the attain· ment of the object of Her Majesty's constant solicitude, the welfare and happiness of her people.

PARLIAMENT VI.—SESSION V.

OPENING OF PARLIAMENT BY COMMISSION.

Date.—February 5th, 1863.

The Lords Commissioners were:—The Lord Chancellor; the Lord of the Privy Seal; the Lord Steward of the Household; the Lord Chamberlain of the Household; the Lord Stanley of Alderley.

The Cabinet.—First Lord of the Treasury, Right Hon. Viscount Palmerston; Lord Chancellor, Right Hon. Lord Westbury; President of the Council, Right Hon. Earl Granville; Lord of the Privy Seal, His Grace the Duke of Argyll; Home Secretary, Right Hon. Sir George Grey, Bart.; Foreign Secretary, Right Hon. Earl Russell; Colonial Secretary, His Grace the Duke of Newcastle; Secretary at War, Right Hon. Sir George Cornewall Lewis, Bart.; Secretary for India, Right Hon. Sir Charles Wood, Bart.; Chancellor of the Exchequer, Right Hon. William Ewart Gladstone; First Lord of the Admiralty, His Grace the Duke of Somerset: President of the Board of Trade, Right Hon. Thomas

Milner Gibson; Postmaster-General, Right Hon. Lord
Stanley of Alderley; Chief Commissioner of the Poor
Law Board, Right Hon. Charles P. Villiers.

The Queen's Speech.

My Lords and Gentlemen,

Her Majesty commands us to inform you that
since you were last assembled she has declared her
consent to a marriage between His Royal Highness the
Prince of Wales and Her Royal Highness the Princess
Alexandra, daughter of Prince Christian of Denmark;
and Her Majesty has concluded thereupon a treaty with
the King of Denmark, which will be laid before you.

The constant proofs which Her Majesty has received
of your attachment to her person and family, persuade
her that you will participate in her sentiments on an
event so interesting to Her Majesty, and which, with
the blessing of God, will, she trusts, prove so conducive
to the happiness of her family, and to the welfare of
her people.

Her Majesty doubts not that you will enable her to
make provision for such an establishment as you may
think suitable to the rank and dignity of the Heir
Apparent to the Crown of these realms.

A revolution having taken place in Greece, by which
the throne of that Kingdom has become vacant, the
Greek nation have expressed the strongest desire that
Her Majesty's son, Prince Alfred, should accept the
Greek crown.

This unsolicited and spontaneous manifestation of
good-will towards Her Majesty and her family, and of a
due appreciation of the benefits conferred by the prin-

ciples and practice of the British Constitution, could
not fail to be highly gratifying, and has been deeply felt
by Her Majesty.

But the diplomatic engagements of Her Majesty's
Crown, together with other weighty considerations,
have prevented Her Majesty from yielding to this general
wish of the Greek nation.

Her Majesty trusts, however, that the same principles
of choice which led the Greek nation to direct their
thoughts in the first instance towards His Royal Highness Prince Alfred, may guide them to the selection of a
Sovereign under whose sway the Kingdom of Greece
may enjoy the blessings of internal prosperity and of
peaceful relations with other States; and if in such a
state of things the Republic of the Seven Islands should
declare a deliberate wish to be united to the Kingdom
of Greece, Her Majesty would be prepared to take such
steps as may be necessary for a revision of the Treaty
of November 1815, by which that Republic was recon-
stituted, and was placed under the protection of the
British Crown.

Her Majesty's relations with foreign Powers continue
to be friendly and satisfactory.

Her Majesty has abstained from taking any step with
a view to induce a cessation of the conflict between the
contending parties in the North American States,
because it has not yet seemed to Her Majesty that any
such overtures could be attended with a probability of
success.

Her Majesty has viewed with the deepest concern the
desolating warfare which still rages in those regions;
and she has witnessed with heartfelt grief the severe

distress and suffering which that war has inflicted upon a large class of Her Majesty's subjects, but which have been borne by them with noble fortitude and with exemplary resignation. It is some consolation to Her Majesty to be led to hope that this suffering and this distress are rather diminishing than increasing, and that some revival of employment is beginning to take place in the manufacturing districts.

It has been most gratifying to Her Majesty to witness the abundant generosity with which all classes of her subjects in all parts of her Empire have contributed to relieve the wants of their suffering fellow-countrymen; and the liberality with which Her Majesty's colonial subjects have on this occasion given their aid has proved that, although their dwelling-places are far away, their hearts are still warm with unabated affection for the land of their fathers.

The Relief Committee have superintended with constant and laborious attention the distribution of the funds entrusted to their charge.

Her Majesty commands us to inform you that she has concluded with the King of the Belgians a Treaty of Commerce and Navigation, and a Convention respecting Joint-Stock Companies. That treaty and that convention will be laid before you.

Her Majesty has likewise given directions that there shall be laid before you papers relating to the affairs of Italy, of Greece, and of Denmark, and that papers shall also be laid before you relating to occurrences which have lately taken place in Japan.

Gentlemen of the House of Commons,

Her Majesty has directed that the estimates for

the ensuing year shall be laid before you. They have been prepared with a due regard to economy, and will provide for such reductions of expenditure as have appeared to be consistent with the proper efficiency of the public service.

My Lords and Gentlemen,

We are commanded by Her Majesty to inform you that, notwithstanding the continuance of the civil war in North America, the general commerce of the country during the past year has not sensibly diminished.

The treaty of commerce which Her Majesty concluded with the Emperor of the French has already been productive of results highly advantageous to both the nations to which it applies; and the general state of the revenue, notwithstanding many unfavourable circumstances, has not been unsatisfactory.

Her Majesty trusts that these results may be taken as proofs that the productive resources of the country are unimpaired.

It has been gratifying to Her Majesty to observe the spirit of order which happily prevails throughout her dominions, and which is so essential an element in the well-being and prosperity of nations.

Various measures of public usefulness and improvement will be submitted for your consideration ; and Her Majesty fervently prays that in all your deliberations the blessing of Almighty God may guide your counsels to the promotion of the welfare and happiness of her people.

Mover of Address in the Lords, Earl of Dudley.
Seconder ,, ,, Earl of Granard.
Mover of Address in the Commons, Mr. Calthorpe.
Seconder ,, ,, Mr. Bazley.

PROROGATION OF PARLIAMENT BY COMMISSION.

Date.—July 28th, 1863.

The Lords Commissioners were:—The Lord Chancellor; the Lord Steward of the Household; the Duke of Newcastle; the Lord Stanley of Alderley; and the Lord Wensleydale.

The Queen's Speech.

My Lords and Gentlemen,

We are commanded by Her Majesty to release you from further attendance in Parliament, and at the same time to convey to you Her Majesty's acknowledgments for the zeal and assiduity with which you have applied yourselves to the performance of your duties during the session now brought to a close.

Her Majesty has seen with deep regret the present condition of Poland. Her Majesty has been engaged, in concert with the Emperor of the French and the Emperor of Austria, in negotiations, the object of which has been to obtain the fulfilment of the stipulations of the Treaty of Vienna of 1815, on behalf of the Poles. Her Majesty trusts that those stipulations will be carried into execution, and that thus a conflict distressing to humanity, and dangerous to the tranquillity of Europe, may be brought to a close.

The civil war between the Northern and Southern States of the North American Union still, unfortunately, continues, and is necessarily attended with much evil, not only to the contending parties, but also to nations which have taken no part in the contest. Her Majesty, however, has seen no reason to depart from that strict neutrality which Her Majesty has observed from the beginning of the contest.

The Greek nation having chosen Prince William of Denmark for their King, Her Majesty is taking steps with a view to the union of the Ionian Islands with the Kingdom of Greece. For this purpose Her Majesty is in communication with the Powers who were parties to the Treaty of 1815, by which those Islands were placed under the protection of the British Crown; and the wishes of the Ionians on the subject of such union will be duly ascertained.

Several barbarous outrages committed in Japan upon British subjects have rendered it necessary for Her Majesty to demand reparation, and Her Majesty hopes that her demands will be conceded by the Japanese Government without its being necessary to resort to coercive measures to enforce them.

The Emperor of Brazil has thought fit to break off his diplomatic relations with Her Majesty, in consequence of Her Majesty not having complied with demands which she did not deem it possible to accede to. Her Majesty has no wish that this estrangement should continue, and would be glad to see her relations with Brazil re-established.

Gentlemen of the House of Commons,

Her Majesty commands us to convey to you her warm acknowledgments for the liberal supplies which you have granted for the services of the present year, and towards the permanent defence of Her Majesty's dockyards and arsenals; and Her Majesty commands us to thank you for the provision you have made for the establishment of His Royal Highness the Prince of Wales.

My Lords and Gentlemen,

The distress which the civil war in North America has inflicted upon a portion of Her Majesty's subjects in the manufacturing districts, and towards the relief of which such generous and munificent contributions have been made, has in some degree diminished, and Her Majesty has given her cordial assent to measures calculated to have a beneficial influence upon that unfortunate state of things.

Symptoms of a renewal of disturbances have manifested themselves in Her Majesty's Colony of New Zealand; but Her Majesty trusts that by wise and conciliatory measures, supported by adequate means of repression, order and tranquillity will be maintained in that valuable and improving colony.

Her Majesty has given her assent to a measure for augmenting the income of a considerable number of small benefices, and she trusts that this measure will be conducive to the interests of the Established Church.

Her Majesty has given her assent to an Act for the revision of a large portion of the Statute Book, by the removal of many Acts, which, although they have become obsolete or unnecessary, obstructed the condensation of the Statute Law.

Her Majesty has felt much pleasure in giving her assent to an Act for placing upon a well-defined footing that Volunteer Force which has added a most important element to the defensive means of the country.

Her Majesty has gladly given her assent to an Act

for carrying into effect the additional treaty concluded by Her Majesty with the President of the United States, for the more effectual suppression of the Slave Trade; and Her Majesty trusts that the honourable co-operation of the Government of the United States will materially assist Her Majesty in those endeavours which Great Britain has long been engaged in making to put an end to the perpetration of that most disgraceful crime. Her Majesty has assented with satisfaction to many other measures of public usefulness, the result of your labours during the present session.

It has been gratifying to Her Majesty to observe that, notwithstanding many adverse circumstances, the general prosperity of her Empire continues unimpaired. Though great local distress has been suffered in Great Britain from the effects of the civil war in America, and in Ireland from the results of three unfavourable seasons, the financial resources of the United Kingdom have been fully maintained, and its general commerce with the world at large has not been materially impaired.

It has been a source of great satisfaction to Her Majesty to find that her East Indian Possessions, rapidly recovering from the disasters which lately overspread them, are entering upon a course of improvement, social, financial, and commercial, which holds out good promise for the growing prosperity of those extensive regions.

On returning to your several counties you will still have important duties to perform ; and Her Majesty fervently prays that the blessing of Almighty God may attend your efforts to promote the welfare and happiness of her subjects, the object of her constant and earnest solicitude.

PARLIAMENT VI.—SESSION VI.

OPENING OF PARLIAMENT BY COMMISSION.

Date.—February 4th, 1864.

The Lords Commissioners were :—The Lord Chancellor; the Lord of the Privy Seal ; the Lord Steward of the Household ; the Lord Chamberlain of the Household ; and the Lord Stanley of Alderley.

The Cabinet.—First Lord of the Treasury, Right Hon. Viscount Palmerston ; Lord Chancellor, Right Hon. Lord Westbury; President of the Council, Right Hon. Earl Granville ; Lord of the Privy Seal, His Grace the Duke of Argyll ; Home Secretary, Right Hon. Sir George Grey, Bart. ; Foreign Secretary, Right Hon. Earl Russell ; Colonial Secretary, His Grace the Duke of Newcastle ; Secretary for War, Right Hon. Earl de Grey and Ripon ; Secretary for India, Right Hon. Sir Charles Wood, Bart.; Chancellor of the Exchequer, Right Hon. William Ewart Gladstone ; First Lord of the Admiralty, His Grace the Duke of Somerset; President of the Board of Trade, Right Hon. Thomas Milner Gibson ; Postmaster-General, Right Hon. Lord Stanley of Alderley ; Chancellor of the Duchy of Lancaster, Right Hon. Edward Cardwell ; Chief Commissioner of the Poor Law Board, Right Hon. C. P. Villiers.

The Queen's Speech.

My Lords and Gentlemen,

We are commanded by Her Majesty to assure you that Her Majesty has great satisfaction in recurring again to the advice and assistance of her Parliament.

Her Majesty is confident that you will share her

feeling of gratitude to Almighty God on account of the Princess of Wales having given birth· to a son, an event which has called forth from her faithful people renewed demonstrations of devoted loyalty and attachment to her person and family.

The state of affairs on the Continent of Europe has been the cause of great anxiety to Her Majesty. The death of the late King of Denmark brought into immediate application the stipulations of the Treaty of May 1852, concluded by Her Majesty, the Emperor of Austria, the Emperor of the French, the King of Prussia, the Emperor of Russia, the King of Sweden, the King of Denmark, and afterwards acceded to by the King of Hanover, the King of Saxony, the King of Wurtemberg, the King of the Belgians, the King of the Netherlands, the Queen of Spain, the King of Portugal, and the King of Sardinia. The treaty declared that it is conducive to the preservation of the balance of power and of the peace of Europe, that the integrity of the Danish Monarchy should be maintained, and that the several territories which have hitherto been under the sway of the King of Denmark should continue so to remain ; and for this purpose it was agreed that in the event of the death of the late King and of his uncle Prince Frederick without issue, His present Majesty, King Christian IX. should be acknowledged as succeeding to all the dominions then united under the sceptre of His Majesty the King of Denmark.

Her Majesty, actuated by the same desire to preserve the peace of Europe, which was one of the declared objects of all the Powers who were parties to that treaty, has been unremitting in her endeavours to

13

bring about a peaceful settlement of the differences
which on this matter have arisen between Germany and
Denmark, and to ward off the dangers which might
follow from a beginning of warfare in the north of
Europe; and Her Majesty will continue her efforts in
the interests of peace.

The barbarous murders and cruel assaults committed
in Japan upon subjects of Her Majesty, rendered it
necessary that demands should be made upon the
Japanese Government, and upon the Daimio by whose
retainers some of those outrages were committed. The
Government of the Tycoon complied with the demand
made upon them by Her Majesty's Government; and full
satisfaction having been made, the friendly relations
between the two Governments have continued unbroken.
But the Daimio Prince of Satsuma refused to comply
with the just and moderate demands which were made
upon him.

His refusal rendered measures of coercion necessary,
and Her Majesty regrets that while those measures have
brought the Daimio to an agreement for compliance,
they led incidentally to the destruction of a considerable
portion of the town of Kagosima.

Papers on this subject will be laid before you.

The insurrection which broke out last year among
some portion of the native inhabitants of New Zealand, still, unfortunately, continues; but there is reason
to hope that it will, before long, be put down.

Her Majesty commands us to inform you that she
has concluded a treaty with the Emperor of Austria,
the Emperor of the French, the King of Prussia, and
the Emperor of Russia, by which Her Majesty consents

to give up the protectorate of the Ionian Islands, and also agrees to the annexation of those islands to the Kingdom of Greece. This treaty shall be laid before you. Her Majesty is also negotiating a treaty with the King of the Hellenes for regulating the arrangements connected with the union of the Ionian Islands with the Kingdom of Greece.

Gentlemen of the House of Commons,

Her Majesty has directed the estimates for the ensuing year to be laid before you. They have been prepared with every attention to economy, and with a due regard to the efficiency of the public service.

My Lords and Gentlemen,

Her Majesty commands us to inform you that the condition of the country is, on the whole, satisfactory. The revenue has fully realised its expected amount, the commerce of the United Kingdom is increasing ; and while the distress in the manufacturing districts has been in some degree lessened, there is reason to look forward to an increased supply of cotton from various countries which have hitherto but scantily furnished our manufacturers with this material for their industry.

Her Majesty has directed that a Commission shall be issued for the purpose of revising the various forms of subscription and declaration required to be made by the clergy of the Established Church. A copy of that Commission will be laid before you.

Various measures of public usefulness will be submitted for your consideration.

Her Majesty commits, with confidence, the great

13 *

interests of the country to your wisdom and care; and she fervently prays that the blessing of Almighty God may attend your deliberations and prosper your counsels for the advancement of the welfare and happiness of her loyal and faithful people.

Mover of Address in the Lords, Marquess of Sligo.
*Seconder   „   „   Lord Abercrombie.
Mover of Address in the Commons, Lord Richard
                                    Grosvenor.
*Seconder   „   „   Mr. Göschen.

PROROGATION OF PARLIAMENT BY COMMISSION.

Date.—July 29th, 1864.

The Lords Commissioners were :—The Lord Chancellor; The Lord Steward of the Household; the Earl de Grey and Ripon; the Lord Chamberlain of the Household; and the Lord Wensleydale.

The Queen's Speech.

My Lords and Gentlemen,

We are commanded by Her Majesty to release you from further attendance in Parliament, and at the same time to convey to you Her Majesty's acknowledgments for the zeal and assiduity with which you have applied yourselves to the discharge of your duties during the session of Parliament now brought to a close.

Her Majesty commands us to inform you that she greatly regrets that the endeavours which she made, in concert with the Emperor of the French, the Emperor of Russia, and the King of Sweden, to bring about a reconciliation between the German Powers and the King of Denmark, were not successful, and that the hostilities which had been suspended (during the negotiations) were again resumed. Her Majesty trusts, however, that the negotiations which have been opened between the belligerents may restore peace to the north of Europe.

Her Majesty having addressed herself to the Powers who were contracting parties to the Treaty by which the Ionian Republic was placed under the protectorate of Great Britain, and having obtained their consent to the annexation of that Republic to the Kingdom of Greece, and the States of the Ionian Republic having agreed thereto, the Republic of the Seven Islands has been formally united to the Kingdom of Greece, and Her Majesty trusts that the union so made will conduce to the welfare and prosperity of all the subjects of His Majesty the King of the Hellenes.

Her Majesty's relations with the Emperor of China continue to be friendly, and the commerce of her subjects with the Chinese Empire is increasing.

Her Majesty has been engaged, in concert with the Emperor of Austria, the Emperor of the French, the King of Prussia, and the Emperor of Russia, in an endeavour to bring to effect an amicable arrangement of differences which have arisen between the Hospodar of Moldo-Wallachia and his Suzerain the Sultan. Her Majesty has the satisfaction to inform you that this endeavour has been successful.

Her Majesty deeply laments that the civil war in North America has not been brought to a close. Her Majesty will continue to observe a strict neutrality between the belligerents, and would rejoice at a friendly reconciliation between the contending parties.

Gentlemen of the House of Commons,

Her Majesty commands us to convey to you her warm acknowledgments for the liberal supplies which you have granted for the service of the present year, and towards the permanent defence of Her Majesty's dockyards and arsenals.

My Lords and Gentlemen,

Her Majesty has observed with satisfaction that the distress which the civil war in North America has created in some of the manufacturing districts has to a great extent abated, and Her Majesty trusts that increased supplies of the raw material of industry may be expected from countries by which it has hitherto been scantily furnished.

The revolt of certain tribes in New Zealand has not yet been quelled, but it is satisfactory to Her Majesty to know that a large portion of the native population of those islands have taken no part in this revolt.

It has been a source of much gratification to Her Majesty to observe the rapid development of the revenues of her East Indian possessions, and the general contentment of the people inhabiting those extensive regions.

Her Majesty has given her cordial assent to many measures of public usefulness, the result of your labours during the session now brought to a close.

The Act for extending to women and children employed in various trades the regulations applicable to factories in general, will tend materially to preserve the health and improve the education of those on whose behalf it was framed.

The Act for authorising the grant of Government annuities will encourage habits of prudence among the working-classes, and will afford them the means of securely investing the results of their industry.

The Act for authorising a further advance for public works in some of the manufacturing districts will contribute to alleviate the distress in these districts, and will afford the means of completing many works of much importance for the health of the population.

The Act for giving increased facilities for the construction of railways will diminish the expenses attendant upon the extension of these important channels of communication.

It has afforded to Her Majesty the most heartfelt satisfaction to observe the general well-being and contentment which prevail throughout her dominions, and to remark the progressive increase and development of the national resources, and to find that, after sufficiently providing for the public service, you have been able to make a material diminution in the taxation of the country.

On returning to your respective counties, you will still have important duties to perform, essentially connected with the linking together of the several classes of the community ; and Her Majesty fervently prays that the blessing of Almighty God may attend your exertions, and guide them to the object of Her Majesty's constant solicitude, the welfare and happiness of her people.

PARLIAMENT VI.—SESSION VII.

Opening of Parliament by Commission.

Date.—February 7th, 1865.

The Lords Commissioners were:—The Lord Chancellor; the First Lord of the Admiralty; the Lord Steward of the Household; the Lord Chamberlain of the Household; and Lord Stanley of Alderley.

The Cabinet.—First Lord of the Treasury, Right Hon. Viscount Palmerston; Lord Chancellor, Right Hon. Lord Westbury; President of the Council, Right Hon. Earl Granville; Lord of the Privy Seal, His Grace the Duke of Argyll; Home Secretary, Right Hon. Sir George Grey, Bart.; Foreign Secretary, Right Hon. Earl Russell; Colonial Secretary, Right Hon. Edward Cardwell; Secretary at War, Right Hon. Earl de Grey and Ripon; Secretary for India, Right Hon. Sir Charles Wood, Bart.; Chancellor of the Exchequer, Right Hon. William Ewart Gladstone; First Lord of the Admiralty, His Grace the Duke of Somerset; President of the Board of Trade, Right Hon. Thomas Milner Gibson; Postmaster-General, Right Hon. Lord Stanley of Alderley; Chancellor of the Duchy of Lancaster, Right Hon. Earl of Clarendon; Chief Commissioner of the Poor Law Board, Right Hon. Charles P. Villiers.

The Queen's Speech.

My Lords and Gentlemen,

We are commanded to assure you that Her Majesty has great satisfaction in recurring again to the advice and assistance of her Parliament.

The negotiations in which the Emperor of Austria
and the King of Prussia were engaged with the King of
Denmark were brought to a conclusion by a Treaty of
Peace, and the communications which Her Majesty
receives from foreign Powers lead her to entertain a
well-founded hope that no renewed disturbance of the
peace of Europe is to be apprehended.

The civil war in North America still, unhappily, continues. Her Majesty remains steadfastly neutral between the contending parties, and would rejoice at a
friendly reconciliation between them.

A Japanese Daimio, in rebellion against his Sovereign,
infringed the rights accorded by treaty to Great Britain,
and to certain other Powers ; and the Japanese Government having failed to compel him to desist from his
lawless proceedings, the Diplomatic Agents and the
naval commanders of Great Britain, France, the Netherlands, and the United States of North America, undertook a combined operation for the purpose of asserting
the rights which their respective Governments have
obtained by treaty. That operation has been attended
with complete success ; and the result has afforded
security for foreign commerce, and additional strength
to the Government of Japan, with which the relations of
Her Majesty are friendly.

Papers on this subject will be laid before you.

Her Majesty regrets that the conflict with some of
the native tribes in New Zealand has not yet been
brought to a close, but the successful efforts of Her
Majesty's regular forces, supported by those raised in
the Colony, have led to the submission of some of the
insurgents ; and those who are still in arms have been

informed of the equitable conditions on which their submission would be accepted.

Her Majesty has great satisfaction in giving her sanction to the meeting of a conference of delegates from her several North American Provinces, who, on invitation from Her Majesty's Governor-General, assembled at Quebec. Those delegates adopted resolutions having for their object a closer union of those Provinces under a central government. If those resolutions shall be approved by the Provincial Legislatures, a Bill will be laid before you for carrying this important measure into effect.

Her Majesty rejoices at the general tranquillity of her Indian dominions; but Her Majesty regrets that long-continued outrages on the persons and property of subjects of Her Majesty, and for which no redress could be had, have rendered it necessary to employ force to obtain satisfaction for the past and security for the future.

Her Majesty deeply laments the calamity which has recently occasioned great loss of life and property in Calcutta, and at other places in India. Prompt assistance was rendered by the officers of the Government, and generous contributions have been made in various parts of India to relieve the sufferings which have thus been occasioned.

Gentlemen of the House of Commons,

Her Majesty has directed the estimates for the ensuing year to be laid before you.

They have been prepared with every attention to economy, and with due regard to the efficiency of the public service.

My Lords and Gentlemen,

Her Majesty commands us to inform you that
the general condition of the country is satisfactory, and
that the revenue realises its estimated amount. The
distress which prevailed in some of the manufacturing
districts has greatly abated, and the Act passed for the
encouragement of public works in those districts has
been attended with useful results.

Ireland, during the past year, has had its share in the
advantage of a good harvest, and trade and manufactures are gradually extending in that part of the
kingdom.

Various measures of public usefulness will be submitted for your consideration.

Bills will be laid before you for the concentration of
all the courts of Law and Equity, with their attendant
offices, on a convenient site; a measure which, Her
Majesty trusts, will promote economy and despatch in
the administration of justice.

The important work for the revision of the Statute
Law, already carried to a considerable extent by recent
Acts of Parliament, will be completed by a Bill that will
be laid before you. Her Majesty hopes that this work
may be a step towards the formation of a digest of the
law.

Bills will also be submitted for your consideration for
for the amendment of the laws relating to Patents for
Inventions, and for conferring on the county courts an
equitable jurisdiction in causes of small amount.

Your assistance will also be invited to give effect to
certain recommendations made to the House of Commons

after inquiry directed by that House, into the operation of the laws regulating the Relief of the Poor.

A Bill will be laid before you founded on the Report of the Commission for inquiring into Public Schools; and Her Majesty has directed that a Commission shall be issued to inquire into endowed and other schools in England which have not been included in the recent inquiries relating to Popular Education.

Her Majesty commits, with confidence, the great interests of the country to your wisdom and care; and she fervently prays that the blessing of Almighty God may attend your counsels, and may guide your deliberations to the attainment of the object of her constant solicitude, the welfare and happiness of her people.

Mover of Address in the Lords, Earl of Charlemont.
Seconder „ „ Lord Houghton.
Mover of Address in the Commons, Sir Hedworth Williamson.
Seconder „ „ Mr. Hanbury Tracy.

PROROGATION OF PARLIAMENT BY COMMISSION.

Date.—July 6th, 1865.

The Lords Commissioners were :—The Lord President; the Lord Steward of the Household; the Lord Chamberlain of the Household; Viscount Eversley; and Lord Wensleydale.

The Queen's Speech.

My Lords and Gentlemen,

We are commanded by Her Majesty to release you from further attendance in Parliament, and at the same time to convey to you Her Majesty's acknowledgments for the zeal and assiduity with which you have applied yourselves to the discharge of your duties in the session now brought to a close.

We are further commanded to inform you that, as the present Parliament has now so nearly lasted the period assigned by law for the duration of Parliaments, that you could not enter upon another yearly session with advantage to the public interest, it is Her Majesty's intention immediately to dissolve the present Parliament, and to issue writs for the calling of a new one.

But Her Majesty cannot take leave of you without commanding us to express to you Her Majesty's deep sense of the zeal and public spirit which, during the six years of your existence as a Parliament, you have constantly displayed in the discharge of important functions, and tendering to you Her Majesty's warm acknowledgments of the many good measures which you have submitted for her acceptance, and which have greatly conduced to the diminution of the public burthens, and to the encouragement of the industry, to the increase of the wealth, and to the promotion of the welfare and happiness of Her Majesty's people.

We are commanded to inform you that Her Majesty's relations with foreign Powers are friendly and satisfactory, and she trusts that there are no questions pending which are likely to lead to any disturbance of the peace of Europe.

Her Majesty rejoices that the civil war in North America has ended, and she trusts that the evils caused by that long conflict may be repaired, and that prosperity may be restored in the States which have suffered from the contest.

Her Majesty regrets that the conferences and communications between Her Majesty's North American Provinces, on the subject of the union of those Provinces in a Confederation, have not yet led to a satisfactory result. Such a union would afford additional strength to those Provinces, and give facilities for many internal improvements. Her Majesty has received gratifying assurances of the devoted loyalty of her North American subjects.

Her Majesty rejoices at the continued tranquillity and increasing prosperity of her Indian dominions ; and she trusts that the large supply which those territories will afford of the raw material of manufacturing industry, together with the termination of the civil war in the United States of North America, will prevent the recurrence of the distress which long prevailed among the manufacturing population of some of the northern counties.

Gentlemen of the House of Commons,

Her Majesty commands us to convey to you her warm acknowledgments for the liberal supplies which you have granted to Her Majesty for the service of the present year, and towards the permanent defence of Her Majesty's dockyards and arsenals.

The commercial treaty, which Her Majesty has recently concluded with Prussia and the other States composing the German Commercial Union, has, by Her Majesty's commands, been laid before you. Her Majesty trusts that this treaty will contribute to the development of commercial relations between this country and Germany, and will promote the interests of the several countries which are parties to it.

Her Majesty commands us to assure you that her attention will continue to be directed to all such measures as may be calculated to extend and to place on a sound footing the trade between Her Majesty's dominions and foreign countries.

My Lords and Gentlemen,

Her Majesty has given her cordial assent to many measures of public usefulness, the result of your labours in the session now brought to a close.

The Act for rendering the expenses incurred for the Support of the Poor chargeable upon the whole of a Union, instead of being confined to separate parishes, will diminish the hardship inflicted upon the labouring poor by reason of removals from parish to parish.

The Partnership Amendment Act will tend to encourage the profitable employment of capital.

The Courts of Justice Building and Concentration Acts will, it is hoped, lessen the expenses and shorten the duration of legal proceedings.

The Clerical Subscription Act, founded on the recommendation of a Royal Commission, will remove objections which have been felt to the number and variety of the forms of subscription and declaration hitherto required of the clergy.

The management and discipline of prisons will be improved by the Act for the consolidation and amendment of the laws on that subject.

The County Court Equitable Jurisdiction Act will give a useful extension to the local administration of justice.

The Act for consolidating the Comptrollership of the Exchequer with the Board of Audit will tend to increase the efficiency of the arrangements for auditing the public accounts.

The Act for establishing the Record of Titles in Ireland will render more easy and secure the transfer of land.

The Act for amending the laws which govern the Constabulary Force in Ireland will tend to prevent the recurrence of such disorders as happened last year at Belfast.

The Colonial Naval Defence Act has removed restrictions which have hitherto prevented the Colonies from taking effectual measures for their own defence against attacks by sea.

Her Majesty has also gladly given her assent to many other useful measures of less general importance.

The electors of the United Kingdom will soon be called upon again to choose their representatives in Parliament; and Her Majesty fervently prays that the blessing of Almighty God may attend their proceedings, and may guide them towards the attainment of the object of Her Majesty's constant solicitude, the welfare and happiness of her people.

PARLIAMENT VII.—SESSION I.

OPENING OF PARLIAMENT BY HER MAJESTY IN PERSON.

Date.—February 5th, 1866.

The Cabinet.—First Lord of the Treasury, Right Hon. Earl Russell, K.G.; Lord Chancellor, Right Hon. Lord Cranworth; President of the Council, Right Hon. Earl Granville, K.G.; Lord of the Privy Seal, His Grace the

Duke of Argyll, K.T.; Home Secretary, Right Hon. Sir George Grey, Bart., G.C.B.; Foreign Secretary, Right Hon. Earl of Clarendon, K.G.; Colonial Secretary, Right Hon. Edward Cardwell; Secretary at War, Most Hon. the Marquess of Hartington; Secretary for India, Right Hon. Earl de Grey and Ripon; Chancellor of the Exchequer, Right Hon. William Ewart Gladstone; First Lord of the Admiralty, His Grace the Duke of Somerset, K.G.; President of the Board of Trade, Right Hon. Robert Milner Gibson; Postmaster-General, Right Hon. Lord Stanley of Alderley; Chancellor of the Duchy of Lancaster, Right Hon. George Joachim Goschen; Chief Commissioner of the Poor Law Board, Right Hon. Charles P. Villiers.

The Queen's Speech.

My Lords and Gentlemen,

It is with great satisfaction that I have recourse to your assistance and advice.

I have recently declared my consent to a marriage between my daughter, Princess Helena, and Prince Christian of Schleswig-Holstein Sonderbourg Augustenbourg. I trust this union may be prosperous and happy.

The death of my beloved uncle, the King of the Belgians, has affected me with profound grief. I feel great confidence, however, that the wisdom which he evinced during his reign will animate his successor, and preserve for Belgium her independence and prosperity.

My relations with foreign Powers are friendly and satisfactory, and I see no cause to fear any disturbance of the general peace.

14

The meeting of the fleets of France and England in the ports of the respective countries has tended to cement the amity of the two nations, and to prove to the world their friendly concert in the promotion of peace.

I have observed with satisfaction that the United States, after terminating successfully the severe struggle in which they were so long engaged, are wisely repairing the ravages of civil war. The abolition of slavery is an event calling forth the cordial sympathies and congratulations of this country, which has always been foremost in showing its abhorrence of an institution repugnant to every feeling of justice and humanity.

I have at the same time the satisfaction to inform you that the exertions and perseverance of my naval squadron have reduced the slave trade on the West Coast of Africa within very narrow limits.

A correspondence has taken place between my Government and that of the United States, with respect to injuries inflicted on American commerce by cruisers under the Confederate flag. Copies of this correspondence will be laid before you.

The renewal of diplomatic relations with Brazil has given me much satisfaction; and I acknowledge with pleasure that the good offices of my Ally, the King of Portugal, have contributed essentially to this happy result.

I have to regret the interruption of peace between Spain and Chili. The good offices of my Government, in conjunction with those of the Government of the Emperor of the French, have been accepted by Spain,

and it is my earnest hope that the causes of disagreement may be removed in a manner honourable and
satisfactory to both countries.

The negotiations which have been long pending in
Japan, and which have been conducted with great ability
by my Minister in that country, in conjunction with the
representatives of my Allies in Japan, have been brought
to a conclusion, which merits my entire approbation.
The existing treaties have been ratified by the Mikado ;
it has been stipulated that the tariff shall be revised in
a manner favourable to commerce, and that the indem-
nity due under the terms of the Convention of October
1864 shall be punctually discharged.

I have concluded a Treaty of Commerce with the
Emperor of Austria, which, I trust, will open to that
Empire the blessings of extended commerce, and be
productive of important benefits to both countries.

The deplorable events which have occurred in the
Island of Jamaica, have induced me to provide at once
for an impartial inquiry, and for the due maintenance of
authority during that inquiry, by appointing a distinguished military officer as Governor and Commander
of the Forces. I have given him the assistance of two
able and learned Commissioners, who will aid him in
examining into the origin, nature, and circumstances of
the recent outbreak, and the measures adopted in the
course of its suppression. The Legislature of Jamaica
has proposed that the present political constitution of
the island should be replaced by a new form of government. A Bill upon this subject will be submitted for
your consideration.

Papers on these occurrences will be laid before you.

14 *

Papers on the present state of New Zealand will be laid before you.

I have given directions for the return to this country of the greater portion of my regular forces employed in that colony.

I watch with interest the proceedings which are still in progress in British North America, with a view to a closer union among the Provinces, and I continue to attach great importance to that object.

I have observed with great concern the extensive prevalence, during the last few months, of a virulent distemper among cattle in Great Britain, and it is with deep regret, and with sincere sympathy for the sufferers, that I have learned the severe losses which it has caused in many counties and districts. It is satisfactory to know that Ireland, and a considerable part of Scotland, are as yet free from this calamity; and I trust that by the precautions suggested by experience, and by the Divine blessing on the means which are now being employed, its further extension may be arrested.

The orders which have been made by the Lords of my Privy Council, by virtue of the powers vested in them by law, with a view to prevent the spreading of this disease, will be laid before you; and your attention will be called to the expediency of the amendment of the law relating to a subject so deeply affecting the interests of my people.

Gentlemen of the House of Commons,

I have directed that the estimates of the ensuing year shall be laid before you. They have been prepared with a due regard to economy, and are at the same time consistent with the maintenance of efficiency in the public service.

The condition of trade is satisfactory.

My Lords and Gentlemen,

A conspiracy, adverse alike to authority, property, and religion, and disapproved and condemned alike by all who are interested in their maintenance, without distinction of creed or class, has unhappily appeared in Ireland. The constitutional power of the ordinary tribunals has been exerted for its repression, and the authority of the law has been firmly and impartially vindicated.

A Bill will be submitted to you, founded on the report of the Royal Commission, on the subject of capital punishment, which I have directed to be laid before you.

Bills will be laid before you for amending and consolidating the laws relating to Bankruptcy, and for other improvements in the law.

Measures will also be submitted to you for extending the system of public audit to branches of receipt and expenditure, which it has not hitherto reached, and for amending the provisions of the law with respect to certain classes of legal pensions.

Your attention will be called to the subject of the oaths taken by Members of Parliament, with a view to avoid unnecessary declarations, and to remove invidious distinctions between members of different religious communities in matters of legislation.

I have directed that information should be procured in reference to the rights of voting in the election of

Members to serve in Parliament for counties, cities, and boroughs.

When that information is complete, the attention of Parliament will be called to the result thus obtained, with a view to such improvements in the laws which regulate the rights of voting in the election of Members of the House of Commons as may tend to strengthen our free institutions and conduce to the public welfare.

In this, and in all other deliberations, I fervently pray that the blessing of Almighty God may guide your counsels to the promotion of the happiness of my people.

Mover of Address in the Lords, Marquess of Normanby.

Seconder ,, ,, Earl of Morley.

Mover of Address in the Commons, Lord Frederick Cavendish.

Seconder ,, ,, Mr. Graham.

PROROGATION OF PARLIAMENT BY COMMISSION.

Date.—August 10th, 1866.

The Lords Commissioners were :—The Lord Chancellor; the Lord of the Privy Seal; the Earl of Malmesbury; the Earl of Bradford; and the Earl of Cadogan.

The Queen's Speech.

My Lords and Gentlemen,

We are commanded by Her Majesty, in releasing you from a protracted session, to convey to you Her Majesty's acknowledgments for the zeal and assiduity with which you have applied yourselves to your Parliamentary duties.

Her Majesty has much satisfaction in informing you that her relations with foreign Powers are on the most friendly footing.

Her Majesty has watched with anxious interest the progress of the war which has recently convulsed a great portion of the continent of Europe. Her Majesty cannot have been an indifferent spectator of events which have seriously affected the position of Sovereigns and Princes with whom Her Majesty is connected by the closest ties of relationship and friendship ; but Her Majesty has not deemed it expedient to take part in a contest in which neither the honour of her Crown nor the interest of her people demanded any active intervention on her part. Her Majesty can only express an earnest hope that the negotiations now in progress between the belligerent Powers may lead to such an arrangement as may lay the foundation of a secure and lasting peace.

A wide-spread treasonable conspiracy, having for its objects the subversion of Her Majesty's authority in Ireland, the confiscation of property, and the establishment of a Republic having its seat in Ireland but deriving its principal support from naturalised citizens of a foreign and friendly State, compelled Her Majesty at the commencement of the present session to assent to a measure, recommended by her representative in Ireland, for the temporary suspension in that part of Her Majesty's dominions of the Habeas Corpus Act. That measure, firmly but temperately acted on by the Irish Executive, had the effect of repressing any outward manifestations of treasonable intentions, and of causing the withdrawal from Ireland of the greater portion of those foreign agents by whom the conspiracy was mainly fostered.

The leaders, however, of this movement were not deterred from prosecuting their criminal designs beyond the limits of Her Majesty's dominions. They even attempted from the territories of the United States of America an inroad upon the peaceful subjects of Her Majesty in her North American provinces. That attempted inroad, however, only served to manifest in the strongest manner the loyalty and devotion of Her Majesty's subjects in those provinces, who, without exception of creed or origin, united in defence of their Sovereign and their country. It served also to show the good faith and scrupulous attention to international rights displayed by the Government of the United States, whose active interference, by checking any attempted invasion of a friendly State, mainly contributed to protect Her Majesty's dominions against the evils of a predatory inroad.

Her Majesty would have been rejoiced, at the close of the present session, to be enabled to put an end to the exceptional legislation which she was compelled to sanction at its commencement; but the protection which Her Majesty owes to her loyal subjects leaves her no alternative but that of assenting to the advice of her Parliament to continue till their next meeting the provisions of the existing law. Her Majesty looks anxiously forward to the time when she may be enabled to revert to the ordinary provisions of the law.

Gentlemen of the House of Commons,

Her Majesty commands us to thank you for the liberal provision which you have made for the public service, and for the naval and military defences of the country.

My Lords and Gentlemen,

Her Majesty has seen with great concern the monetary pressure which, for a period of unprecedented duration, has weighed upon the interests of the country. The consequent embarrassment appeared at one moment to be aggravated by so general a feeling of distrust and of alarm, that Her Majesty, in order to restore confidence, authorised her Ministers to recommend to the Directors of the Bank of England a course of proceeding suited to the emergency.

This, though justifiable under the circumstances, might have led to an infringement of the law, but Her Majesty has the satisfaction of being able to inform you that no such infringement has taken place, and that, although the monetary pressure is not yet sensibly mitigated, alarm is subsiding; and the state of trade being sound, and the condition of the people generally prosperous, Her Majesty entertains a sanguine hope that confidence will soon be restored.

Her Majesty has observed with satisfaction, and with deep gratitude to Almighty God, that He has so far favoured the measures which have been adopted for staying the fearful pestilence which has visited our herds and flocks, that its destructive effects have been in a great measure checked, and that there is reason to hope for its entire extinction at no distant period. In the meantime, Her Majesty has given her willing assent to a measure which has been introduced for the relief of those districts which have suffered the most severely from its visitation.

Her Majesty regrets that this country has at length been subjected to the fearful visitation of cholera which has prevailed in other European countries, but from which it has hitherto been happily exempt. Her Majesty has directed that a Form of Prayer to Almighty God, suitable to the present exigency, should be offered up in all the churches of this realm; and Her Majesty has given her cordial approval to legislative measures sanctioning the adoption by local authorities of such steps as science and experience have shown to be most effectual for the check of this fearful malady.

Her Majesty hopes that those in whose hands so large and beneficial an authority is left will not be slow to execute the powers entrusted to them, and that they will be seconded in their endeavours by all who have at heart the safety and well-being of her people. In connection with this subject, Her Majesty hopes that a Bill, to which she has given her ready assent, for improving the navigation of the river Thames, may incidentally be conducive to the public health.

Her Majesty has great satisfaction in congratulating the country, and the world at large, on the successful accomplishment of the great design of connecting Europe and America by the means of an electric telegraph. It is hardly possible to anticipate the full extent of the benefits which may be conferred on the human race by this signal triumph of scientific enterprise; and Her Majesty has pleasure in expressing her deep sense of what is due to the private energy which, in spite of repeated failure and discouragement, has at length, for the second time, succeeded in establishing direct communication between the two continents.

Her Majesty trusts that no impediment may occur to interrupt the success of this great undertaking, calculated, as it undoubtedly is, to cement yet closer the ties which bind Her Majesty's North American colonies to their mother country, and to promote the unrestricted intercourse and friendly feeling which it is most desirable should subsist between Her Majesty's dominions and the great Republic of the United States.

Her Majesty is aware that, in returning to your respective homes, many of you have duties to perform hardly less important than those which belong to you in your legislative capacity. Her Majesty places full reliance on the loyalty and devotion with which you will discharge those duties; and Her Majesty earnestly prays that your influence and efforts may, under the blessing of Divine Providence, tend to the general welfare, prosperity, and contentment of her people.

PARLIAMENT VII.—SESSION II.

OPENING OF PARLIAMENT BY HER MAJESTY IN PERSON.

Date.—February 5th, 1867.

The Cabinet.—First Lord of the Treasury, Right Hon. Earl of Derby, K.G.; Lord Chancellor, Right Hon. Lord Chelmsford; President of the Council, His Grace the Duke of Buckingham and Chandos, K.G.; Lord of the Privy Seal, Right Hon. Earl of Malmesbury, G.C.B.; Home Secretary, Right Hon. Spencer Horatio Walpole; Foreign Secretary, Right Hon. Lord Stanley; Colonial Secretary, Right Hon. Earl of Carnarvon;

Secretary at War, Right Hon. General Peel; Secretary for India, Right Hon. Viscount Cranbourne; Chancellor of the Exchequer, Right Hon. Benjamin Disraeli; First Lord of the Admiralty, Right. Hon. Sir J. Somerset Pakington, Bart., G.C.B.; President of the Board of Trade, Right Hon. Sir Stafford Henry Northcote, Bart., C.B.; Chief Commissioner of Works and Public Buildings, Right Hon. Lord John James Robert Manners; Chief Commissioner of the Poor Law Board, Right Hon. Gathorne Hardy; Chief Secretary for Ireland, Right Hon. Lord Naas.

The Queen's Speech.

My Lords and Gentlemen,

In again recurring to your advice and assistance, I am happy to inform you that my relations with foreign Powers are on a friendly and satisfactory footing.

I hope that the termination of the War in which Prussia, Austria, and Italy have been engaged may lead to the establishment of a durable peace in Europe.

I have suggested to the Government of the United States a mode by which questions pending between the two countries, arising out of the late civil war, may receive amicable solution, and which, if met, as I trust it will be, in a corresponding spirit, will remove all grounds of possible misunderstanding, and promote relations of cordial friendship.

The war between Spain and the Republics of Chili and Peru still continues, the good offices of my Government, in conjunction with that of the Emperor of the French, having failed to effect a reconciliation. If, either by agreement between the parties themselves, or by the mediation of any other friendly Power, peace shall be restored, the object which I have had in view will equally be attained.

Discontent, prevailing in some provinces of the Turkish Empire, has broken out in actual insurrection in Crete. In common with my Allies, the Emperor of the French and the Emperor of Russia, I have abstained from any active interference in these internal disturbances, but our joint efforts have been directed to bringing about improved relations between the Porte and its Christian subjects, not inconsistent with the sovereign rights of the Sultan.

The protracted negotiations which arose out of the acceptance by Prince Charles of Hohenzollern of the government of the Danubian Principalities have been happily terminated by an arrangement to which the Porte has given its ready adhesion, and which has been sanctioned by the concurrence of all the Powers signitaries of the Treaty of 1856.

Resolutions in favour of a more intimate union of the provinces of Canada, Nova Scotia, and New Brunswick have been passed by their several Legislatures; and delegates duly authorised, and representing all classes of Colonial party and opinion, have concurred in the conditions upon which such an Union may be best effected. In accordance with their wishes a Bill will be submitted to you, which, by the consolidation of Colonial interests and resources, will give strength to the several provinces as members of the same Empire and animated by feelings of loyalty to the same Sovereign.

I have heard with deep sorrow that the calamity of

famine has pressed heavily on my subjects in some parts of India. Instructions were issued to my Government in that country to make the utmost exertions to mitigate the distress which prevailed during the autumn of last year. The blessing of an abundant harvest has since that time materially improved the condition of the suffering districts.

The persevering efforts and unscrupulous assertions of treasonable conspirators abroad have, during the last autumn, excited the hopes of some disaffected persons in Ireland, and the apprehensions of the loyal population; but the firm yet temperate exercise of the powers entrusted to the Executive, and the hostility manifested against the conspiracy by men of all classes and creeds, have greatly tended to restore public confidence, and have rendered hopeless any attempt to disturb the general tranquillity. I trust that you may consequently be enabled to dispense with the continuance of an exceptional legislation for that part of my dominions.

I acknowledge, with deep thankfulness to Almighty God, the great decrease that has taken place in the cholera, and in the pestilence which has attacked our cattle; but the continued prevalence of the latter in some foreign countries, and its occasional re-appearance in this, will still render necessary some special measures of precaution; and I trust that the visitation of the former will lead to increased attention to those sanitary measures which experience has shown to be the best preventive.

Estimating as of the highest importance an adequate supply of pure and wholesome water, I have directed the issue of a Commission to inquire into the best means of permanently securing such a supply for the metropolis, and for the principal towns in densely-peopled districts of the Kingdom.

Gentlemen of the House of Commons,

I have directed the estimates for the ensuing year to be laid before you. They have been prepared with a due regard to economy, and to the requirements of the public service.

You will, I am assured, give your ready assent to a moderate expenditure calculated to improve the condition of my soldiers, and to lay the foundation of an efficient army of reserve.

My Lords and Gentlemen,

Your attention will again be called to the state of the representation of the people in Parliament; and I trust that your deliberations, conducted in a spirit of moderation and mutual forbearance, may lead to the adoption of measures which, without unduly disturbing the balance of political power, shall freely extend the elective franchise.

The frequent occurrence of disagreements between employers of labour and their workmen, causing much private suffering and public loss, and occasionally leading, as is alleged, to acts of outrage and violence, has induced me to issue a Commission to inquire into and report upon the organisation of trades' unions and other associations, whether of workmen or employers, with power to suggest any improvement of the law for their mutual benefit. Application will be made to you for Parliamentary powers which will be necessary to make this inquiry effective.

I have directed Bills to be laid before you for the extension of the beneficial provisions of the Factory Acts to other trades specially reported on by the Royal Commission on the Employment of Children, and for the better regulation, according to the principles of those Acts, of workshops where women and children are largely employed.

The condition of the mercantile marine has attracted my serious attention. Complaints are made that the supply of seamen is deficient, and that the provisions for their health and discipline on board ship are imperfect. Measures will be submitted to you with a view to increase the efficiency of this important service.

I have observed with satisfaction the regulations recently introduced into the Navigation Laws of France. I have expressed to the Emperor of the French my readiness to submit to Parliament a proposal for the extinction, on equitable terms, of the exemptions from local charges on shipping which are still enjoyed by a limited number of individuals in British ports ; and His Imperial Majesty has, in anticipation of this step, already admitted British ships to the advantage of the new law. A Bill upon this subject will forthwith be laid before you.

A Bill will also be submitted to you for making better provision for the arrangement of the affairs of railway companies which are unable to meet their engagements.

Measures will be submitted to you for improving the management of sick and other poor in the metropolis, and for a redistribution of some of the charges of relief therein.

Your attention will also be called to the amendment of the Law of Bankruptcy; to the consolidation of the Courts of Probate and Divorce and Admiralty; and to the means of disposing with greater despatch and frequency of the increasing business in the superior courts of common law, and at the assizes.

The relations between landlord and tenant in Ireland have engaged my anxious attention, and a Bill will be laid before you which, without interfering with the rights of property, will offer direct encouragement to occupiers of land to improve their holdings, and provide a simple mode of obtaining compensation for permanent improvements.

I commend to your careful consideration these and other measures which will be brought before you; and I pray that your labours may, under the blessing of Providence, conduce to the prosperity of the country and the happiness of my people.

Mover of Address in the Lords, Earl Beauchamp.
Seconder   „   „   Lord Delamere.
Mover of Address in the Commons, Mr. De Grey.
Seconder   „   „   Mr Graves.

PROROGATION OF PARLIAMENT BY COMMISSION.
Date.—August 21st, 1867.

The Lords Commissioners were:—The Lord Chancellor; the Duke of Richmond; the Lord Chamberlain; the Duke of Beaufort; and the Earl of Devon.

The Queen's Speech.

My Lords and Gentlemen,

I am happy to be enabled to release you from the labours of a long and more than usually eventful session, and to offer you my acknowledgments for the successful diligence with which you have applied your-selves to your Parliamentary duties.

My relations with foreign countries continue on a friendly footing.

At the commencement of the present year great fears were entertained that differences which have arisen between France and Prussia might have led to a war of which it was impossible to foresee the ultimate result. Happily, the advice tendered by my Government, and by those of the other neutral States, aided by the moderation of the two Powers chiefly interested, sufficed to avert the threatened calamity; and I trust that no ground at present exists for apprehending any disturb-ance of the general peace.

The communications which I have made to the reigning Monarch of Abyssinia, with a view to obtain the release of the British subjects whom he detains in his dominions, have, I regret to say, thus far proved in-effectual. I have therefore found it necessary to address to him a peremptory demand for their immediate libe-ration, and to take measures for supporting that demand should it ultimately be found necessary to resort to force.

The treasonable conspiracy in Ireland, to which I have before called your attention, broke out in the early part of the present year in a futile attempt at insurrec-tion. That it was suppressed, almost without blood-shed, is due not more to the disciplined valour of my troops and to the admirable conduct of the police, than to the general loyalty of the population and the absence of any token of sympathy with the insurgents on the part of any considerable portion of my subjects. I rejoice that the supremacy of the law was vindicated without imposing on me the painful necessity of sacrificing a single life.

The Bill for the abolition of certain local exemptions from taxation enabled me to avail myself of a liberal concession made, in anticipation, by the Emperor of the French, whereby several taxes were removed which pressed heavily upon British shipping.

I have concluded a Postal Convention with the United States of America, whereby the rate of postage between the two countries will be diminished by one half, and further arrangements are in progress for increasing the intercourse between this country and the continent of North America.

The Act for the Union of the British North American Provinces is the final accomplishment of a scheme long contemplated, whereby those Colonies, now combined in one dominion, may be expected not only to gain additional strength for the purpose of defence against external aggression, but may be united among themselves by fresh ties of mutual interest, and attached to the mother country by the only bonds which can effectually secure such important dependencies, those of loyalty to the Crown and attachment to the British connection.

Gentlemen of the House of Commons,

I thank you for the liberal supplies which you have voted for the public service.

My Lords and Gentlemen,

I have had great satisfaction in giving my assent to a Bill for amending the representation of the people

15 *

in Parliament. I earnestly trust that the extensive and liberal measure which you have passed may effect a durable settlement of a question which has long engaged public attention ; and that the large number of my subjects who will be for the first time admitted to the exercise of the Elective Franchise may, in the discharge of the duties thereby devolved upon them, prove themselves worthy of the confidence which Parliament has reposed in them.

It is gratifying to me to find that the lengthened consideration which you have necessarily given to this important question has not prevented your entering on many subjects to which your attention was directed at the commencement of the session, and particularly to such as have immediate reference to the well-being of the industrial classes.

I have had especial pleasure in giving my assent to Bills for extending to various trades, with such modifications as have been found necessary, the provisions of the Factory Acts, the success of which has proved the possibility of combining effectual protection to the labour of women and children with a due consideration for the interests of the trades immediately concerned.

I confidently anticipate from the operation of the present Acts the same improvement in the physical, social, and moral condition of the working classes, which has been found to accompany the application of the Acts to those trades to which they have been hitherto confined.

The restraints alleged to be imposed on workmen and their employers by trade unions and other associations appeared to me to call for inquiry ; and the revelations derived from the examination before the Commission, to which you gave your legislative sanction, have disclosed a state of things which will demand your most earnest attention.

The administration of the Poor Laws, which generally has conferred great benefit on the community, and especially on the poor themselves, requires constant supervision ; and I have readily assented to a Bill which, applied to the Metropolis alone, will tend to equalise the pressure of taxation and improve the treatment of the sick poor, whose condition will be greatly benefited by your well-considered legislation.

The Bill for the regulation of the merchant shipping contains important provisions calculated to add to the health and comfort of those engaged in the mercantile marine.

These and other valuable amendments of the law have been the result of your labours during the present session ; and in returning to your homes you will carry with you the gratifying consciousness that your time and pains have not been misapplied, and that they have resulted in a series of measures which I hope and earnestly pray may contribute to the welfare of the country and the contentment and happiness of my people.

PARLIAMENT VII.—SESSION III.

OPENING OF PARLIAMENT BY COMMISSION.

Date.—November 19th, 1867.

The Lords Commissioners were :—The Lord Chancellor ; the Lord President of the Council ; the Lord of the Privy Seal; the Duke of Buckingham; and the Earl of Cadogan.

The Cabinet.—First Lord of the Treasury, Right Hon. Earl of Derby, K.G.; Lord Chancellor, Right Hon. Lord Chelmsford; President of the Council, His Grace the Duke of Marlborough; Lord of the Privy Seal, Right Hon. Earl of Malmesbury, G.C.B.; Home Secretary, Right Hon. Gathorne Hardy; Foreign Secretary, Right Hon. Lord Stanley; Colonial Secretary, His Grace the Duke of Buckingham and Chandos, K.G.; Secretary at War, Right Hon. Sir John Somerset Pakington, Bart.; Secretary for India, Right Hon. Sir Stafford Henry Northcote, Bart., C.B.; Chancellor of the Exchequer, Right Hon. Benjamin Disraeli; First Lord of the Admiralty, Right Hon. Henry Thomas Lowry Corry; President of the Board of Trade, His Grace the Duke of Richmond; Chief Commissioner of Works and Public Buildings, Right Hon. Lord John James Robert Manners; Chief Secretary for Ireland, Right Hon. Lord Naas.

The Queen's Speech.

My Lords and Gentlemen,

In again applying to you for your advice and assistance, I regret that I have found it necessary to call for your attendance at an unusually and, probably, to many of you, an inconvenient season.

The Sovereign of Abyssinia, in violation of all international law, continues to hold in captivity several of my subjects, some of whom have been especially accredited to him by myself; and his persistent disregard of friendly representations has left me no alternative but that of making a peremptory demand for the liberation of my subjects, and supporting it by an adequate force.

I have accordingly directed an expedition to be sent for that purpose alone, and I confidently rely upon the support and co-operation of my Parliament in my endeavour at once to relieve their countrymen from an unjust imprisonment, and to vindicate the honour of my Crown.

I have directed that papers on the subject shall be forthwith laid before you.

I receive from all foreign Powers assurances of their friendly feelings, and I see no reason to apprehend the disturbance of the general peace of Europe.

A band of Italian volunteers, without authority from their own Sovereign, having invaded the Papal territory, and threatened Rome itself, the Emperor of the French felt himself called upon to despatch an expedition for the protection of the Sovereign Pontiff and his dominions ; that object having been accomplished, and the defeat and dispersion of the volunteer force having relieved the Papal territory from the danger of external invasion, I trust that His Imperial Majesty will find himself enabled, by an early withdrawal of his troops, to remove any possible ground of misunderstanding between His Majesty's Government and that of the King of Italy.

The treasonable conspiracy, commonly known as Fenianism, baffled and repressed in Ireland, has assumed in England the form of organised violence and assassination. These outrages require to be rigorously put down, and I rely for their effectual suppression upon the firm administration of the law, and the loyalty of the great mass of my subjects.

Gentlemen of the House of Commons,

The estimates for the ensuing year are in course of preparation, and will in due time be laid before you. They will be framed with a view to economy, and to the necessary requirements of the public service.

My Lords and Gentlemen,

As a necessary sequel to the legislation of the last session, Bills will be laid before you for amending the representation of the people in Scotland and Ireland.

I have reason to believe that the Commissioners appointed to inquire into and report upon the boundaries of existing boroughs, as well as of the proposed division of counties and newly-enfranchised boroughs, have made considerable progress in their inquiries, and no time will be lost after the receipt of their report in laying before you their recommendations for your consideration and decision.

A Bill will also be presented to you for the more effectual prevention of bribery and corruption at Elections.

The Public Schools Bill, which has already been more than once submitted to Parliament, will again be laid before you.

The general question of the education of the people requires your most serious attention, and I have no doubt you will approach the subject with a full appreciation both of its vital importance and of its acknowledged difficulty.

Measures will be submitted to you during the present session for amending and consolidating the various Acts relating to the mercantile marine.

The exemption which the country has now for some time enjoyed from the cattle plague, affords a favourable opportunity for considering such permanent enactments as may relieve the home trade from vexatious restrictions, and facilitate the introduction, under due regulation, of foreign cattle for home consumption.

Measures for the amendment of the law, which have been deferred under the pressure of more urgent business, will be submitted for your consideration.

Other questions, apparently calling for legislative action, have been referred to Commissions, whose reports, as they shall be received, shall, without delay, be laid before Parliament.

Mover of Address in the Lords, Earl Brownlow.
Seconder ,, ,, Lord Hylton.
Mover of Address in the Commons, Mr. Hart Dyke.
Seconder ,, ,, Colonel Hogg.

PROROGATION OF PARLIAMENT BY COMMISSION.

Date.—July 31st, 1868.

The Lords Commissioners were:—The Lord Chancellor; the Lord of the Privy Seal; the Duke of Beaufort; the Duke of Buckingham; and the Earl of Devon.

The Queen's Speech.

My Lords and Gentlemen,

I am happy to be enabled to release you from your labours, and to offer you my acknowledgments for the diligence with which you have applied yourselves to your Parliamentary duties.

My relations with foreign Powers remain friendly and satisfactory. I have no reason to apprehend that Europe will be exposed to the calamity of war, and my policy will continue to be directed to secure the blessings of peace.

I announced to you at the beginning of this session that I had directed an expedition to be sent to Abyssinia to liberate my envoy and other of my subjects, detained by the ruler of that country in an unjust captivity.

I feel sure that you will share in my satisfaction at the complete success which has attended that expedition. After a march of 400 miles through a difficult and unexplored country, my troops took the strong place of Magdala, freed the captives, and vindicated the honour of my Crown; and by their immediate return, without one act of oppression or needless violence, proved that the expedition had been undertaken only in obedience to the claims of humanity, and in fulfilment of the highest duties of my sovereignty.

The cessation of the long-continued efforts to promote rebellion in Ireland, has for some time rendered unnecessary the exercise by the Executive of exceptional powers. I rejoice to learn that no person is now detained under the provisions of the Act for the Suspension of the Habeas Corpus, and that no prisoner awaits trial in Ireland for an offence connected with the Fenian conspiracy.

Gentlemen of the House of Commons,

I have to thank you for the liberal supplies which you have voted for the public service.

My Lords and Gentlemen,

I have had much satisfaction in giving my assent to a series of measures completing the great work of the amendment of the representation of the people in Parliament, which has engaged your attention for two sessions.

I have seen with satisfaction that the time necessarily occupied by this comprehensive subject has not prevented you dealing with other questions of great public interest, and I have gladly given my sanction to Bills for the better government of Public Schools, the regulation of Railways, the amendment of the law relating to British Sea Fisheries, and for the acquisition and maintenance of Electric Telegraphs by the Postmaster-General; and to several important measures, having for their object the improvement of the law, and of the civil and criminal procedures in Scotland.

By the appointment of a Comptroller-in-Chief in the War Office, a considerable reform in army administration has been commenced, which, by combining at home and abroad the various departments of military supply under one authority, will conduce to greater economy and efficiency both in peace and war.

It is my intention to dissolve the present Parliament at the earliest day that will enable my people to reap the benefit of the extended system of representation which the wisdom of Parliament has provided for them. I look with entire confidence to their proving themselves worthy of the high privilege with which they have thus been invested ; and I trust that, under the blessing of Divine Providence, the expression of their opinion on those great questions of public policy which have occupied the attention of Parliament and remain undecided, may tend to maintain unimpaired that civil and religious freedom which has been secured to all my subjects by the institutions and settlement of my realm.

It is my earnest prayer that all your deliberations may be so guided as to conduce to the general contentment and happiness of my people.

PARLIAMENT VIII.—SESSION I.

OPENING OF PARLIAMENT BY COMMISSION.

Date.—December 16th, 1868.

The Lords Commissioners were:—The Lord Chancellor; the Lord President of the Council; the Lord of the Privy Seal; the Lord Chamberlain of the Household; and the Marquess of Ailesbury.

The Cabinet.—First Lord of the Treasury, Right Hon. William Ewart Gladstone; Lord Chancellor, Right Hon. Lord Hatherley; President of the Council, Right Hon. Earl de Grey and Ripon; Lord of the Privy Seal, Right Hon. Earl of Kimberley; Home Secretary, Right Hon. Henry Austin Bruce; Foreign Secretary, Right Hon. Earl of Clarendon, K.G.; Colonial Secretary, Right Hon. Earl Granville, K.G.; Secretary at War, Right Hon. Edward Cardwell; Secretary for India, His Grace the Duke of Argyll, K.G.; Chancellor of the Exchequer, Right Hon. Robert Lowe; First Lord of the Admiralty, Right Hon. H. C. Eardley Childers; Postmaster-General, Right Hon. Marquess of Hartington; President of the Board of Trade, Right Hon. John Bright; Chief Secretary for Ireland, Right Hon. Chichester Samuel Fortescue; Chief Commissioner of the Poor Law Board, Right Hon. G. J. Göschen.

The Queen's Speech.

My Lords and Gentlemen,

I recur to your advice at the earliest period permitted by the arrangements consequent upon the retirement of the late administration.

And it is with special interest that I commend to you the resumption of your labours at a time when the popular branch of the Legislature has been chosen with the advantage of a greatly enlarged enfranchisement of my faithful and loyal people.

I am able to inform you that my relations with all foreign Powers continue to be most friendly; and I have the satisfaction to believe that they cordially share in the desire by which I am animated for the maintenance of peace. I shall at all times be anxious to use my best exertions for the promotion of this most important object.

In concurrence with my Allies I have endeavoured, by friendly interposition, to effect a settlement of the differences which have arisen between Turkey and Greece; and I rejoice that our joint efforts have aided in preventing any serious interruption of tranquillity in the Levant.

I have been engaged in negotiations with the United States of North America for the settlement of questions which affect the interests and the international relations of the two countries; and it is my earnest hope that the result of these negotiations may be to place on a firm and durable basis the friendship which should ever exist between England and America.

I have learned with grief that disturbances have

occurred in New Zealand, and that on one spot they have been attended with circumstances of atrocity. I am confident that the Colonial Government and people will not be wanting either in energy to repress the outbreaks, or in the prudence and moderation which, I trust, may prevent their recurrence.

Gentlemen of the House of Commons,

The estimates for the expenditure of the coming financial year will be submitted to you. They have been framed with a careful regard to the efficiency of the services, and they will exhibit a diminished charge upon the country.

My Lords and Gentlemen,

The ever-growing wants of diversified interests of the Empire will necessarily bring many questions of public policy under your review.

The condition of Ireland permits me to believe that you will be spared the painful necessity which was felt by the late Parliament for narrowing the securities of personal liberty in that country by the suspension of the Habeas Corpus Act.

I recommend that you should inquire into the present modes of conducting Parliamentary and Municipal elections, and should consider whether it may be possible to provide any further guarantees for their tranquillity, purity, and freedom.

A measure will be brought under your notice for the relief of some classes of occupiers from hardships in respect of rating, which appears to be capable of remedy.

You will also be invited to direct your attention to Bills for the extension and improvement of education in

Scotland; and for rendering the considerable revenues of the endowed schools of England more widely effectual for the purpose of instruction.

A measure will be introduced for applying the principle of representation to the control of the county rate, by the establishment of Financial Boards for counties.

It will be proposed to you to recur to the subject of Bankruptcy, with a view to the more effective distribution of assets, and to the abolition of imprisonment for debt.

The ecclesiastical arrangements of Ireland will be brought under your consideration at a very early date, and the legislation which will be necessary in order to their final adjustment will make the largest demands upon the wisdom of Parliament.

I am persuaded that, in the prosecution of the work, you will bear a careful regard to every legitimate interest which it may involve, and that you will be governed by the constant aim to promote the welfare of religion through the principles of equal justice, to secure the action of the undivided feeling and opinion of Ireland on the side of loyalty and law, to efface the memory of former contentions, and to cherish the sympathies of an affectionate people.

In every matter of public interest, and especially in one so weighty, I pray that the Almighty may never cease to guide your deliberations, and may bring them to a happy issue.

Mover of Address in the Lords, Earl of Carysfort.
Seconder   ,,   ,, Lord Monck.
Mover of Address in the Commons, Mr. H. Cowper.
Seconder,   ,,   ,, Mr. Mundella.

PROROGATION OF PARLIAMENT BY COMMISSION.

Date.—August 11th, 1869.

The Lords Commissioners were:—The Lord Chancellor; the Lord of the Privy Seal; Earl Granville; the Lord Chamberlain of the Household; and Lord Foley.

The Queen's Speech.

My Lords and Gentlemen,

We are commanded by Her Majesty to dispense with your further attendance in Parliament.

Her Majesty announces to you with pleasure that she continues to receive from all foreign Powers the strongest assurances of their friendly disposition, and that her confidence in the preservation of peace has been continued and confirmed during the present year.

The negotiations in which Her Majesty was engaged with the United States of North America have, by mutual consent, been suspended; and Her Majesty earnestly hopes that this delay may tend to maintain the relations between the two countries on a durable basis of friendship.

Her Majesty has a lively satisfaction in acknowledging the untiring zeal and assiduity with which you have prosecuted the arduous labours of the year.

In the Act for putting an end to the Establishment of the Irish Church, you carefully kept in view the several considerations which, at the opening of the session, were commended to your notice.

It is the hope of Her Majesty that this important measure may hereafter be remembered as a conclusive proof of the paramount anxiety of Parliament to pay reasonable regard, in legislating for each of the three kingdoms, to the special circumstances by which it may be distinguished, and to deal on principles of impartial justice with all interests and all portions of the nation.

Her Majesty firmly trusts that the Act may promote the work of peace in Ireland, and may help to unite all classes of its people in that fraternal concord with their English and Scottish fellow-subjects which must ever form the chief source of strength to her extended Empire.

Her Majesty has observed with pleasure your general and cordial readiness to unite in the removal, through the Assessed Rates Act, of a practical grievance which was widely felt.

Her Majesty congratulates you on having brought your protracted labours on the subjects of Bankruptcy and of Imprisonment for Debt to a legislative conclusion which is regarded with just satisfaction by the trading classes and by the general public.

The law which you have framed for the better government of Endowed Schools in England, will render the large resources of these establishments more accessible to the community and more efficient for their important purpose.

It may reasonably be expected that the Act for the Supervision of Habitual Criminals will contribute further to the security of life and property.   . . .

The measure which has been passed with respect to the contagious diseases of animals will, as Her Majesty believes, add confidence and safety to the important trades of breeding and feeding cattle at home, without unnecessarily impeding the freedom of import from abroad.

16

By the repeal of the tax on fire insurance you have met a long-cherished wish of the community; and in the removal of the duty on corn Her Majesty sees new evidence of your desire to extend industry and commerce and to enlarge to the uttermost those supplies of food which our insular position in a peculiar degree both encourages and requires.

Her Majesty trusts that the measure for the purchase and management of the electric telegraphs by the State may be found to facilitate the great commercial and social object of rapid, easy, and certain communication, and may prove no unworthy sequel to that system of cheap postage which has passed with much advantage into so many countries of the civilised world.

Gentlemen of the House of Commons,

We are commanded to state that Her Majesty thanks you for the liberal supplies which you have granted for the service of the year, and for the measures by which you have enabled her at once to liquidate the charge of the Abyssinian Expedition.

My Lords and Gentlemen,

Her Majesty reflects with pleasure that in returning to your several homes you may contemplate with thankfulness the fruit of your exertions in the passing of many important laws, a portion of which we have now had it in command to notice.

During the recess you will continue to gather that practical knowledge and experience which form the solid basis of legislative aptitude; and Her Majesty invokes the blessing of the Almighty alike upon your present and your future labours for the public weal.

PARLIAMENT VIII.—SESSION II.

OPENING OF PARLIAMENT BY COMMISSION.

Date.—February 8th, 1870.

The Lords Commissioners were :—The Lord Chancellor ; the Lord President of the Council ; the Lord Privy Seal ; the Lord Steward of the Household ; and the Lord Chamberlain of the Household.

The Cabinet.—First Lord of the Treasury, Right Hon. William Ewart Gladstone ; Lord Chancellor, Right Hon. Lord Hatherley ; President of the Council, Right Hon. Earl de Grey and Ripon, K.G. ; Lord of the Privy Seal, Right Hon. Earl of Kimberley ; Home Secretary, Right Hon. Henry Austin Bruce ; Foreign Secretary, Right Hon. Earl of Clarendon, K.G. ; Colonial Secretary, Right Hon. Earl Granville, K.G. ; Secretary at War, Right Hon. Edward Cardwell ; Secretary for India, His Grace the Duke of Argyll ; Chancellor of the Exchequer, Right Hon. Robert Lowe ; First Lord of the Admiralty, Right Hon. Hugh C. Eardley Childers ; Postmaster-General, Right Hon. Marquis of Hartington ; President of the Board of Trade, Right Hon. John Bright ; Chief Secretary for Ireland, Right Hon. Chichester S. Fortescue ; Chief Commissioner of the Poor Law Board, Right Hon. G. J. Göschen.

The Queen's Speech.

My Lords and Gentlemen,

We have it in command from Her Majesty again to invite you to resume your arduous duties, and to express the regret of Her Majesty that recent indis-

16 *

position has prevented her from meeting you in person, as had been her intention, at a period of remarkable public interest.

The friendly sentiments which are entertained in all quarters towards this country, and which Her Majesty cordially reciprocates, the growing disposition to resort to the good offices of allies in cases of international difference, and the conciliatory spirit in which several such cases have recently been treated and determined, encourage Her Majesty's confidence in the continued maintenance of the general tranquillity.

Papers will be laid before you with reference to recent occurrences in New Zealand.

Gentlemen of the House of Commons,

The estimates for the services of the approaching financial year are in a forward state of preparation. Framed with a view, in the first place, to the effective maintenance of the public establishments, they will impose a diminished charge upon the subjects of Her Majesty.

The condition of the revenue has answered to the expectations which were formed during the past session.

Her Majesty trusts that you will be disposed to carry to its completion the inquiry which you last year instituted into the mode of conducting Parliamentary and Municipal elections, and thus to prepare the materials for useful and early legislation.

My Lords and Gentlemen,

It will be proposed to you to amend the laws respecting the occupation and acquisition of land in Ireland, in a manner adapted to the peculiar circumstances of that country, and calculated, as Her Majesty believes, to bring about improved relations between the several classes concerned in Irish agriculture, which collectively constitute the great bulk of the people. These provisions when matured by your impartiality and wisdom, as Her Majesty trusts, will tend to inspire among persons with whom such sentiments may still be wanting, that steady confidence in the law and that desire to render assistance in its effective administration which mark her subjects in general ; and thus will aid in consolidating the fabric of the Empire.

We are further directed by Her Majesty to state that many other subjects of public importance appear to demand your care ; and among these especially to inform you that a Bill has been prepared for the enlargement, on a comprehensive scale, of the means of national education.

In fulfilment of an engagement to the Government of the United States, a Bill will be proposed to you for the purpose of defining the status of subjects or citizens of foreign countries who may desire naturalisation, and of aiding them in the attainment of that object.

You will further be invited to consider Bills, prepared in compliance with the Report of the Commission on Courts of Judicature, for the improvement of the constitution and procedure of the superior tribunals of both original and appellate jurisdiction.

The question of religious test in the Universities and Colleges of Oxford and Cambridge, has been under discussion for many years. Her Majesty recommends such a legislative settlement of this question as may contribute to extend the usefulness of these great institutions and to heighten the respect with which they are justly regarded.

Bills have been prepared for extending the incidence of rating, and for placing the collection of the large sums locally raised for various purposes on a simple and uniform footing.

Her Majesty has likewise to recommend that you should undertake the amendment of the laws which regulate the grant of licenses for the sale of fermented and spirituous liquors.

Measures will also be brought under your consideration for facilitating the transfer of land, for regulating the succession to real property in case of intestacy, for amending the laws as to the disabilities of members of trade combinations, and for both consolidating and improving the body of statutes which relate to merchant shipping.

While commending to you these weighty matters of legislation, Her Majesty commands us to add that the recent extension of agrarian crime in several parts of Ireland, with its train of accompanying evils, has filled Her Majesty with painful concern.

The Executive Government has employed freely the means at its command for the prevention of outrage, and a partial improvement may be observed; but although the number of offences, within this class of crime, has been by no means so great as at some former periods, the indisposition to give evidence in aid of the administration of justice has been alike remarkable and injurious.

For the removal of such evils, Her Majesty places her main reliance on the permanent operation of wise and necessary changes in the law. Yet she will not hesitate to recommend to you the adoption of special provisions, should such a policy appear, during the course of the session, to be required by the paramount interest of peace and order.

Upon these and all other subjects Her Majesty devoutly prays that your labours may be constantly attended by the blessing of Almighty God.

Mover of Address in the Lords, Marquess of Huntly.
Seconder   ,,   ,,   Earl of Fingall.
Mover of Address in the Commons, Captain Egerton.
Seconder   ,,   ,,   Sir Charles W. Dilke.

Prorogation of Parliament by Commission.

Date.—August 10th, 1870.

The Lords Commissioners were :—The Lord Chancellor; the Lord of the Privy Seal; the Colonial Secretary; the Marquess of Normanby; and the Lord Chamberlain of the Household.

The Queen's Speech.

My Lords and Gentlemen,

The state of public business enables me to release you from further attendance in Parliament.

I continue to receive from foreign Powers assurances of good-will and friendship; but I have witnessed with grief and pain, on domestic as well as public grounds, the recent outbreak of war between two powerful nations, both of them allied with this country.

My best exertions had been used to avert this great calamity.

I shall now direct a constant and anxious attention to the strict observance of the duties and the maintenance of the rights of neutrality.

I have cheerfully assented to the measure, matured by your wisdom, to enlarge the power of the Executive, not only for the discharge of international duties, but for the prevention of acts which, in times of war, might be injurious to the interests of the country.

I shall make every fitting endeavour to check the operation of causes which might lead towards enlarging the area of the present conflict, and to contribute, if opportunity shall be afforded me, to the restoration of an early and honourable peace.

I have tendered to the two belligerent powers treaties identical in form to give additional security to Belgium against the hazards of a war waged upon her frontiers. This treaty has been signed by Count Bernstorff on the part of the North German Confederation, and the French Ambassador has signified that he has authority to sign the corresponding instrument as soon as his full powers arrive. Other Powers, which were parties to the Treaty of 1839, have been invited to accede, if they should think fit, to this engagement.

The shocking murders recently perpetrated in Greece produced a painful impression throughout Europe, and have drawn attention to serious evils existing in that country. My unremitting efforts will be directed to securing the complete and searching character of the inquiry which has been instituted.

Gentlemen of the House of Commons,

I thank you for the liberal provision which was made by you for the ordinary service of the year, and for the additional supplies of men and money which you have voted in view of the altered state of things on the continent of Europe.

The condition of the revenue gives ground for the hope that it may be able to meet the new charge which has been created, without reversing the proper balance of income and expenditure.

My Lords and Gentlemen,

In regard to domestic legislation, I may fitly congratulate you on the close of a session marked by an assiduous devotion to labours of the utmost national importance.

The temporary Act for the repression of Agrarian Crimes, and the maintenance of order in Ireland, has up to the present time answered the purpose for which it was passed.

From the Act for regulating the occupation and ownership of land, I anticipate the gradual establishment both of harmonious relations between owners and occupiers of land, and of general confidence in the provisions and administration of the law, and in the just and benevolent intentions of the Legislature.

In consequence of the efforts which have been made in matters of capital moment, to remove from the Statute Book whatever might seem inequitable to Ireland, I trust that the discharge of the first duty of Government in providing for the security of life and property will become more easy; and I shall rely with confidence upon the loyalty and affection of my Irish subjects.

It has given me pleasure to concur with you in the passage of the important law providing for national education in England. I perceive in it a new guarantee for the moral and social well-being of the nation, and for its prosperity and power.

The Naturalisation Act and the Act for the Extradition of Criminals will tend to confirm our friendly relations with foreign Powers.

The Act which regulates enlistment for a shortened term of service in the ranks of the army will, I trust, tend to increase the efficiency of the soldier; and to provide for the nation a reserve of men well trained to arms, and ready in any case of emergency to return to the standards.

I bid you farewell for the recess, with the earnest prayer that when you are again summoned to your duties I may be enabled to rejoice with you in the re-establishment of peace on the continent of Europe.

PARLIAMENT VIII.—SESSION III.

OPENING OF PARLIAMENT BY HER MAJESTY IN PERSON.
The Prince of Wales, in his robes, sitting on her right hand.

Date.—February 9th, 1871.

The Cabinet.—First Lord of the Treasury, Right Hon. William Ewart Gladstone ; Lord Chancellor, Right Hon. Lord Hatherley ; President of the Council, Right Hon. Earl de Grey and Ripon, K.G. ; Lord of the Privy Seal, Right Hon. Viscount Halifax, G.C.B. ; Home Secretary, Right Hon. Henry Austin Bruce ; Foreign Secretary, Right Hon. Earl Granville, K.G. ; Colonial Secretary, Right Hon. Earl of Kimberley ; Secretary at War, Right Hon. Edward Cardwell ; Secre-

tary for India, His Grace the Duke of Argyll, K.G.;
Chancellor of the Exchequer, Right Hon. Robert
Lowe; First Lord of the Admiralty, Right Hon. H. C.
Eardley Childers; Postmaster-General, Right Hon.
William Monsell; President of the Board of Trade,
Right Hon. Chichester S. Fortescue; Chief Secretary
for Ireland, Right Hon. Marquess of Hartington; Chief
Commissioner of the Poor Law Board, Right Hon.
George J. Göschen.

The Queen's Speech.

My Lords and Gentlemen,

At an epoch of such moment to the future
fortunes of Europe, I am especially desirous to avail
myself of your counsels.

The war which broke out, in the month of July,
between France and Germany, has raged, until within
the last few days, with unintermitted and likewise with
unexampled force, and its ravages may be renewed after
but a few days more, unless moderation and forethought,
prevailing over all impediments, shall sway the councils
of both the parties whose well-being is so vitally concerned.

At the time when you separated, I promised a constant attention to the subject of neutral obligations,
and I undertook to use my best endeavours to prevent
the enlargement of the area of the war, and to contribute,
if opportunity should offer, to the restoration of an early
and honourable peace.

In accordance with the first of these declarations, I
have maintained the rights and strictly discharged the
duties of neutrality.

The sphere of the war has not been extended beyond the two countries originally engaged.

Cherishing with care the cordiality of my relations with each belligerent, I have forborne from whatever might have been construed as gratuitous or unwarranted interference between parties, neither of whom had shown a readiness to propose terms of accommodation such as to bear promise of acceptance by the other.

I have been enabled, on more than one occasion, to contribute towards placing the representatives of the two contending countries in confidential communication ; but, until famine compelled the surrender of Paris, no further result had been obtained.

The armistice now being employed for the Convocation of an Assembly in France, has brought about a pause in the constant accumulation, on both sides, of human suffering, and has rekindled the hope of a complete accommodation. I pray that this suspension may result in a peace compatible for the two great and brave nations involved, with security and with honour, and likely therefore to command the approval of Europe, and to give reasonable hope of a long duration.

It has been with concern that I have found myself unable to accredit my Ambassador in a formal manner to the Government of Defence which has subsisted in France since the revolution of September ; but neither the harmony nor the efficiency of the correspondence of the two States has been in the smallest degree impaired.

The King of Prussia has accepted the title of Emperor of Germany at the instance of the chief authorities of the nation.

I have offered my congratulations on an event which

bears testimony to the solidity and independence of Germany, and which, I trust, may be found conducive to the stability of the European system.

I have endeavoured, in correspondence with other Powers of Europe, to uphold the sanctity of treaties, and to remove any misapprehension as to the binding character of their obligations.

It was agreed by the Powers which had been parties to the Treaty of 1856 that a Conference should meet in London. This Conference has now been for some time engaged in its labours, and I confidently trust that the result of its deliberations will be to uphold both the principles of public right and the general policy of the Treaty, and at the same time, by the revision of some of its conditions in a fair and conciliatory spirit, to exhibit a cordial co-operation among the Powers with regard to the Levant.

I greatly regret that my earnest efforts have failed to procure the presence at the Conference of any representative of France, which was one of the chief parties to the Treaty of 1856, and which must ever be regarded as a principal and indispensable member of the great commonwealth of Europe.

At different times, several questions of importance have arisen which are not yet adjusted, and which materially affect the relations between the United States and the territories and people of British North America. One of them in particular, which concerns the Fisheries, calls for early settlement, lest the possible indiscretion of individuals should impair the neighbourly understanding which it is on all grounds so desirable to cherish and maintain.

I have, therefore, engaged in amicable communications with the President of the United States. In order to determine the most convenient mode of treatment for these matters, I have suggested the appointment of a joint Commission ; and I have agreed to a proposal of the President that this Commission shall be authorised at the same time, and in the same manner, to resume the consideration of the American claims growing out of the circumstances of the late war. This arrangement will, by common consent, include all claims for compensation which have been or may be made by each Government, or by its citizens, upon the other.

The establishment of a Prince of the House of Savoy on the throne of Spain, by the free choice of the popularly-elected representatives of the Spanish nation, will, I trust, insure for a country which has passed, with so much temperance and self-control, through a prolonged and trying crisis, the blessings of a stable Government.

I am unhappily not able to state that the inquiry which was instituted by the Government of Greece into the history of the shocking murders perpetrated during the last spring at Dilessi has reached a termination answerable in all respects to my just expectations, but I shall not desist from my endeavours to secure the complete attainment of the objects of the inquiry. Some valuable results, however, have in the meantime been obtained for the exposure and repression of a lawless and corrupting system, which has too long afflicted the Greek Peninsula.

The anxiety which the massacre at Tien-tsin on the

21st of June last called forth has happily been dispelled; and while it will be my earnest endeavour to provide for the security of my subjects and their trade in those remote quarters, I count on your concurrence in the policy that I have adopted of recognising the Chinese Government as entitled to be dealt with in its relations with this country in a conciliatory and forbearing spirit.

The Parliamentary recess has been one of anxious interest in regard to foreign affairs. But I rejoice to acquaint you that my relations are, as heretofore, those of friendship and good understanding with the Sovereigns and States of the civilised world.

Papers illustrative of the conduct of my Government in relation to the several matters on which I have now summarily touched, will be duly laid before you.

In turning to domestic affairs, I have first to inform you that I have approved of a marriage between my daughter, Princess Louise, and the Marquess of Lorne, and I have declared my consent to this union in Council.

Gentlemen of the House of Commons,

The revenue of the country flourishes, and the condition of trade and industry may, though with partial drawbacks, be declared satisfactory.

The estimates for the coming year will be promptly laid before you.

My Lords and Gentlemen,

The lessons of military experience afforded by the present war have been numerous and important.

The time appears appropriate for turning such lessons

to account by efforts, more decisive, than heretofore, at practical improvement. In attempting this, you will not fail to bear in mind the special features in the position of this country so favourable to the freedom and security of the people; and if the changes from a less to a more effective and elastic system of defensive military preparation shall be found to involve, at least for a time, an increase of various charges, your prudence and patriotism will not grudge the cost, as long as you are satisfied that the end is important, and the means judicious. No time will be lost in laying before you a Bill for the better regulation of the army and the auxiliary land forces of the Crown, and I hardly need commend it to your anxious and impartial considera- tion.

I trust that the powerful interest at present attaching to affairs abroad, and to military questions, will not greatly abate the energy with which you have heretofore applied yourselves to the work of general improvement in our domestic legislation.

I commend anew to your attention several measures on subjects which I desired to be brought before you during the last session of Parliament, but which the time remaining at your disposal, after you had dealt with the principal subjects of the year, was not found sufficient to carry to a final issue.

I refer especially to the Bills on religious tests in the Universities of Oxford and Cambridge, on eccle- siastical titles, on the disabilities of trade combinations, on the Courts of Justice and Appeal, on the adjustment of local burdens, and on the licensing of houses for the sale of intoxicating liquors.

The inquiry made by a Committee of the Commons House being now complete, a measure will be placed before you on an early day for the establishment of secret voting.

A proposal is anxiously expected in Scotland for the adjustment of the question of primary education. With reference to the training of the young in schools on a national scale and basis, that portion of the country has especial claims on the favourable consideration of Parliament; and I trust the year may not pass by without your having disposed of this question by the enactment of a just and effective law.

The condition of Ireland with reference to agrarian crime has, in general, afforded a gratifying contrast with the state of that island in the preceding winter; but there have been painful though very partial exceptions.

To secure the best results for the great measures of the two last sessions, which have so recently passed into operation, and which involve such direct and pressing claims upon the attention of all classes of the community, a period of calm is to be desired; and I have thought it wise to refrain from suggesting to you at the present juncture the discussion of any political question likely to become the subject of new and serious controversy in that country.

The burdens devolving upon you as the great Council of the nation, and of this ancient and extended Empire, are, and must long continue to be, weighty. But you labour for a country whose laws and institutions have stood the test of time, and whose people, earnestly attached to them, and desiring their continuance, will

17

unite with their Sovereign in invoking upon all your designs the favour and aid of the Most High.

Mover of Address in the Lords, Marquess of West-
minster.

Seconder „ „ Earl of Rosebery.

Mover of Address in the Commons, Mr. J. G. C.
Hamilton.

Seconder „ „ Mr. Morley.

PROROGATION OF PARLIAMENT BY COMMISSION.

Date.—August 21st, 1871.

The Lords Commissioners were:—The Lord Chancellor; the Lord of the Privy Seal; the Duke of St.
Albans; the Earl Cowper; and the Earl of Cork.

The Queen's Speech

My Lords and Gentlemen,

The time has now arrived when I am enabled to release you from your attendance in Parliament, and to commend your unwearied labours for the public good.

I acknowledge with satisfaction the loyal readiness with which you have made provision to my beloved children, Princess Louise and Prince Arthur.

The great events and important changes which have recently occurred on the continent of Europe have not compromised the friendly relations subsisting between the Crown of the United Kingdom and foreign Powers. Whatever part I may take in those international questions which from time to time may arise, will continue to be taken with no other view than the maintenance of general concord and public right.

The Conference which was sitting in London at the commencement of the session, was joined during its deliberations by a French plenipotentiary, and it considered and agreed upon a revision of those stipulations of the Treaty of 1856 which concerned the Black Sea and the Bosphorus. I trust that the unanimous decision of the Powers, which has been recorded in a new treaty, may assist in securing the tranquillity and welfare of the East.

It is with a special satisfaction that I refer on the present occasion to our relations with the United States of America. By the Treaty of Washington, modes of settlement have been fixed for several questions which had long remained in dispute.

My communications with the American Government have not been without the promise of advantage to other countries. The President has concurred with me in an application of that principle of amicable reference which was proclaimed by the Treaty of Paris, and which I rejoice to have now an opportunity of recommending by example. And we have also agreed in the adoption of certain rules for guiding the maritime conduct of neutrals, which may, I trust, ere long obtain general recognition, and form a valuable addition to the code of international law.

I place full reliance upon the disposition of the American Government to carry forward with cordiality and zeal the subsidiary arrangements which have been determined on for the execution of the treaty.

I shall apprise the Parliament of Canada that the provisions which require its consent are, in my view, highly conducive to the interests of the Dominion. On

17 *

these provisions, however, that Parliament will pass an independent and final judgment.

The Government of France has signified its desire to after some of the provisions of the Commercial Treaty of 1860, which is now terminable upon a notice of twelve months by either of the contracting States. I am anxious to meet the wishes of a friendly Power, and to give scope for any measures calculated to meet its fiscal exigencies; but I should witness with concern any change of a nature to restrict that commercial intercourse between the two countries which has done so much for their closer union.

Gentlemen of the House of Commons,

I thank you for the liberal supplies which, under the circumstances of the year, I directed my Government to ask from you; and for the sum of money you have voted in order to meet the charge of the compensations required by the abolition of purchase in the army.

My Lords and Gentlemen,

I observe with concern that you have not been able to bring to a definitive issue the treatment of some of the subjects which were recommended to you in the Speech from the Throne at the opening of the session.

But several important laws have been added to the statute book.

By the Army Regulation Bill you have made a liberal provision for the officers of the army, who will no longer be permitted on retirement to sell their commissions to their successors; and by transferring to the Executive

Government powers in respect to the auxiliary forces, which have hitherto been vested in the lords-lieutenants of counties, you have laid the foundation for measures calculated to effect a closer union among the various land forces of the kingdom.

The Act by which, after a full examination of the facts, you conferred extraordinary powers on the Viceroy of Ireland for the repression of agrarian outrage in Westmeath, has thus far answered its purpose. Elsewhere in that portion of the United Kingdom there is a gratifying immunity from crime, and agriculture and trade are prosperous.

By the measure relating to university tests, to the repeal of the Ecclesiastical Titles Act, and to the laws which affect trades unions, you have brought to a conclusion long continued and serious controversies.

The Local Government Board Act will, I trust, prepare the way for important sanitary and administrative improvements; and the Act relating to the Judicial Committee will supply a much-needed element of strength to an important tribunal, and afford a prospect of clearing away a serious arrear of appeals now before the Privy Council.

But there is every likelihood that, for a long time to come, the great and varied interests of the United Kingdom, and of the Empire at large, together with the extending demands of modern society, may prevent any lightening of the honourable but arduous burdens of legislation.

The condition of the revenue, the revived activity of trade, and the prospects of the harvest, are subjects for congratulation; and I trust that these and all other bounties of Providence will ever meet their fitting acknowledgment in the hearts of a grateful people.

PARLIAMENT VIII.—SESSION IV.

OPENING OF PARLIAMENT BY COMMISSION.

Date.—February 6th, 1872.

The Lords Commissioners were :—The Lord Chancellor; the Lord President of the Council; the Lord of the Privy Seal; the Lord Chamberlain of the Household; and the Lord Steward of the Household.

The Cabinet.—First Lord of the Treasury, Right Hon. William Ewart Gladstone; Lord Chancellor, Right Hon. Lord Hatherley; President of the Council, Most Hon. the Marquess of Ripon, K.G.; Lord of the Privy Seal, Right Hon. Viscount Halifax, G.C.B.; Home Secretary, Right Hon. Henry Austin Bruce; Foreign Secretary, Right Hon. Earl Granville, K.G.; Colonial Secretary, Right Hon. Earl of Kimberley; Secretary at War, Right Hon. Edward Cardwell; Secretary for India, His Grace the Duke of Argyll; Chancellor of the Exchequer, Right Hon. Robert Lowe; First Lord of the Admiralty, Right Hon. George Joachim Göschen; Postmaster-General, Right Hon. William Monsell; President of the Board of Trade, Right Hon. Chichester S. Fortescue; Chief Secretary for Ireland, Right Hon. Marquess of Hartington ; Chief Commissioner of the Poor Law Board, Right Hon. James Stansfeld.

The Queen's Speech.

My Lords and Gentlemen,

I avail myself of the opportunity afforded by your re-assembling for the discharge of your momentous duties to renew the expression of my thankfulness to the Almighty for the deliverance of my dear son, the Prince of Wales, from the most imminent danger, and of my lively recollection of the profound and universal sympathy shown by my loyal people during the period of anxiety and trial.

I propose that on Tuesday, the 27th instant, conformably to the good and becoming usage of former days, the blessing thus received shall be acknowledged on behalf of the nation by a thanksgiving in the Metropolitan Cathedral. At this celebration it is my desire and hope to be present.

Directions have been given to provide the necessary accommodation for the Members of the two Houses of Parliament.

The assurances of friendship which I have received from foreign Powers continue to be in all respects satisfactory. I need hardly assure you that my endeavours will at all times be steadily directed to the maintenance of these friendly relations.

The Slave Trade, and practices scarcely to be distinguished from slave-trading, still pursued in more than one quarter of the world, continue to attract the attention of my Government. In the South Sea Islands the name of the British Empire is even now dishonoured by the connection of some of my subjects with these nefarious practices; and in one of them the murder of an exem-

plary Prelate has cast fresh light upon some of their
baneful consequences A Bill will be presented to you
for the purpose of facilitating the trial of offences of this
class in Australasia; and endeavours will be made to
increase, in other forms, the means of counteraction.

Various communications have passed between my
Government and the Government of France on the
subject of the commercial treaty concluded in 1860.
From a divergence of the views respectively entertained
in relation to the value of protective laws, this correspondence has not brought about any agreement to
modify that important convention. On both sides,
however, there has been uniformly declared an earnest
desire that nothing shall occur to impair the cordiality
which has long prevailed between the two nations.

Papers relating to these subjects will be laid before
you.

The arbitrators, appointed pursuant to the Treaty of
Washington, for the purpose of settling amicably certain
claims known as the "Alabama" claims, have held their
first meeting at Geneva.

Cases have been laid before the arbitrators on behalf
of each party to the treaty. In the case so submitted
on behalf of the United States, large claims have been
included which are understood on my part not to be
within the province of the arbitrators. On this subject
I have caused a friendly communication to be made to
the Government of the United States.

The Emperor of Germany has undertaken to arbitrate
on the San Juan Water Boundary; and the cases of the
two Governments have been presented to His Imperial
Majesty.

The Commission at Washington has been appointed, and is in session. The provisions of the treaty which require the consent of the Parliament of Canada, awaiting its assembling.

Turning to domestic affairs, I have to apprize you that, with very few exceptions, Ireland has been free from serious crime. Trade in that part of the United Kingdom is active, and the advance of agricultural industry is remarkable.

I am able also to congratulate you, so far as present experience allows a judgment to be passed, upon the perceptible diminution of the number both of the graver crimes and of habitual criminals in Great Britain.

Gentlemen of the House of Commons,

The principal estimates for the coming year have been prepared. They will at once be laid before you; and I trust that you will find them suitable to the circumstances of the country.

The state of the revenue affords favourable indications of the demand for employment and the general condition, indications which are corroborated by a decline of pauperism not inconsiderable.

My Lords and Gentlemen,

Your attention will be invited to several measures of acknowledged national interest. Among these there will be Bills for the improvement of public education in Scotland, for the regulation of mines, for the amendment of what is known as the Licensing System, and in relation to the Superior Courts of Justice and Appeal.

In particular, a Bill, having for its main object the establishment of secret voting, together with a measure relating to corrupt practices at Parliamentary elections, will be immediately presented to you.

Several measures of administrative improvement for Ireland will also be laid before you.

There will likewise be laid before you legislative provisions founded on the report of the Sanitary Commission.

You, my Lords and Gentlemen, will, I am confident, again apply your well-known assiduity to that work of legislation which, from the increasing exigencies of modern society, still seems to grow upon your hands. And I shall continue to rely, under Divine Providence, alike on the loyalty of my people, and on your energy and wisdom, to sustain the constant efforts of the Crown to discharge the duties, to uphold the rights, and to defend the honour of the Empire.

Mover of Address in the Lords, Earl de la Warr.
Seconder „ „ Viscount Powerscourt.
Mover of Address in the Commons, Mr. Strutt.
Seconder „ „ Mr. Colman.

PROROGATION OF PARLIAMENT BY COMMISSION.

Date.—August 10th, 1872.

The Lords Commissioners were:—The Lord Chancellor; the Marquess of Ailesbury; the Foreign Secretary; the Colonial Secretary; and the Lord Bishop of London.

The Queen's Speech.

My Lords and Gentlemen,

The time has now arrived when you may properly relinquish the performance of your arduous duties for a

term of repose which has been honourably earned by
your devoted assiduity.

I rejoice to inform you that the controversy which
had arisen between my Government and the Government
of the United States, in consequence of the presentation
of the American claims for indirect losses under the
Treaty of Washington, has been composed by a spontaneous declaration of the arbitrators entirely consistent
with the views which I announced to you at the opening
of the session. In concurrence with your action on the
part of the United Kingdom, the Parliament of Canada
has passed the Acts necessary to give effect to the
treaty within the Dominion. All the arrangements
contemplated by that instrument are, therefore, now
in progress ; and I reflect with satisfaction that the
subjects with which it has dealt no longer offer any impediment to a perfect concord between two kindred
nations.

Since I addressed you at the commencement of the
session, I have received from the Government of France
the formal notice which would bring to an end the Commercial Treaty of 1860. That Government, however,.
has indicated a desire for further communications. In
any correspondence on this subject I shall be guided by
an earnest anxiety to secure attention to the just claims
of my subjects, by the friendly feeling which has so long
united the two countries, and by my conviction of the
moral as well as material benefits to be derived by each
from a free intercourse between them.

I have had great satisfaction in concluding with the
Emperor of Germany a treaty, in conformity with the
provisions of the Act of 1870, for the mutual surrender

of fugitive criminals. I am engaged in framing similar arrangements with other powers.

My Government has taken steps to prepare the way for dealing more effectually with the slave trade on the East Coast of Africa.

I have cheerfully given my assent to an Act of the Legislature of the Cape Colony for the establishment in that Colony of what is known as responsible government.

Gentlemen of the House of Commons,

My acknowledgments are due to you for the ample provision which you have made for the varied exigencies of the public service.

My Lords and Gentlemen,

Although the wants and expectations of the country seem to outstrip every effort of Parliament in its career of legislative improvement, I notice with satisfaction the main additions which you have been enabled to make during the present year to our laws.

The Act having reference to the outrages upon natives in the islands of the Pacific is well designed, by providing for the more easy and effectual prevention and punishment of the offences at which it is aimed, to promote the ends of humanity and the honour of the Empire.

The Act for the localisation of the army, while it strengthens the defensive system of the country, will lend an indispensable aid in effecting those important reforms which have been approved by Parliament.

Although you have been unable during the present session to mature any measures directed against corrupt practices in the choice of Members of Parliament, I observe with pleasure that the cognate subject of Municipal elections has had your attention, and that you have presented to me a law which is well calculated to check existing evils, and which provides a tribunal for trying the validity of such elections.

By the Scottish Education Act, you have made provision for the further extension and greater efficacy of the training of the young throughout Scotland, in accordance with the conscientious and deep-rooted convictions of the people and with the principles of religious freedom.

The Act for establishing a Board of Local Government in Ireland, modelled on the English Statute of 1871, supplies a machinery for giving effect to many useful laws, and promises to extend within that portion of the United Kingdom the solid benefits of popular local institutions

The measure for the amendment of the Act of Uniformity, based as it is upon careful inquiry and on a large amount of ascertained consent, has, without offence or shock, introduced useful modification into an ancient system of Divine worship to which a large portion of my people are warmly attached.

The Public Health Act, though it does not embrace all the enactments which have been desired, has, by the establishment of efficient and duly organised local authorities, done much both for the enforcement of the present sanitary laws, and for rendering more easy what yet remains to be accomplished in the way of legislative provision on the subject.

The Act for regulating the custody and management

of the large funds held by the Court of Chancery, will relieve the numerous class of suitors in that Court from risks and inconveniences to which they may heretofore have been more or less exposed, and will likewise tend to an increased stability in our finance.

I am gratified to find that by the Acts for the regulation of mines you have been enabled to supply new securities for the safety and advantage of large bodies of my subjects engaged in this great branch of industry.

The enactments embodied in the measure for the regulation of the licensing system constitute a sensible improvement in the existing law, and I trust that the several regulations of police, which they include, will be found conducive to public order.

I am able to speak favourably both of the tranquillity and of the growing prosperity of Ireland.

The revenue is in a flourishing condition.

While I cordially congratulate you on the activity of trade and industry, I hope it will be borne in mind that periods of unusually rapid changes in the prices of commodities, and in the value of labour, are likewise periods in which there is more than ever a call for the exercise of moderation and forethought.

In bidding you farewell, I ask you to join with me in acknowledging the abundant mercies of the Almighty and in imploring their continuance.

PARLIAMENT VIII.—SESSION V.

Opening of Parliament by Commission.

Date.—February 6th, 1873.

The Lords Commissioners were:—The Lord Chancellor; the Lord President of the Council; the Lord of

the Privy Seal; the Earl of Kimberley; and the Earl
of Cork and Ossery.

The Cabinet.—First Lord of the Treasury, Right
Hon. William Ewart Gladstone ; Lord Chancellor, Right
Hon. Lord Selborne ; President of the Council,
Most Hon. Marquess of Ripon, K.G. ; Lord of the
Privy Seal, Right Hon. Viscount Halifax, G.C.B. ;
Home Secretary, Right Hon. Henry Austin Bruce;
Foreign Secretary, Right Right Hon. Earl Granville,
K.G.; Colonial Secretary, Right Hon. Earl of Kim-
berley ; Secretary at War, Right Hon. Right Hon.
Edward Cardwell ; Secretary for India, His Grace the
Duke of Argyll, K.G. ; Chancellor of the Exchequer,
Right Hon. Robert Lowe ; Chancellor of the Duchy of
Lancaster, Right Hon. Hugh Culling Eardley Childers ;
First Lord of the Admiralty, Right Hon. George J.
Goschen; President of the Board of Trade, Right Hon.
Chichester S. Fortescue ; Chief Secretary for Ireland,
Right Hon. Marquess of Hartington ; Chief Commis-
sioner to the Poor Law Board, Right Hon. James
Stansfeld.

The Queen's Speech.

My Lords and Gentlemen,

I greet you cordially on your reassembling for
the discharge of your momentous duties.

I have the satisfaction of maintaining relations of
friendship with foreign Powers throughout the world.

You were informed, when I last addressed you, that
steps had been taken to prepare the way for dealing
more effectually with the slave trade on the east coast
of Africa. I have now despatched an envoy to Zanzi-

bar, furnished with such instructions as appear to me best adapted for the attainment of the object in view. He has recently reached the place of his destination, and has entered into communication with the Sultan.

My Ally, the German Emperor, who had undertaken to pronounce judgment as arbiter on the line of water-boundary so long in dispute under the terms of the Treaty of 1846, has decided, in conformity with the contention of the Government of the United States, that the Haso Channel presents the line most in accordance with the true interpretation of that treaty.

I have thought it the course most befitting the spirit of international friendship and the dignity of the country, to give immediate execution to the award by withdrawing promptly from my partial occupation of the island of San Juan.

The proceedings before the tribunal of arbitration at Geneva, which I was enabled to prosecute in consequence of the exclusion of the indirect claims preferred on behalf of the Government of the United States, terminated in an award which in part established and in part repelled the claims allowed to be relevant. You will, in due course, be asked to provide for the payment of the sum coming due to the United States under this award.

My acknowledgments are due to the German Emperor, and likewise to the tribunal at Geneva, for the pains and care bestowed by them on the peaceful adjustment of the controversies, such as could not but impede the full prevalence of national good-will in a case where it was especially to be cherished.

In further prosecution of a well-understood and

established policy, I have concluded a treaty for the extradition of criminals with my Ally the King of the Belgians.

The Government of France has, during the recess, renewed its communications with my Government for the purpose of concluding a commercial treaty to replace that of 1860, which is about to expire.

In prosecuting these communications, I have kept in view the double object of an equitable regard to existing circumstances, and of securing a general provision more permanent in its character, and resting on a reciprocal and equal basis, for the commercial and maritime transactions of the two countries. I hope to be enabled within a short period to announce to you the final result.

It has been for some years felt by the Governments of Russia and the United Kingdom respectively, that it would be conducive to the tranquillity of Central Asia if the two Governments should arrive at an identity of view regarding the line which describes the northern frontier of the dominions of Afghanistan; accordingly a correspondence has passed, of which this is the main subject. Its tenour, no less than its object, will, I trust, be approved by the public opinion of both nations.

Papers will be laid before you with relation to the awards delivered under the Treaty of Washington, to the commercial negotiations with France, and to the northern frontier of the dominions of Afghanistan.

Gentlemen of the House of Commons,

The estimates for the coming financial year will

18

be presented to you. They have been framed with a view to the efficiency and moderation of our establishments, under circumstances of inconvenience entailed by variations of an exceptional nature in the prices of some important commodities.

My Lords and Gentlemen,

Although the harvest has been to some extent deficient, the condition of the three kingdoms with reference to trade and commerce, to the sufficiency of the revenue for meeting the public charge, to the decrease of pauperism, and to the relative amount of ordinary crime, may be pronounced generally satisfactory.

A measure will be submitted to you, on an early day, for settling the question of university education in Ireland. It will have for its object the advancement of learning in that portion of my dominions, and will be framed with a careful regard to the rights of conscience.

You will find ample occupation in dealing with other legislative subjects of importance, which, for the most part, have already been under notice in various forms and at different periods. Among these, your attention will speedily be asked to the formation of a Supreme Court of Judicature, including provision for the trial of appeals.

Among the measures which will be brought before you, there will also be proposals for facilitating the transfer of land ; and for the amendment of our system of local taxation, of certain provisions of the Education Act of 1870, and of the general Acts regulating railways and canals ; together with various Bills for the improvement of the law.

I earnestly commend your deliberations to the guidance and favour of Almighty God.

Mover of Address in the Lords, Earl of Clarendon.
Seconder „ „ Lord Monteagle.
Mover of Address in the Commons, Mr. Lyttelton.
Seconder „ „ Mr. Stone.

PROROGATION OF PARLIAMENT BY COMMISSION.

Date.—August 5th, 1873.

The Lords Commissioners were:—The Lord Chancellor; Earl Granville; Earl Cowper; the Lord Chamberlain of the Household; and the Lord Steward of the Household.

The Queen's Speech.

My Lords and Gentlemen,

I am now released from the necessity of calling upon you for the further prosecution of your arduous occupations.

In bidding you farewell for the recess, I make it my first duty to thank you for the loyal promptitude with which you have made further provision for my son, the Duke of Edinburgh, on the occasion of his approaching marriage with the Grand Duchess Marie Alexandrowna of Russia.

This marriage will, I trust, form a new tie of amity between two great Empires.

The best relations continue to subsist between myself and all foreign Powers.

I am able to announce the successful termination of the mission to Zanzibar, made known to you at the beginning of the session. Treaties have been concluded

18 *

with the Sultan of Zanzibar, with the Imaun of Muscat, and with other native Powers, which provide means for the more effectual repression of the slave trade on the east coast of Africa.

I have been enabled to bring to a satisfactory issue the commercial negotiations with France, in which my Government has for some time been engaged. Under the provisions of an instrument signed on the 23rd of July, and awaiting ratification, the Treaties of 1860 are again put in force, with a comprehensive engagement contracted between the two countries for mutual treatment on the footing of the most favoured nation ; and the differential tax on the British flag has been removed. Separate provisions are contained in the treaty for the adjustment of the question of mineral oils, and otherwise for the relief and extension of trade.

I have likewise concluded treaties of extradition with Italy, Denmark, Sweden, and Brazil. The ratifications of the two last-named treaties have not yet been exchanged, but I anticipate no difficulty in this final step ; and I am engaged in negotiations for agreements of a similar character with other States, both in Europe and beyond it.

I am still occupied in giving effect to those provisions of the Treaty of Washington which relate to British claims against the Government of the United States, and to the interests of my possessions in North America.

Gentlemen of the House of Commons,

I am very sensible of the liberality with which you have provided for the various charges of the State, and have likewise enabled me promptly to meet the obligations imposed upon me by the award of the arbitrators at Geneva during the past year.

My Lords and Gentlemen,

I have observed with satisfaction the progress you have been enabled to make in the remission of public burdens, by reducing both the sugar duties and the income-tax to points lower than any at which they have previously stood.

The Act for the establishment of the Supreme Court of Judicature forms a distinguished record of your persevering labour, and will be found, as I hope, to confer corresponding benefits on the country in the more cheap, certain, expeditious, and effectual administration of justice.

The Acts for the amendment of the Education Act of 1870, and of the Endowed Schools Act of 1869, will, as I trust, tend to accelerate the attainment of solid national advantages through the extension of education, both in the middle and the most numerous classes of the community.

The Act relating to the regulation of railways and canals promises to conduce to the more harmonious working of the railway system of the country.

I have with pleasure assented to the Act relating to merchant shipping, from which, and from the labours of the Commission recently appointed, I hope for a diminution of the risks to which the sea-faring population is exposed.

The revenue has, up to this time, fully answered my expectations; and although the activity of trade in some of its branches may have been somewhat restrained by a variety of causes, the general condition of the people continues to exhibit evidences of improvement.

These, and all mercies of Divine Providence, will, I trust, find their suitable acknowledgments alike in our words and in our hearts.

PARLIAMENT IX.—SESSION I.

OPENING OF PARLIAMENT BY COMMISSION.

Date.—March 19th, 1874.

The Lords Commissioners were:—The Lord Chancellor; the Lord Chamberlain of the Household; the Lord Steward of the Household; the Earl of Bradford; and Lord Skelmersdale.

The Cabinet.—First Lord of the Treasury, Right Hon. Benjamin Disraeli; Lord Chancellor, Right Hon. Lord Cairns; President of the Council, His Grace the Duke of Richmond; Lord of the Privy Seal, Right Hon. Earl of Malmesbury; Chancellor of the Exchequer, Right Hon. Sir Stafford H. Northcote; Home Secretary, Right Hon. R. Assheton Cross; Foreign Secretary, Right Hon. Earl of Derby; Colonial Secretary, Right Hon Earl of Carnarvon; Secretary at War, Right Hon. Gathorne Hardy; Secretary for India, Most Hon. Marquess of Salisbury; First Lord of the Admiralty, Right Hon. George Ward Hunt; Postmaster-General, Right Hon Lord John James Robert Manners.

The Queen's Speech.

My Lords and Gentlemen,

I recur to your advice at the earliest period

permitted by the arrangements consequent on the retirement of the late Administration.

My relations with all foreign Powers continue to be most friendly. I shall not fail to exercise the influence arising from these cordial relations for the maintenance of European peace, and the faithful observance of international obligations.

The marriage of my son the Duke of Edinburgh with the Grand Duchess Marie Alexandrowna of Russia is at once a source of happiness to myself, and a pledge of friendship between two great Empires.

The war with the King of Ashantee has terminated in the capture and destruction of his capital, and in negotiations which, I trust, may lead to a more satisfactory condition of affairs than has hitherto prevailed on the West Coast of Africa.

The courage, discipline, and endurance displayed by my forces, both of land and sea service, together with the energy and skill evinced in the conduct of the expedition, have brilliantly maintained, under the most trying circumstances, the traditionary reputation of the British arms.

I deeply regret that the drought of last summer has affected the most populous provinces of my Indian Empire, and has produced extreme scarcity, in some parts amounting to actual famine, over an area inhabited by several millions. I have directed the Governor-General of India to spare no cost in striving to mitigate this terrible calamity.

Gentlemen of the House of Commons,

The estimates for the coming financial year will forthwith be submitted to you.

My Lords and Gentlemen,

The delay and expense attending the transfer of land have long been felt to be a reproach to our system of law and a serious obstacle to dealings in real property. This subject has, in former sessions, occupied the attention of Parliament, and I trust that the measures which will now be submitted for your consideration will be found calculated to remove much of the evil of which complaint has been made.

You will probably be of opinion that the re-arrangement of the Judicature and the blending of the administration of law and equity, which were effected for England by the enactment of last session, ought, on the same principles, to be extended to Ireland, and you will be asked to devote some part of your time to the accomplishment of this object.

The greater part of these changes would be inapplicable to the tribunals of Scotland, but you will be invited, as to that part of my Kingdom, to consider the most satisfactory mode of bringing the procedure upon appeals into harmony with recent legislation; and, among other measures relating to her special interests, a Bill for amending the law relating to land rights, and for facilitating the transfer of land, will be laid before you.

Serious differences have arisen, and remonstrances have been made by large classes of the community, as to the working of the recent Act of Parliament affecting the relationship of master and servant, of the Act of, 1871, which deals with offences connected with trade, and of the law of conspiracy, more especially as connected with these offences. On these subjects I am desirous that, before attempting any further legislation,

you should be in possession of all material facts, and of
the precise questions in controversy, and for this purpose
I have issued a Royal Commission to inquire into the
state and working of the present law with a view to its
early amendment.

A Bill will be introduced dealing with such parts of
the Acts relating to intoxicating liquors as have given
rise to complaints which appear to deserve the interference of Parliament.

Your attention will also be directed to the laws
affecting Friendly and Provident Societies.

All these matters will require your grave consideration, and I pray that the Almighty may guide your
deliberations for the welfare of my realm.

Mover of Address in the Lords, Marquess of Lothian.
Seconder „ „ Earl Cadogan.
Mover of Address in the Commons, Sir William Stir-
ling Maxwell.
Seconder „ „ Mr. Callender.

PROROGATION OF PARLIAMENT BY COMMISSION.

Date.—August 7th, 1874.

The Lords Commissioners were:—The Lord Chancellor; the Lord Steward of the Household; the Foreign
Secretary; the Earl of Bradford; and Lord Skelmersdale.

The Queen's Speech.

My Lords and Gentlemen,

The time has arrived when I am enabled to release
you from your attendance in Parliament.

In doing so, my first wish is to thank you for the

readiness with which you have made provision for my son Prince Leopold, on his attaining his majority.

My relations with all foreign Powers continue to be friendly, and the influence arising from those cordial relations will be employed, as heretofore, in maintaining the obligations imposed by treaties, and in promoting and consolidating the peace of Europe.

The Emperor of Russia having made proposals for a Conference to be held at Brussels, the object of which is to lessen, by judicious regulations, the severities of war, I have, in common with other Powers, authorised a delegate to attend that Conference ; but before doing so, I have thought it right to obtain assurances from all the Powers thus represented that no proposal shall be brought forward either to alter the recognised rules of international law, or to place restrictions on the conduct of naval operations.

The recommendations which may issue from the Conference will have my careful consideration, but I have reserved to myself full freedom of action in regard to their acceptance or rejection.

Negotiations have been undertaken for the renewal of the Reciprocity Treaty formerly in force between the Dominion of Canada and the United States of North America. These negotiations, commenced at the desire and in the interest of the Dominion, have been temporarily suspended by the adjournment of the American Senate. They will be revived at an early date, and it is my hope that they may lead to an increase of commercial intercourse between my Colonial subjects and the citizens of the United States.

I deeply lament the continuance in Spain of disturbances which form a single exception to the general tranquillity of Europe ; but, while earnestly desiring the restoration of peace or civil order in that country, I believe that this result will be most surely brought about by a rigid abstinence from interference in the internal affairs of an independent and friendly State.

The treaty recently concluded with the Sultan of Zanzibar, having for its object the suppression of the East African slave trade, has been faithfully observed, and has already done much to put an end to that traffic as carried on by sea. The exertions of my naval and consular servants in that part of the world will not be relaxed until complete success has been obtained.

I am thankful to say that the famine in India has, as yet, been attended with little mortality—a result mainly attributable, under Providence, to the precautions taken by my Indian Government. The strenuous exertions of my Viceroy, and of the officers serving under him, merit my high approbation.

Since the close of hostilities on the Gold Coast, steady progress has been made in the task of pacifying the country and organising its administration. Treaties of Peace have been concluded with important tribes, and the King of Ashantee has persevered in the discharge of his obligations to this country.

Gentlemen of the House of Commons,

   I acknowledge the liberality with which you have provided for the charges of the State.

My Lords and Gentlemen,

   I have seen with pleasure the considerable reductions which you have been able to make in taxa-

tion. The total abolition of the sugar duties will not
only confer a benefit on the consumers of an article in
universal demand, but will also prove of much commercial advantage to the nation. The removal of the duty
on horses is another measure well calculated to encourage the trade and industry of the country. Concur-
rently with these remissions, and with a further reduction
of the Income Tax to a rate which is little more than
nominal, you have been enabled to make important
grants from the general revenue towards services which,
though of Imperial concern, have hitherto been defrayed
either exclusively or in an undue proportion, out of
local rates. I trust that these measures, when their
full effect has been felt, will conduce to the general
prosperity of the country and will impart increased
elasticity to the revenue.

Although the session has been unavoidably cur-
tailed of a third of its usual duration, I observe with
satisfaction that you have been able to carry measures
of general interest and importance.

I have cordially given my consent to the Act for
improving the health of women, young persons, and
children employed in manufactures. By this measure I
anticipate that not only will the health and education
of the classes affected by it be promoted, but that the
relations between the employers and employed in those
important branches of industry will be maintained on a
footing of enduring harmony and mutual good-will.

I have readily sanctioned the Act for the reform of
the system of patronage in the Church of Scotland. I
trust that the removal of this ancient cause of controversy may both strengthen the Church and conduce

to the religious welfare of a large number of my subjects.

The Act for the better regulation of Public Worship in the Church of England, will, I hope, tend to prevent or allay the unhappy controversies which sometimes arise from the difficulty experienced in obtaining an early decision on doubtful points of law, and a definite interpretation of the authorised form of Public Worship. Such controversies, even when they occur between people loyally desirous to conform to the doctrine and discipline of the Established Church, beget serious evils, and their speedy termination by competent authority is a matter of grave importance to the interests of religion.

The legal measures which you have passed with reference to the limitation of actions for real property, the law of vendors and purchasers, and land rights and conveyancing in Scotland, as well as Acts for regulating the sale of intoxicating liquors and for carrying forward sanitary legislation in the United Kingdom, may be expected to be productive of public advantage and satisfaction.

The Commission issued by me for inquiring into the state and working of the law as to offences connected with trade, has been unable to complete its labours in time to admit of legislation during the session now about to terminate ; and I regret that the pressure of business in the House of Commons has made it necessary to suspend the consideration of the measures for facilitating the transfer of land in England, for re-arranging' the ʲudicature of England and Ireland, and for establishing an Imperial Court of Appeal. These subjects will naturally claim your earliest attention in a future session.

In returning to your counties and constituencies, you will have the opportunity of beneficially exercising that influence which is the happy result of our local institutions, and I pray that the blessing of the Almighty may accompany you in the discharge of all your duties.

PARLIAMENT IX.—SESSION II.

OPENING OF PARLIAMENT BY COMMISSION.

Date.—February 5th, 1875.

The Lords Commissioners were:—The Lord Chancellor; the Lord of the Privy Seal; the Lord Chamberlain of the Household; the Lord Steward of the Household; and Lord Skelmersdale.

The Cabinet.—First Lord of the Treasury, Right Hon. Benjamin Disraeli; Lord Chancellor, Right Hon. Lord Cairns; President of the Council, His Grace the Duke of Richmond; Lord of the Privy Seal, Right Hon. Earl of Malmesbury; Chancellor of the Exchequer, Right Hon. Sir Stafford Henry Northcote; Home Secretary, Right Hon. R. Assheton Cross; Foreign Secretary, Right Hon. Earl of Derby; Colonial Secretary, Right Hon. Earl of Carnarvon; Secretary at War, Right Hon. Gathorne Hardy; Secretary for India, Most Hon. Marquess of Salisbury; First Lord of the Admiralty, Right Hon. George Ward Hunt; Postmaster-General, Right Hon. Lord John J. R. Manners.

The Queen's Speech.

My Lords and Gentlemen,

It is with great satisfaction that I again meet

you, and resort to the advice and assistance of my Parliament.

I continue to receive assurances of friendship from all foreign Powers. The peace of Europe has remained, and I trust will remain unbroken. To preserve and consolidate it will ever be a main object of my endeavours.

The Conference held at Brussels on the Laws and Usages of War has concluded its sittings. My Government have carefully examined the reports of its proceedings; but bearing in mind, on the one hand, the importance of the principles involved, and on the other, the widely divergent opinions which were there expressed, and the improbability of their being reconciled, I have not thought it right to accede to proposals which have been made for further negotiations on the subject. The correspondence which has passed will be presented to you.

The Government of Spain presided over by Marshal Serrano has ceased to exist, and the Prince of Asturias has been called to the throne under the title of King Alfonso XII. The question of formally recognising, in concert with other Powers, the newly restored Monarchy, is at this moment before my Government, and its decision will not be long delayed. It is my earnest hope that internal peace may be speedily restored to a great but unfortunate country.

The exertions of my naval and consular servants in the repression of the East African Slave Trade have not been relaxed, and I confidently trust that they will bring about the complete extinction of a traffic equally repugnant to humanity and injurious to legitimate commerce.

The differences which had arisen between China and Japan, and which at one time threatened to lead to war between those States, have been happily adjusted. I have learnt with pleasure that the good offices of my Minister at Pekin have been largely instrumental in bringing about this result.

The past year has been one of general prosperity and progress throughout my Colonial Empire.

On the Gold Coast a steady advance has been made in the establishment of civil government, peace has been maintained, and I have procured the assent of the protected tribes to the abolition of slavery. Henceforth, I trust, freedom will exist there as in every part of my dominions.

In Natal I have found myself under the necessity of reviewing the sentence which has been passed upon a native chief, and of considering the condition of the tribes and their relation to the European settlers and my Government. I doubt not that I shall have your concurrence in any measures that it may become my duty to adopt for ensuring a wise and humane system of native administration in that part of South Africa.

Papers will be laid before you on these several matters.

The King and Chiefs of Fiji having made a new offer of their Islands, unfettered by conditions, I have thought it right to accept the cession of a territory which, independently of its large natural resources, offers important maritime advantages to my fleets in the Pacific.

An ample harvest has restored prosperity to the Provinces of my Eastern Empire which last year were visited with famine. By the blessing of Providence my Indian Government has been able entirely to avert the loss of life which I had reason to apprehend from that great calamity.

Gentlemen of the House of Commons,

I have directed the estimates of the year to be prepared and presented to you without delay.

My Lords and Gentlemen,

The condition of the finances is satisfactory. The trade of the country in the past year has somewhat fallen short of that of the year before; but the general prosperity of the people, supported as it has been by an excellent harvest, as well as by the great reductions lately made in taxation, has led to a steady increase in the consumption of all the necessaries of life, and of those articles which contribute to the revenue.

The various statutes of an exceptional or temporary nature now in force for the preservation of peace in Ireland will be brought to your notice, with a view to determine whether some of them may not be dispensed with.

Several measures which were unavoidably postponed at the end of last session will be again introduced. Among the most important are those for simplifying the transfer of land, and completing the reconstruction of the Judicature.

Bills will also be laid before you for facilitating the improvement of the dwellings of the working classes in large towns, for the consolidation and amendment of

19

the sanitary laws, and for the prevention of the pollution of rivers.

A measure has been proposed for consolidating and amending the laws relating to Friendly Societies. Its object will be to assist, without unnecessarily interfering with, the laudable efforts of my people to make provision for themselves against some of the calamities of life.

A Bill for the amendment of the Merchant Shipping Act will be laid before you.

Your attention will be moreover directed to legislation for the better security of my subjects from personal violence, and for more effectually providing for the trial of offences by establishing the office of a Public Prosecutor.

Although the report of the Commission issued by me, to inquire into the state and working of the law as to offences connected with trade, has not yet been made to me, I trust that any legislation on this subject which may be found to be expedient may take place in the present session.

You will also be invited to consider a measure for improving the law as to agricultural tenancies.

I commend to your careful consideration these and other measures which may be submitted to you; and I pray that your deliberations may, under the Divine blessing, result in the happiness and contentment of my people.

Mover of Address in the Lords, Earl of Donoughmore.
Seconder   „   „   Lord Rayleigh.
Mover of Address in the Commons, Mr. E. Stanhope.
Seconder   „   „   Mr. Whitelaw.

PROROGATION OF PARLIAMENT BY COMMISSION.

Date.—August 13th, 1875.

The Lords Commissioners were :—The Lord Chancellor; the Lord President of the Council; the Lord Steward of the Household; the Earl of Shrewsbury; and the Earl of Hardwicke.

The Queen's Speech.

My Lords and Gentlemen,

I am happy to be enabled to release you from your attendance in Parliament.

The relations between myself and all foreign Powers continue to be cordial, and I look forward with hope and confidence to the uninterrupted maintenance of European peace.

The visit paid to this country, on the invitation of my Government, by the Ruler of Zanzibar, has led to the conclusion of a supplementary convention, which, I trust, may be efficacious for the more complete suppression of East African Slave Trade.

I have learned with deep regret that the expedition despatched by my Indian Government from Burmah, with a view to open communications with the Western Provinces of China, has been treacherously attacked by an armed force while on Chinese territory. This outrage, unhappily involving the death of a young and promising member of my Consular Service, is the subject of careful inquiry; and no effort shall be spared to secure the punishment of those by whom it was instigated and committed.

19 *

The condition of my Colonial Empire is generally prosperous.

Progress has been made in the settlement of questions affecting the Constitution and Government of Natal; and I confidently look for important and valuable results from the proposal for a Conference of the South African Colonies and States.

Gentlemen of the House of Commons,

I thank you for the liberal supplies which you have voted for the public service.

My Lords and Gentlemen,

It is gratifying to me to find that the lengthened considerations you have given to the various statutes which have from time to time been passed for the preservation of peace in Ireland, has resulted in a measure which, while relaxing the stringency of former enactments, is calculated to maintain the tranquillity of that country.

I have, with pleasure, given my assent to an Act for facilitating the improvement of the dwellings of the working classes in large towns, which will, I trust, lead to the decrease of many of the principal causes of disease, misery, and crime. I feel sure that this legislation, together with that relating to the consolidation and amendment of the Sanitary Laws, and the laws relating to Friendly Societies, will greatly promote the moral and physical welfare of my people.

It has afforded me much satisfaction to give my assent to two important statutes for the amendment of the Acts relating to master and servant and trade offences, and the law of conspiracy as connected with these offences—statutes which will, I trust, place the relations of employers and employed on a just and equal footing, and add to the contentment and good-will of large classes of my subjects.

Among the enactments which you have passed for the improvement of the law, I am well pleased to observe that a comprehensive measure for simplifying the title and facilitating the transfer of land in England has taken its place in the Statute Book; that an Act has been passed for the amendment of the Law of Entail in Scotland; and that you have made provision, by amending the Judicature Act of 1873, for bringing the great changes in my Civil Courts, and their procedure which it inaugurated, into immediate and practical effect.

The state of public business, and the differences of opinion naturally arising on a varied and comprehensive scheme, have unfortunately prevented you from completing the consideration of the Merchant Shipping Bill; but I rejoice that you have been able, by a temporary enactment, to diminish considerably the dangers to which my seafaring subjects are exposed.

By the Agricultural Holdings Act you have greatly and beneficially enlarged the powers of owners, limited in interest, to offer to their tenants a sufficient security for judicious outlay upon the farms they occupy; and while maintaining absolute freedom of contract, you have raised a presumption of rights, under which a new inducement will be given to expend capital upon the improvement of land.

I have every reason to hope that the progress of the revenue which has marked recent years will be fully sustained in the present. The arrangements which you have made with respect to the reduction of the National Debt, and those for the better regulation of loans for public works, will lead to valuable improvements in our system of Imperial and local finance.

The enactments for a registration of trade marks will supply a deficiency that has for some time been felt in our commercial system.

I trust that the Act constituting a new Bishopric at St. Albans may prove advantageous to the vast population of the dioceses affected by the measure.

In bidding you farewell for the recess, I pray that the blessing of Providence may fall on your recent labours, and accompany you in the discharge of all your duties.

PARLIAMENT IX.—SESSION III.

OPENING OF PARLIAMENT BY HER MAJESTY IN PERSON.

Date.—February 8th, 1876.

The Cabinet.—First Lord of the Treasury, Right Hon. Benjamin Disraeli ; Lord Chancellor, Right Hon. Lord Cairns ; President of the Council, His Grace the Duke of Richmond and Gordon ; Lord of the Privy Seal, Right Hon. Earl of Malmesbury ; Chancellor of the Exchequer, Right Hon. Sir Stafford H. Northcote, Bart. ; Home Secretary, Right Hon. Richard Assheton Cross ; Foreign Secretary, Right Hon. Earl of Derby ; Colonial Secretary, Right Hon. Earl of Carnarvon ; Secretary at War, Right Hon. Gathorne Hardy ; Secretary for India, Most Hon. Marquess of Salisbury ; First Lord of the Admiralty, Right Hon. George Ward

Hunt ; Postmaster-General, Right Hon. ¡Lord John
J. R· Manners.

The Queen's Speech.

My Lords and Gentlemen,

It is with much satisfaction that I again resort
to the advice and assistance of my Parliament.

My relations with all foreign Powers continue to be
of a cordial character.

The insurrectionary movement which, during the last
six months, has been maintained in the Turkish
provinces of Bosnia and Herzegovina, and which the
troops of the Sultan have, up to the present time, been
unable to repress, has excited the attention and interest
of the Great European Powers. I have considered it
my duty not to stand aloof from the efforts now being
made by allied and friendly Governments to bring about
a pacification of the disturbed districts, and I have
accordingly, while respecting the independence of the
Porte, joined in urging on the Sultan the expediency of
such measures of administrative reform as may remove
all reasonable cause of discontent on the part of his
Christian subjects.

I have agreed to purchase, subject to your ·sanction,
the shares which belong to the Khedive of Egypt in the
Suez Canal, and I rely with confidence on your enabling
me to complete a transaction in which the public
interests are deeply involved.

The representations which I addressed to the Chinese
Government, as to the attack made in the course of last
year on the expedition sent from Burmah to the western
provinces of China, have been received in a friendly

spirit, The circumstances of that lamentable outrage are now the subject of an inquiry, in which I have thought it right to request that a member of my diplomatic service should take part. I await the result of this inquiry in the firm conviction that it will be so conducted as to lead to the discovery and punishment of the offenders.

Papers on all these subjects will be laid before you.

I am deeply thankful for the uninterrupted health which my dear son, the Prince of Wales, has enjoyed during his journey through India. The hearty affection with which he has been received by my Indian subjects, of all classes and races, assures me that they are happy under my rule and loyal to my throne. At the time that the direct government of my Indian Empire was transferred to the Crown no formal addition was made to the style and titles of the Sovereign. I have deemed the present a fitting opportunity for supplying this omission, and a Bill upon the subject will be presented to you.

The humane and enlightened policy consistently pursued by this country in putting an end to slavery within her own dependencies, and in suppressing the slave trade throughout the world, makes it important that the action of British national ships in the territorial waters of foreign States should be in harmony with these great principles. I have, therefore, given directions for the issue of a Royal Commission to inquire into all treaty engagements and other international obligations bearing upon this subject, and all instructions from time to time issued to my naval officers, with a view to ascertain whether any steps ought to be taken to secure for my ships and their commanders abroad greater power for the maintenance of the right of personal liberty.

A Bill will be laid before you for punishing slave-traders who are subjects of Native Indian Princes.

The affairs of my Colonial Empire, the general prosperity of which has continued to advance, have received a large share of my attention. Papers of importance and interest will soon be in your hands, showing the proceedings with respect to a conference of the South African Colonies and States.

The murder of a high officer of the Straits Settlements whilst acting as Resident in a neighbouring Malay State, and the disorders ensuing on that outrage, have demanded the interference of my troops. I trust that the operations, which have been ably and energetically conducted, though not without loss of some valuable lives, have restored order, and re-established the just influence and authority of this country.

Gentlemen of the House of Commons,

I have directed the estimates of the year to be prepared and presented to you without delay.

My Lords and Gentlemen,

Bills for regulating the ultimate tribunal of appeal for the United Kingdom, and for the amendment of the merchant shipping laws, will be immediately submitted to you.

Legislation will be proposed relating to the universities and to primary education.

Your attention will also be called to the Acts relating to the enclosure of commons, and to a measure for promoting economy and efficiency in the management of prisons, and at the same time effecting a relief of local burthens.

Other important measures, as the time of the session permits, will be introduced to your notice; and I pray that your deliberations may, under the Divine blessing, result in the happiness and contentment of my people.

Mover of Address in the Lords, Earl of Aberdeen.
Seconder „ „ Earl of Ellesmere.
Mover of Address in the Commons, Mr. Ridley.
Seconder „ „ Mr. Mulholland.

PROROGATION OF PARLIAMENT BY COMMISSION.

Date.—August 15th, 1876.

The Lords Commissioners were :—The Lord Chancellor ; the Lord President of the Council ; the Lord Chamberlain of the Household ; the Earl of Hardwicke ; and the Earl of Bradford.

The Queen's Speech.

My Lords and Gentlemen,

I am happy to be able to release you from your attendance in Parliament.

My relations with all foreign Powers are of a friendly character, and I look forward confidently to the maintenance of the good understanding which now prevails.

The efforts which, in common with other Powers, I have made to bring about a settlement of the differences unfortunately existing between the Porte and its Christian subjects in Bosnia and Herzegovina have hitherto been unsuccessful, and the conflict begun in those provinces has extended to Servia and Montenegro. Should a favourable opportunity present itself, I shall be ready, in concert with my Allies, to offer my good offices for the purpose of mediation between the contending parties, bearing in mind alike the duties imposed upon me by treaty obligations, and those which arise from considerations of humanity and policy.

A difference has arisen between my Government and that of the United States as to the proper construction of that article of the Treaty of 9th August 1842, which relates to the mutual surrender of persons accused of certain offences. The inconvenience to both countries which would follow on a cessation of the practice of extradition are great and obvious, and I entertain a hope that a new arrangement may soon be arrived at, by which this matter may be placed on a satisfactory footing.

I am deeply thankful that my dear son, the Prince of Wales, has returned in good health from his lengthened journey through India. His presence in that part of my dominions has given occasion for the expression of feelings of loyalty and devotion to my throne, which I highly value.

In pursuance of the power conferred upon me, I have by proclamation assumed the title of Empress of India. In making, as regards India, this addition to the ancient style of my Crown, I have desired to record, on an occasion of peculiar interest to me, the earnest solicitude which I feel for the happiness of my Indian people.

I trust that peace and order are re-established in the Malay Peninsula, and that the rulers of the Native States will cheerfully accept the recommendations and assistance of my officers for the better government of their territories.

The visit to this country of the President of the Orange Free State has resulted in a satisfactory settlement of the long controversy which has existed with reference to the province of Griqualand, and an important advance has thus been made towards that friendly and cordial co-operation of neighbouring States, which is essential to the interests of South Africa.

The Conference on South African affairs, with regard to which papers have already been laid before you, is now sitting in London, and cannot fail to contribute largely to the settlement of various important questions.

Gentlemen of the House of Commons,

I thank you for the liberal supplies you have voted for the public service.

The additional outlay required to place my army and navy upon a proper footing of efficiency, and the check which has been given to the advance of the revenue by the comparative stagnation of trade, have compelled me to propose to you an increase in taxation. I desire to acknowledge the readiness with which you have responded to that appeal, and at the same time to assure you that no effort shall be wanting to keep the expenditure of the country within the bounds of moderation.

I notice with satisfaction the increased attention paid by you to the subject of local finance, and your greater watchfulness over the cost of services which are every year becoming more important, and the consideration of which ought not to be dissevered from that of imperial expenditure.

My Lords and Gentlemen,

The Act which you have passed for the amendment of the laws relating to merchant shipping will, I trust, promote the safety of our ships and seamen without imposing unnecessary restrictions upon the conduct of a service in the prosperity of which our national interests are in so many ways involved.

The measure for making further provision respecting the elementary education of the country is one of great importance, and will complete the work on which successive Parliaments have for many years been engaged, by securing a due attendance at school of the children for whose benefit the means and machinery of education have been so largely supplied.

I have readily given my consent to a Bill for facilitating the regulation and improvement of commons, and for making such amendments in the Inclosure Acts as will, I hope, tend to the preservation of open spaces in the neighbourhoods of large towns, and to the increase of the health and comfort of my people.

The serious evils arising from the pollution of rivers have long been the subject of public complaint, and I rejoice that you have passed a measure which, by checking those evils, will improve the sanitary condition of the country.

I have observed with much satisfaction the arrangements which you have made for maintaining and increasing the efficiency of the tribunal of ultimate appeal for the United Kingdom, by which, at the same time, the Judicial Committee of my Privy Council and my Intermediate Court of Appeal will be improved and strengthened.

I anticipate the best results from the Act which you have passed providing safeguards against painful experiments upon living animals.

I regret that pressure of other business has prevented the completion of your labours upon several measures of much importance. Among these I specially notice the Bills relating to the Universities of Oxford and Cambridge, to the administration of prisons, and to the law affecting maritime contracts. I trust, however, that the attention which you have given to these questions in the past session may facilitate their settlement in the next.

In bidding you farewell, I pray that the blessing of Providence may rest on your recent labours, and accompany you in the discharge of all your duties.

PARLIAMENT IX.—SESSION IV.

OPENING OF PARLIAMENT BY HER MAJESTY IN PERSON.

Date.—February 8th, 1877.

The Cabinet.—First Lord of the Treasury and Lord of the Privy Seal, Right Hon. Earl of Beaconsfield; Lord Chancellor, Right Hon. Lord Cairns; President of the Council, His Grace the Duke of Richmond and Gordon; Chancellor of the Exchequer, Right Hon. Sir Stafford H. Northcote; Home Secretary, Right Hon. Richard Assheton Cross; Foreign Secretary, Right Hon. Earl of Derby; Colonial Secretary, Right Hon.

Earl of Carnarvon; Secretary at War, Right Hon.
Gathorne Hardy; Secretary for India, Most Hon. Mar-
quess of Salisbury; First Lord of the Admiralty, Right
Hon. George Ward Hunt; Postmaster-General, Right
Hon. Lord John J. R. Manners; Chief Secretary for
Ireland, Right Hon. Sir Michael E. Hicks-Beach.

The Queen's Speech.

My Lords and Gentlemen,

It is with much satisfaction that I again resort
to the advice and assistance of my Parliament.

The hostilities which, before the close of last session,
had broken out between Turkey on the one hand and
Servia and Montenegro on the other, engaged my most
serious intention, and I anxiously waited for an opportunity when my good offices, together with those of my
Allies, might be usefully interposed.

This opportunity presented itself by the solicitation
of Servia for our mediation, the offer of which was
ultimately entertained by the Porte.

In the course of the negotiations I deemed it expedient
to lay down and, in concert with the other Powers, to
submit to the Porte certain bases upon which I held
that not only peace might be brought about with the
Principalities, but the permanent pacification of the
disturbed provinces, including Bulgaria, and the amelioration of their condition, might be effected.

Agreed to by the Powers, they required to be expanded
and worked out by negotiation or by conference, accompanied by an armistice.

The Porte, though not accepting the bases and proposing other terms, was willing to submit them to the equitable consideration of the Powers.

While proceeding to act in this mediation, I thought it right, after inquiry into the facts, to denounce to the Porte the excesses ascertained to have been committed in Bulgaria, and to express my reprobation of their perpetrators.

An armistice having been arranged, a Conference met at Constantinople for the consideration of extended terms in accordance with the original bases, in which Conference I was represented by a Special Envoy, as well as by my Ambassador.

In taking these steps, my object has throughout been to maintain the peace of Europe, and to bring about the better government of the disturbed provinces without infringing upon the independence and integrity of the Ottoman Empire.

The proposals recommended by myself and my Allies have not, I regret to say, been accepted by the Porte ; but the result of the Conference has been to show the existence of a general agreement among the European Powers which cannot fail to have a material effect upon the condition and Government of Turkey.

In the meantime, the armistice between Turkey and the Principalities has been prolonged, and is still unexpired, and may, I trust, yet lead to the conclusion of an honourable peace.

In these affairs I have acted in cordial co-operation with my Allies, with whom, as with other foreign Powers, my relations continue to be of a friendly character.

Papers on these subjects will be forthwith laid before you.

My assumption of the Imperial title at Delhi was welcomed by the chiefs and people of India with professions of affection and loyalty most grateful to my feelings.

It is with deep regret that I have to announce a calamity in that part of my dominions, which will demand the most earnest watchfulness on the part of my Government there. A famine not less serious than that of 1873 has overspread a large portion of the Presidencies of Madras and Bombay.

I am confident that every resource will be employed, not merely in arrest of this present famine, but in obtaining fresh experience for the prevention or mitigation of such visitations for the future.

The prosperity and progress of my Colonial Empire remain unchecked, although the proceedings of the Government of the Transvaal Republic, and the hostilities in which it has engaged with the neighbouring tribes, have caused some apprehension for the safety of my subjects in South Africa.

I trust, however, that the measures which I have taken will suffice to prevent any serious evil.

Gentlemen of the House of Commons,

I have directed the estimates of this year to be prepared and presented to you without delay.

My Lords and Gentlemen,

Bills relating to the Universities of Oxford and Cambridge, and for amending the law as to bankruptcy and letters patent for inventions, will be laid before you.

20

Your attention will be again called to measures for promoting economy and efficiency in the management of the prisons of the United Kingdom, which will at the same time effect a relief of local burthens.

Bills will also be laid before you for amending the laws relating to the valuation of property in England, for simplifying and amending the law relating to factories and workshops, and for improving the law relating to the summary jurisdiction of magistrates.

Legislation will be proposed with reference to roads and bridges in Scotland, and the Scotch Poor Law.

You will be asked to constitute one Supreme Court of Judicature in Ireland, and to confer an equitable jurisdiction on the county courts in that country.

I commend to you these and other measures which may be submitted for your consideration, and trust that the blessing of the Almighty will attend your labours and direct your efforts.

Mover of Address in the Lords, Viscount Grey de
Wilton.
Seconder ,, ,, Earl of Haddington.
Mover of Address in the Commons, Viscount Galway.
Seconder ,, ,, Mr. Torr.

PROROGATION OF PARLIAMENT BY COMMISSION.

Date.—August 14th, 1877.

The Lords Commissioners were :—The Lord Chancellor; the Lord President of the Council; the Secretary of State for India; the Earl of Harrowby; and Lord Skelmersdale.

The Queen's Speech.

My Lords and Gentlemen,

I am happy to be able to release you from your attendance in Parliament.

My relations with all foreign Powers continue to be friendly.

The exertions which, since the commencement of disturbances in Eastern Europe, I have not ceased to make for the maintenance of the public peace, have, unfortunately, not been successful.

On the outbreak of war between the Russian and the Ottoman Empires, I declared my intention of preserving an attitude of neutrality so long as the interests of this country remained unaffected. The extent and nature of those interests were further defined in a communication which I caused to be addressed to the Government of Russia, and which elicited a reply indicating friendly dispositions on the part of that State.

I shall not fail to use my best efforts, when a suitable opportunity occurs, for the restoration of peace, on terms compatible with the honour of the belligerents and with the general safety and welfare of other nations.

If in the course of the contest the rights of my Empire should be assailed or endangered, I should confidently rely upon your help to vindicate and maintain them.

The apprehensions of a serious famine in Southern India, which I communicated to you at the opening of the session, have, I grieve to say, been fully verified. The visitation which has fallen upon my subjects in Madras and Bombay, and upon the people of Mysore,

20 *

has been of extreme severity, and its duration is likely to be prolonged.

No exertion will be wanting on the part of my Indian Government to mitigate this terrible calamity.

The proclamation of my sovereignty in the Transvaal has been received throughout the province with enthusiasm. It has also been received with marked satisfaction by the native chiefs and tribes; and the war, which threatened in its progress to compromise the safety of my subjects in South Africa, is happily brought to a close.

I trust that the measure which has been passed to enable the European communities of South Africa to unite upon such terms as may be agreed on, will be the means of preventing the recurrence of similar dangers, and will increase and consolidate the prosperity of this important part of my dominions.

Gentlemen of the House of Commons,

I thank you for the liberal supplies which you have voted for the public service.

I have issued a royal warrant to give effect to the provision which you have made for ensuring adequate promotion for the officers of my army.

My Lords and Gentlemen,

The measures which have been passed relating to the prisons of the United Kingdom, will secure economy and efficiency in their management, and at the same time effect a considerable reduction in local burthens.

The Universities of Oxford and Cambridge, under the Act to which I have gladly given my assent, will obtain power to extend more generally the benefit of the higher education.

The Acts for reorganising the Superior Courts of Justice in Ireland, and for reforming and conferring an extensive equitable jurisdiction on the county courts, will largely improve the administration of the law in that part of the United Kingdom.

I anticipate the best results from the Act which extends to the Sheriff Courts of Scotland jurisdiction in regard to veritable rights.

In bidding you farewell, I pray that the blessing of Almighty God may rest on your recent labours, and accompany you in the discharge of all your duties.

PARLIAMENT IX.—SESSION V.

OPENING OF PARLIAMENT BY COMMISSION.

Date.—January 17th, 1878.

The Lords Commissioners were :—The Lord Chancellor ; the Lord President of the Council; the Lord Chamberlain of the Household ; the Lord Steward of the Household ; and Lord Skelmersdale.

The Cabinet.—First Lord of the Treasury and Lord of the Privy Seal, Right Hon. Earl of Beaconsfield ; Lord Chancellor, Right Hon. Lord Cairns ; President of the Council, His Grace the Duke of Richmond and Gordon ; Chancellor of the Exchequer, Right Hon. Sir Stafford H. Northcote ; Home Secretary, Right Hon. Richard Assheton Cross ; Foreign Secretary, Right Hon. Earl of Derby ; Colonial Secretary, Right Hon. Earl of Carnarvon ; Secretary at War, Right Hon.

Gathorne Hardy; Secretary for India, Most Hon. Marquess of Salisbury; First Lord of the Admiralty, Right Hon. William Henry Smith; Postmaster-General, Right Hon. Lord John J. R. Manners; Chief Secretary for Ireland, Right Hon. Sir Michael E. Hicks-Beach.

The Queen's Speech.

My Lords and Gentlemen,

I have thought fit to assemble you before the usual period of your meeting, in order that you might become acquainted with the efforts I have made to terminate the war now devastating Eastern Europe and Armenia, and that I might have the advice and assistance of my Parliament in the present state of public affairs.

You are aware that, after having unsuccessfully striven to avert that war, I declared my intention to observe strict neutrality in a contest which I lamented, but had failed to prevent, so long as the interests of my Empire, as defined by my Government, were not threatened.

I expressed, at the same time, my earnest desire to avail myself of any opportunity which might present itself for promoting a peaceful settlement of the questions at issue between the belligerent Powers.

The successes obtained by the Russian arms, both in Europe and Asia, convinced the Porte that it should endeavour to bring to a close hostilities which were causing immense suffering to its subjects. The Government of the Sultan accordingly addressed to the neutral Powers, parties to the treaties relating to the Turkish Empire, an appeal for their good offices.

It did not, however, appear to the majority of the Powers thus addressed that they could usefully comply with the request, and they communicated this opinion to the Porte.

The Porte then determined to make a separate appeal to my Government, and I at once agreed to make an inquiry of the Emperor of Russia whether His Imperial Majesty would entertain overtures for peace.

The Emperor expressed, in reply, his earnest desire for peace, and stated, at the same time, his opinion as to the course which should be pursued for its attainment.

Upon this subject communications have taken place between the Governments of Russia and Turkey through my good offices, and I earnestly trust that they may lead to a pacific solution of the points at issue, and to a termination of the war. No efforts on my part will be wanting to promote that result.

Hitherto, so far as the war has proceeded, neither of the belligerents has infringed the conditions on which my neutrality is founded, and I willingly believe that both parties are desirous to respect them so far as it may be in their power. So long as these conditions are not infringed, my attitude will continue the same. But I cannot conceal from myself that, should hostilities be unfortunately prolonged, some unexpected occurrence may render it incumbent on me to adopt measures of precaution. Such measures could not be effectually taken without adequate preparation, and I trust to the liberality of my Parliament to supply the means which may be required for that purpose.

Papers on these affairs will be forthwith laid before you.

My relations will all foreign Powers continue to be friendly.

I am thankful that the terrible famine which has ravaged Southern India is nearly at an end. Strenuous and successful exertions have been made by my local governments to relieve the sufferings of the population, and in that duty they have been powerfully seconded by the liberal aid of my people at home, and in my Colonies. I have directed that an inquiry shall be made into the measures most proper to diminish the danger of such calamities for the future.

The condition of native affairs in South Africa has of late caused me some anxiety, and has demanded the watchful attention of my Government. I have thought it expedient to reinforce my troops in that part of my Empire. I trust that a peaceable and satisfactory settlement of all differences may be shortly obtained.

Gentlemen of the House of Commons,

I have directed the estimates of the year to be prepared and presented to you without delay.

My Lords and Gentlemen,

A Bill will be laid before you upon the subject of county government, and your attention will be again called to the consolidation of the factory law, and to the summary jurisdiction of magistrates.

You will be asked at an early period of the session to take into your consideration a Bill on the subject of cattle disease in this country.

The questions of Scottish roads and bridges, and of endowed schools and hospitals in Scotland, will also be brought before you.

Your attention will be invited to the subject of intermediate education in Ireland, and to the grand jury law in that country.

Among other measures for the amendment of the law, a Bill will be laid before you to simplify and express in one Act the whole law and procedure relating to indictable offences.

I commend these subjects to your most careful consideration, and pray that the blessing of the Almighty may attend and guide your deliberations.

Mover of Address in the Lords, Earl of Wharncliffe.
Seconder ,, ,, Earl of Loudoun.
Mover of Address in the Commons, Mr. Wilbraham
                                   Egerton.
Seconder ,, ,, Mr. Tennant.

PROROGATION OF PARLIAMENT BY COMMISSION.

Date.—August 16th, 1878.

The Lords Commissioners were:—The Lord Chancellor; the Lord President of the Council; the Lord of the Privy Seal; the Lord Chamberlain of the Household; and Lord Skelmersdale.

The Queen's Speech.

My Lords and Gentlemen,

When, in a critical condition of public affairs, you assembled at the commencement of the year, I pointed out to you that, in the interests of my Empire, precautions might become necessary, for which I appealed to your liberality to provide. At the same time I assured you that no efforts in the cause of peace should be wanting on my part.

Your response was not ambiguous, and contributed largely to a pacific solution of the difficulties which then existed. The terms of agreement between Russia and the Porte, so far as they affected pre existing treaties, were, after an interval of discussion, submitted to a Congress of the Powers ; and their councils have resulted in a peace which I am thankful to believe is satisfactory and likely to be durable. The Ottoman Empire has not emerged from a disastrous war without severe loss ; but the arrangements which have been made, while favourable to the subjects of the Porte, have secured to it a position of independence which can be upheld against aggression.

I have concluded a defensive convention with the Sultan, which has been laid before you. It gives, as regards his Asiatic Empire, a more distinct expression to the engagements I, together with other Powers, accepted in 1856, but of which the form has not been found practically effectual. The Sultan has, on the other hand, bound himself to adopt and carry into effect the measures necessary for securing the good government of those provinces. In order to promote the objects of this agreement, I have undertaken the occupation and administration of the island of Cyprus.

In aiding to bring about the settlement which has taken place, I have been assisted by the discipline and high spirit of my forces by sea and by land, by the alacrity with which my reserves responded to my call, by the patriotic offers of military aid by my people in the Colonies, and by the proud desire of my Indian army to be reckoned among the defenders of the British Empire—a desire justified by the soldierly qualities of the force recently quartered at Malta.

The spontaneous offers of troops made by many of the Native Governments in India were very gratifying to me, and I recognise in them a fresh manifestation of that feeling towards my Crown and person which has been displayed in many previous instances.

My relations with all foreign Powers continue to be friendly.

Although the condition of affairs in South Africa still affords some ground for anxiety, I have learnt with satisfaction, from the reports of my civil and military officers, that the more serious disturbances which had arisen among the native population on the frontiers of the Cape Colony are now terminated.

Gentlemen of the House of Commons,

I thank you for the liberal supplies which you have voted for the public service.

My Lords and Gentlemen,

The Act which has been passed for amending and greatly simplifying the law relating to factories and workshops will, I trust, still further secure the health and education of those who are employed in them.

I have had much pleasure in giving my assent to a measure relating to the contagious diseases of cattle, which, by affording additional securities against the introduction and spread of these diseases, will tend to encourage the breeding of live stock in the country, and to increase the supply of food to my people.

You have amended the law as to highways in a

manner which cannot but improve their classification and management, and at the same time relieve inequalities in the burden of their maintenance.

I trust that advantage will be taken of the means which you have provided for dividing bishoprics in the more populous districts of the country, and thus increasing the efficiency of the Church.

I anticipate the best results from the wise arrangements which you have made for the encouragement of intermediate education in Ireland.

The measure for amending and consolidating the public health laws in that country is well calculated to promote the important object at which it aims.

The measure passed in regard to roads and bridges in Scotland and for the abolition of tolls, will greatly improve the management of highways in that part of the United Kingdom; while the Acts relating to education, and to endowed schools and hospitals, cannot fail to extend the benefits of education and improve the administration of charitable endowments in that country.

In bidding you farewell, I pray that the blessing of Almighty God may rest on your recent labours, and accompany you in the discharge of all your duties.

PARLIAMENT IX.—SESSION VI.

OPENING OF PARLIAMENT BY COMMISSION.

Date.—December 5th, 1878.

The Lords Commissioners were:—The Lord Chancellor; the Lord President of the Council; the Lord of the Privy Seal; the Lord Steward of the Household; and Lord Skelmersdale.

The Cabinet.—First Lord of the Treasury, Right Hon. Earl of Beaconsfield, K.G. ; Lord Chancellor, Right Hon. Lord Cairns ; President of the Council, His Grace the Duke of Richmond and Gordon ; Lord of the Privy Seal, His Grace the Duke of Northumberland ; Chancellor of the Exchequer, Right Hon. Sir Stafford H. Northcote ; Home Secretary, Right Hon. Richard Assheton Cross ; Foreign Secretary, Most Hon. Marquess of Salisbury ; Colonial Secretary, Right Hon. Sir Michael Edward Hicks-Beach ; Secretary at War, Right Hon. Frederick Arthur Stanley ; Secretary for India, Right Hon. Viscount Cranbrook ; First Lord of the Admiralty, Right Hon. William Henry Smith ; Postmaster-General, Right Hon. Lord John J. R. Manners ; President of the Board of Trade, Right Hon. Viscount Sandon.

The Queen's Speech.

My Lords and Gentlemen,

I regret that I have been obliged to call for your attendance at an unusual and, probably to most of you, an inconvenient season.

The hostility towards my Indian Government manifested by the Ameer of Afghanistan, and the manner in which he repulsed my friendly mission, left me no alternative but to make a peremptory demand for redress.

This demand having been disregarded, I have directed an expedition to be sent into his territory, and I have taken the earliest opportunity of calling you together and making to you the communication required by law.

I have directed that papers on the subject shall be laid before you.

I receive from all foreign Powers assurances of their friendly feelings, and I have every reason to believe that the arrangements for the pacification of Europe, made by the Treaty of Berlin, will be successfully carried into effect.

Gentlemen of the House of Commons,

The estimates of the ensuing year are in course of preparation, and will in due time be submitted to you.

My Lords and Gentlemen,

I propose that, after full deliberation upon the matters which have led me to anticipate your usual time of meeting, and after a suitable recess, you should proceed to the consideration of various measures for the public benefit which will then be laid before you.

I confidently commit to your wisdom the interests of my Empire, and I pray that the blessing of Almighty God may attend your counsels.

Mover of Address in the Lords, Earl of Ravensworth.
Seconder   ,,   ,, Lord Inchiquin.
Mover of Address in the Commons, Viscount Castle-
reagh.
Seconder   ,,   ,, Mr. Hall.

PROROGATION OF PARLIAMENT BY COMMISSION.

Date.—August 15th, 1879.

The Lords Commissioners were :—The Lord Chancellor ; the Lord of the Privy Seal ; the Lord Steward of the Household ; the Earl of Hardwicke ; and Lord Skelmersdale.

The Queen's Speech.

My Lords and Gentlemen,

I am happy to be able to relieve you from your laborious duties.

My relations with other Powers continue to be cordial, and my influence with them will be employed in maintaining the obligations imposed by treaties, and in promoting and consolidating the general peace.

The territorial arrangements stipulated in the Treaty of Berlin have been faithfully executed, and the delimitation of the two frontiers is nearly completed. The Balkan Peninsula has been evacuated by the Russian army in accordance with the treaty.

Under the unanimous sanction of the signatory Powers, suitable provision has been made for the government of the Ottoman Province of Eastern Roumelia, and I have with great satisfaction given my approval to the election of Prince Alexander of Battenburg as Prince of Bulgaria.

The calamities inflicted by the late war have hitherto precluded the adoption of those reforms by the Ottoman Government, of which it has acknowledged the necessity, but I have urged, and shall continue to urge, the importance of a timely compliance with its engagements in this respect.

At the suggestion of my Government, in conjunction with that of France, a change has taken place in the Viceroyalty of Egypt, which the past misgovernment of that country had rendered necessary.

The treaty concluded with the Ameer of Afghanistan, which has been laid before you, has happily terminated

the war which his predecessor compelled me to undertake. By it my friendly relations with that State are
re-established, guarantees for its peace and safety given,
and the frontiers of India strengthened.

The ability displayed in this war by those in command
of my troops, British and native, and the gallantry and
endurance of the troops themselves, well deserved the
thanks bestowed upon them by both Houses of Parliament. My acknowledgments are especially due to the
many native princes who made offers of assistance, as
well as to those whose forces were actually brought into
the field, and I recognise in such zealous co-operation
their attachment and good-will to my Indian Empire.

Since I last addressed you, my forces have been
engaged in a serious conflict with the most powerful
native ruler in South Africa. While I have pleasure in
thanking them for vindicating the honour of the British
arms, I must mourn over the sacrifice of many a
precious life. I trust that the decisive success which
has recently attended their operations will lead to an
early establishment of peace on an enduring basis, and
that my subjects in that part of the world, being thus
relieved from the danger to which they have hitherto
been exposed, may readily join in such arrangements as
may best secure their safety and prosperity in the future.

Gentlemen of the House of Commons,

I thank you for the liberal supplies which you
have voted for the public service.

My Lords and Gentlemen,

By the Army Discipline Act you have for the
first time placed upon the Statute Book in a complete

code the laws relating to service in my army and my other military forces. You have arranged in a clear and comprehensive form the provisions for the due maintenance of discipline ; you have improved the system under which enlistment takes place ; and you have amended the regulations under which the reserves can be recalled to the colours.

The Acts providing for the appointment of a Public Prosecutor, and amending the law relating to summary jurisdiction of magistrates, will, I trust, greatly improve the administration of the criminal law.

The alterations which you have made in the law relating to banking and joint stock companies are well calculated to conduce to the prosperity of this important portion of our mercantile and commercial system.

The depressed condition of the agricultural interest has naturally engaged your attention, and I have much pleasure in complying with the Address of the House of Commons requesting me to appoint a Commission to inquire into the causes to which the depression is owing, and how far they can be remedied by legislation.

I observe with satisfaction that you have been able to consider the important subject of Education in Ireland, and that you have agreed to measures which will form a fitting supplement to the enactment of last session as to intermediate education. The primary education of the country cannot but be stimulated by the careful provision you have made for improving the position of the teachers ; and the Bill you have passed for University Education will, I trust, supply what is needed for the advancement of learning in its higher branches.

21

In bidding farewell, I pray that the blessing of Providence may rest on the labours with which you have been occupied during the session.

PARLIAMENT IX.—SESSION VII.

OPENING OF PARLIAMENT BY COMMISSION.

' *Date.*—February 5th, 1880.

The Lords Commissioners were:—The Lord Chancellor; the Lord Steward of the Household; the Lord Chamberlain of the Household ; the Secretary of State for the Colonies; and the Earl of Cork and Orrery.

The Cabinet.—First Lord of the Treasury, Right Hon. Earl of Beaconsfield, K.G.; Lord Chancellor, Right Hon. Lord Cairns ; President of the Council, His Grace the Duke of Richmond and Gordon; Lord of the Privy Seal, His Grace the Duke of Northumberland ; Chancellor of the Exchequer, Right Hon. Sir Stafford H. Northcote ; Home Secretary, Right Hon. Richard Assheton Cross ; Foreign Secretary, Most Hon. Marquess of Salisbury ; Colonial Secretary, Right Hon. Sir Michael E. Hicks-Beach; Secretary at War, Right Hon. Frederick Arthur Stanley; Secretary for India, Right Hon. Viscount Cranbrook ; First Lord of the Admiralty, Right Hon. W. H. Smith; Postmaster-General, Right Hon. Lord John J. R. Manners; President of the Board of Trade, Right Hon. Viscount Sandon.

The Queen's Speech.

My Lords and Gentlemen,

It is with much satisfaction that I again resort to the advice and assistance of my Parliament.

My relations with all the Powers continue to be friendly. The course of events since the prorogation of Parliament has tended to furnish additional security to the maintenance of European peace, as laid down by the Treaty of Berlin. Much, however, remains to be done to repair the disorder with which the late war has affected many parts of the Turkish Empire.

A Convention for the suppression of the slave trade has been concluded between my Government and that of His Imperial Majesty the Sultan.

At the close of your last session I expressed my hope that the Treaty of Gundamak had happily terminated the war in Afghanistan. In conformity with its provisions, my envoy, with his retinue, were honourably received and entertained by the Ameer of Cabul. While engaged, however, in the exercise of their duty, he, and those connected with the embassy, were treacherously attacked by overwhelming numbers, and, after a heroic defence, were almost all massacred. An outrage so intolerable called for condign chastisement, and my troops which, pursuant to the stipulations of the treaty, either had withdrawn or were withdrawing from the territories governed by the Ameer, were ordered to retrace their steps. The skill exhibited in the rapid march upon Cabul, and in the advances upon the other line of action, reflects the highest credit upon the officers and men of my British and Native forces, whose bravery has shone with its wonted lustre in every collision with the enemy.

The abdication of the Ameer, and the unsettled condition of the country, renders the recall of my troops impossible for the present; but the principle on which

21 *

my Government has hitherto acted remains unchanged, and while determined to make the frontiers of my Indian Empire strong, I desire to be in friendly relations alike with those who may rule in Afghanistan and with the people of that country.

My anticipations as to the early establishment of peace in South Africa have been fulfilled. The capture and deposition of the Zulu King, and the breaking up of the military organisation on which his dynasty was based, have relieved my possessions in that part of the world from a danger which has seriously impeded their advancement and consolidation.

In Basutoland a native outbreak of considerable importance has been effectively quelled by my Colonial forces; while the Transvaal has been freed from the depredations of a powerful chief, who, having successfully resisted the former Government of the country, had persistently resisted our attempts at conciliation. I have reason to hope that the time is now approaching when an important advance may be made towards the establishment of a union or confederation, under which the powers of self-government already enjoyed by the inhabitants of the Cape Colony may be extended to my subjects in other parts of South Africa.

Papers on these and other matters will be forthwith laid before you.

Gentlemen of the House of Commons,

I have directed the estimates of this year to be prepared and laid before you without delay.

My Lords and Gentlemen,

The Commission which, at the close of the

session, I informed you I had issued to inquire into the cause of agricultural depression throughout the Kingdom, is pursuing its labours. In the meantime the serious deficiency in the usual crops in some parts of Ireland has rendered necessary special precautions on the part of my Government to guard against the calamities with which those districts were threatened.

With this view they have called upon the authorities charged with the duty of administering relief to make ample preparation for the distribution of food and fuel, should such a step become necessary; and they have also stimulated the employment of labour by advances more liberal than those prescribed by the existing law.

I feel assured that you will give your sanction to the course which has been adopted, where it may have exceeded the power entrusted by Parliament to the Executive Government.

A proposal will be submitted to you for providing the funds required for these exceptional advances on the security of the property administered by the Church Temporalities Commissioners.

I trust you will be able to resume the consideration of the Criminal Code, and of the improvement of the law of bankruptcy.

Bills will be laid before you for enlarging the power of owners of settled land, of consolidating and amending the lunacy laws, and for simplifying the practice of conveyancing.

I commend to you these and other measures which may be submitted for your consideration, and I trust that the blessing of the Almighty will attend and direct your labours.

Mover of Address in the Lords, Earl of Onslow.
Seconder ,, ,, Earl of Rosse.
Mover of Address in the Commons, Col. Drummond Moray.
Seconder ,, ,, Mr. J. P. Corry.

DISSOLUTION OF PARLIAMENT BY COMMISSION.

Date.—March 24th, 1880.

The Lords Commissioners were :—The Lord Chancellor ; the Earl of Hardwicke ; the Earl of Bradford ; the Secretary of State for India ; and Lord Skelmersdale.

The Queen's Speech.

My Lords and Gentlemen,

As the time assigned by law for the termination of the present Parliament is near at hand, I am induced by considerations of public policy and convenience to select this period of the session for releasing you from your legislative duties, with a view to an immediate dissolution and the issue of writs for a general election.

I cannot part from you without expressing my deep sense of the zeal and ability which during more than six years you have consistently displayed in exercising your important functions, nor without tendering to you my warm acknowledgments for the useful measures which you have submitted for my acceptance, and especially for the manner in which you have upheld a policy, the object of which was at once to defend my Empire, and secure the general peace.

My relations with foreign Powers are friendly, and favourable to the maintenance of tranquillity in Europe.

I entertain the confident hope that the measures adopted in Afghanistan will lead to a speedy settlement of that country.

I have had much satisfaction in assenting to the Acts you have passed for the relief of the distress unhappily prevalent in Ireland; and trusting that these measures will be accepted by my Irish subjects as a proof of the ready sympathy of the Imperial Parliament, I look forward with confidence to the restored prosperity of their country.

I rejoice to observe the indication of a general improvement in trade, and that the commercial depression which I have had to lament appears to be passing away.

I have witnessed with the greatest sympathy the heavy losses sustained by the various classes connected with the cultivation of the soil, and have viewed with admiration the patience and high spirit with which they have contended against an almost unprecedented series of disastrous seasons.

I trust that, with the blessing of Providence, a more favourable harvest may be looked for, and that, from the Commission which I issued to inquire into the causes of agricultural depression, suggestions will come which will lead to the more profitable use of agricultural land, and to a higher development of this branch of national industry.

The electors of the United Kingdom will be called upon forthwith to choose their representatives in Parliament; and I fervently pray that the blessing of Almighty God may guide them to promote the object of my constant solicitude, the happiness of my people.

PARLIAMENT X.—SESSION I.

OPENING OF PARLIAMENT BY COMMISSION.

Date.—May 20th, 1880.

The Lords Commissioners were:—The Lord Chancellor; the Lord President of the Council; the Lord Chamberlain of the Household; the Lord Steward of the Household; and the Earl of Cork.

The Cabinet.—First Lord of the Treasury and Chancellor of the Exchequer, Right Hon. William Ewart Gladstone; Lord Chancellor, Right Hon. Lord Selborne; President of the Council, Right Hon. Earl Spencer; Lord of the Privy Seal, His Grace the Duke of Argyll; Home Secretary, Right Hon. Sir W. V. Harcourt; Foreign Secretary, Right Hon. Earl Granville; Colonial Secretary, Right Hon. Earl of Kimberley; Secretary at War, Right Hon. H. C. E. Childers; Secretary for India, Right Hon. Marquess of Hartington; First Lord of the Admiralty, Right Hon. Earl of Northbrook; Chancellor of the Duchy of Lancaster, Right Hon. John Bright; President of the Board of Trade, Right Hon. Joseph Chamberlain; Chief Secretary for Ireland, Right Hon. W. E. Forster; President of the Local Government Board, Right Hon. J. G. Dodson.

The Queen's Speech.

My Lords and Gentlemen,

I avail myself of the earliest opportunity of meeting you after the recent General Election, and the arrangements required upon a change of Administration.

The cordial relations which I hold with all the other Powers of Europe, will, I trust, enable me to promote, in concert with them, the early and complete fulfilment of the Treaty of Berlin, with respect to effectual reforms and equal laws in Turkey, as well as to such territorial questions as have not yet been settled in conformity with the provisions of that treaty. I regard such a fulfilment as essential for the avoidance of further complications in the East.

In accordance with this view, I have deemed it expedient to despatch an Ambassador Extraordinary to the Court of the Sultan.

On the last occasion of my addressing you, I expressed my hope that the measures adopted in Afghanistan would lead to a speedy settlement of that country. Since that period the gallantry of my troops has continued to be conspicuous, and the labours of my Government in India have been unremitting But I have to lament that the end in view has not yet been attained. My efforts will, however, be unceasingly directed towards the pacification of Afghanistan, and toward the establishment of such institutions as may be found best fitted to secure the independence of its people, and to restore their friendly relations with my Indian Empire,

The condition of Indian finance, as it has recently been made known to me, has required my special attention. I have directed that you shall be supplied with the fullest information on this weighty subject

I invite your careful notice to the important questions of policy connected with the future of South Africa. I have continued to commend to the favourable consideration of the authorities, and of the people of the various settlements, the project of confederation. In maintaining my supremacy in the Transvaal, with its diversified population, I desire both to make provision for the security of the indigenous races, and to extend to the European settlers institutions based on large and liberal principles of self-government.

Gentlemen of the House of Commons,

I notice with satisfaction that the imports and exports of the country, as well as other signs, indicate some revival in trade ; but the depression which has lately been perceived in the revenue continues without abatement.

The estimates of income which were laid before the last Parliament were framed with moderation, but the time which has since elapsed exhibits no promise that they will be exceeded.

The annual estimates of charge, so far as they have not been already voted, will be promptly laid before you.

My Lords and Gentlemen,

The late season of the year at which you commence your labours will, I fear, seriously abridge the time available for useful legislation, but I make no doubt you will studiously turn it to the best account.

The Peace Preservation Act for Ireland expires on the 1st of June. You will not be asked to renew it. My desire to avoid the evils of exceptional legislation in abridgment of liberty would not induce me to forego in any degree the performance of the first duty of every Government in providing for the security of life and property ; but while determined to fulfil this sacred obligation, I am persuaded that the loyalty and good sense of my Irish subjects will justify me in relying on the provisions of the ordinary law, firmly administered, for the maintenance of peace and order.

The provisions enacted before the dissolution of the late Parliament, for the mitigation of distress in Ireland, have been serviceable for that important end. The question of the sufficiency of the advances already authorised by Parliament is under my consideration.

A measure will at an early day be submitted to you for putting an end to the controversies which have arisen with respect to burials in churchyards and cemeteries.

It will be necessary for you to renew the Act for secret voting.

Among the chief subjects which will be brought under your notice, as time may permit, will be Bills for giving more effectual protection to occupiers of land against injury from ground game, for determining on a just principle the liabilities of employers for accidents sustained by workmen, and for the extension of the borough franchise in Ireland.

These and all your labours I heartily commend to the blessing of God.

Mover of Address in the Lords, Earl of Elgin.
Seconder ,, ,, Lord Sandhurst.
Mover of Address in the Commons, Mr. A. Grey.
Seconder ,, ,, Mr. Hugh Mason.

PROROGATION OF PARLIAMENT BY COMMISSION.

Date.—September 7th, 1880.

The Lords Commissioners were:—The Lord Chancellor ; the Lord Steward of the Household ; the Lord

Chamberlain of the Household ; the Secretary of State
for the Colonies ; and the Earl of Cork and Orrery.

The Queen's Speech.

My Lords and Gentlemen,

It is with great satisfaction that I find myself at
length enabled to release you from your arduous
labours.

I continue to receive assurances of the most friendly
character from all foreign Powers.

The failure of the Sublime Porte to execute, according
to its engagement, a plan which was agreed upon in
April last for the determination of the Ottoman frontier
lying towards Montenegro, has caused unfortunate
delays in the settlement of that question, and the Treaty
of Berlin has not yet taken effect in other points of
importance which remained open at the commencement
of the session

The Governments which were parties to that treaty
have communicated to the Sultan their judgment on the
means of bringing to a satisfactory settlement the Greek
and Montenegrin frontier questions, on the administrative organisation of the European provinces of Turkey,
and on the principal reforms required in the Asiatic
provinces inhabited by Armenians.

For the attainment of the object in view, I continue
to place reliance on the fact that the concert of Europe
has been steadily maintained in regard to the Eastern
Question, and that the Powers which signed the Treaty
of Berlin are pressing upon the Sublime Porte, with all
the authority which belongs to their united action, the

measures which, in their belief, are best calculated to ensure tranquillity in the East.

I have not been unmindful, during the few months[1] which have elapsed since I last addressed you, of the considerations which I have stated would guide my policy on the north-western frontier of my Indian Empire. Measures have already been taken for the complete military evacuation of Northern Afghanistan, and some progress has been made towards the pacification and settlement of the country.

A renewal of hostilities by the Afghans, under Ayoub Khan, has rendered necessary further military operations in South Afghanistan. The prompt measures taken by the Indian Government for the relief of the garrison of Candahar, and the conspicuous ability and energy displayed by my officers and troops in the execution of those measures, resulting in the brilliant victory recently gained by the gallant force under the command of Sir Frederick Roberts, will, I trust, speedily bring to an honourable termination the war in that division of the country.

I regret it has not hitherto been possible to give you such information on the general state of Indian finance, and the recent miscarriages in presenting the accounts of military expenditure, as you would justly require before entering on a practical consideration of the subject. You may, however, rest assured that I shall redeem my pledge to supply you with this information at the earliest period in my power.

No advance has recently been made in the project of a South African Confederation; nor could advantage arise from endeavours to press it forward, except in proportion to the favourable movement of public opinion in that portion of the Empire. The general state of affairs in South Africa is, however, on the whole satis-'factory, except in Basutoland, where I trust that a moderate and conciliatory policy may allay the agitation caused by the enforcement of the Disarmament Act.

Gentlemen of the House of Commons,

I tender to you my thanks for the liberal pro-vision which you have made to meet the charges of the public service.

My Lords and Gentlemen,

I acknowledge, with thankfulness to the Almighty, the happy continuance, during several weeks, of fine weather for securing a harvest, which gives in many places a reasonable promise of abundance. I am enabled to anticipate both a further revival of trade and some addition to the revenue of the country for the year; and I dwell with especial pleasure upon the probable improvement in the condition of the people of Ireland, who have so seriously suffered from previous failure of the crops.

I rejoice also to observe that, notwithstanding the lateness of the period at which you began your labours, your indefatigable zeal and patience have enabled you to add to the Statute Book some valuable laws.

I refer particularly to your settlement of the long-contested questions relating to the subject of burials, to the Education Act, and the Act for the better deter-mining the liability of employers ; and to these I would add the Act relating to ground game, the repeal of the malt duty, the Savings' Bank Act, and the Post Office

Money Orders Act, and the measures for bettering the condition of merchant seamen, and for providing for the safer carriage of grain cargoes.

I trust these measures may, under Divine Providence, contribute to the welfare and prosperity of my people.

PARLIAMENT X.—SESSION II.

OPENING OF PARLIAMENT BY COMMISSION.

Date.—January 6th, 1881.

The Lords Commissioners were:—The Lord Chancellor; the Lord President of the Council; the Lord Steward of the Household; the Earl of Cork; and Lord Monson.

The Cabinet.—First Lord of the Treasury and Chancellor of the Exchequer, Right Hon. William Ewart Gladstone; Lord Chancellor, Right Hon. Lord Selborne; President of the Council, Right Hon. Earl Spencer; Lord of the Privy Seal, His Grace the Duke of Argyll; Home Secretary, Right Hon. Sir W. V. Harcourt; Foreign Secretary, Right Hon. Earl Granville; Colonial Secretary, Right Hon. Earl of Kimberley; Secretary at War, Right Hon. H. C. E. Childers; Secretary for India, Right Hon. Marquess of Hartington; First Lord of the Admiralty, Right Hon. Earl of Northbrook; Chancellor of the Duchy of Lancaster, Right Hon. John Bright; President of the Board of Trade, Right Hon. Joseph Chamberlain; Chief Secretary for Ireland, Right Hon. W. E. Forster; President of the Local Government Board, Right Hon. J. G. Dodson.

The Queen's Speech.

My Lords and Gentlemen,

I have called you, at a period earlier that usual, to the resumption of your labours, as some affairs of more than common urgency demand your attention.

My relations with foreign Powers continue to be friendly and harmonious.

The main question relating to the frontier between Turkey and Montenegro has been settled.

The Powers are now engaged in communications which have in view the determination of the frontier between Turkey and Greece.

Some important portions of the Treaty of Berlin, which have so long remained without fulfilment, continue to form an object of my anxious attention.

⌈A rising in the Transvaal has recently imposed upon me the duty of taking military measures, with a view to the prompt vindication of my authority; and has, of necessity, set aside for the time any plan for securing to the European settlers that full control over their own local affairs, without' prejudice to the interests of the natives, which I have been desirous to confer.

I regret that the war in Basutoland still continues, notwithstanding the efforts of the Cape Government. It would cause me much satisfaction if a suitable occasion should present itself for friendly action on my part with a view to the restoration of peace.

The war in Afghanistan has been brought to a close, and, with the exception of the Candahar force, my troops have been recalled within the Indian frontier. It is not my intention that the occupation of Candahar shall be permanently maintained, but the still unsettled condition of the country, and the consequent difficulty of establishing a Native Government, have delayed for a time the withdrawal of the army from that position.

Papers on the several subjects to which I have adverted, as well as further correspondence on the military estimates of India, will be presented to you.

Gentlemen of the House of Commons,

The estimates for the services of the coming year are in a forward state of preparation, and will be speedily laid before you.

My Lords and Gentlemen,

There has been a gradual, though not very rapid, improvement in the trade of the country, and I am now able to entertain a more favourable expectation of the revenue for the year than I could form at its commencement.

The anticipation, with which I last addressed you, of a great diminution of the distress in Ireland, owing to an abundant harvest, was realised; but I grieve to state that the social condition of the country has assumed an alarming character. Agrarian crimes in general have multiplied far beyond the experience of recent years. Attempts upon life have not grown in the same proportion as other offences; but I must add that efforts have been made for personal protection, far beyond all former precedent, by the police, under the direction of the Executive. I have to notice other evils yet more widely spread. The administration of justice has been frustrated, with respect to these offences, through the impossibility of procuring evidence; and an extended

22

system of terror has thus been established in various
parts of the country, which has paralysed almost alike
the exercise of private rights and the performance of
civil duties.

In a state of things new in some important respects,
and hence with little of available guidance from former
precedent, I have deemed it right steadily to put in
use the ordinary powers of the law before making any
new demand. But a demonstration of their insufficiency,
amply supplied by the present circumstances of the
country, leads me now to apprise you that proposals will
be immediately submitted to you for entrusting me with
additional powers, necessary, in my judgment, not only
for the vindication of order and public law, but likewise
to secure, on behalf of my subjects, protection for life
and property, and personal liberty of action.

Subject to the primary and imperious obligations to
which I have just referred, I continued to desire not
less than heretofore, to prosecute the removal of
grievance and the work of legislative improvement in
Ireland, as well as in Great Britain.

The Irish Land Act of 1870 has been productive of
great benefits, and has much contributed to the security
and comparative well-being of the occupiers of the
soil, without diminishing the value or disturbing the
foundations of property. In some respects, however,
and more particularly under the strain of recent and
calamitous years, the protection which it supplied has
not been found sufficient, either in Ulster or the other
provinces.

I recommend you to undertake the further development of its principles, in a manner conformable to the

special wants of Ireland, both as regards the relation of landlord and tenant, and with a view to effective efforts for giving to a large portion of the people, by purchase, a permanent proprietary interest in the soil. This legislation will require the removal, for the purposes in view, of all obstacles arising out of limitations on the ownership of property, with a due provision for the security of the interests involved.

A measure will be submitted to you for the establishment of county government in Ireland, founded upon representative principles, and framed with the double aim of confirming popular control over expenditure, and of supplying a yet more serious want, by extending the formation of habits of local self-government.

Bills will be laid before you for the abolition of corporal punishment in the army and in the navy.

You will be asked to consider measures for the further reform of the law of bankruptcy, for the conservancy of rivers and the prevention of floods, for revising the constitution of endowed schools and hospitals in Scotland, for the renewal of the Act which established secret voting, and for repressing the corrupt practices of which, in a limited number of towns, there were lamentable examples at the last General Election.

I trust that your labours, which will be even more than usually arduous, may be so guided by Divine Providence as to promote the happiness of my people.

Mover of Address in the Lords, Lord Carington.
Seconder,   „   „   Earl of Yarborough.
Mover of Address in the Commons, Mr. Stuart Rendel.
Seconder   „   „   Mr. Slagg.

PROROGATION OF PARLIAMENT BY COMMISSION.

Date.—August 27th, 1881.

The Lords Commissioners were :—The Lord Chancellor ; the President of the Council ; the Earl of Kenmare ; the Earl of Cork ; and Lord Monson.

The Queen's Speech.

My Lords and Gentlemen,

The time has arrived when I am at length enabled to release you from your unusually severe and protracted labours.

My relations with all foreign Powers continue to be amicable and cordial.

Progress has been made since I last addressed you in the territorial arrangements of the Levant. A treaty has been concluded, with the sanction of all the Great Powers, for the cession of Thessaly to the Greek kingdom ; and its peaceful execution has begun.

Recent events in Tunis have led to communications between my Government and the Government of France ; and I have received satisfactory assurances from the Republic as to the rights secured to me by treaty with the Bey, and as to the relations between the Regency and the neighbouring Ottoman territory of Tripoli.

The Convention has been signed which secures to the European population of the Transvaal, subject to important conditions therein set forth, a complete internal self-government. It awaits ratification by a representative assembly of the people. I trust that, when confirmed, it will contribute effectually to the tranquillity of South Africa, and to stability in its affairs.

The hopes in which I indulged on the last occasion
of my addressing you, with respect to the war in Basutoland, have been fulfilled ; and I have to notice, with
much satisfaction, the termination of hostilities in that
country

In the month of April my troops were withdrawn from
Candahar, and the government of Southern Afghanistan
was assumed by the Ameer Abdur Rahman.

I have no reason to anticipate any disturbance of
peace on the North-West Frontier of my Indian dominions from the contest with the Ameer into which
Ayoub Khan has since entered.

It will be my object, while respecting the independence
of the Afghan people, to promote, by my friendly offices,
as opportunity may arise, the restoration of peace.

Gentlemen of the House of Commons,

I thank you for the supplies which you have
provided to meet the public charge, and for the contribution you have liberally made towards the expenses of
the recent war in Afghanistan.

My Lords and Gentlemen,

The commercial negotiations with France have
been suspended ; but I continue desirous on every ground
to use my best efforts for the conclusion of a treaty on
terms favourable to extended intercourse between the
two nations, to whose close amity I attach so great a
value.

The Act for the regulation of the forces gives full
legislative effect to the plans approved by Parliament
for connecting regiments with the districts in which they
will be mainly raised, and for combining together more

closely the several branches of my land forces. This
completion of the series of arrangements adopted by a
former Parliament cannot fail to render more efficient
the military organisation of the country.

I warmly appreciate the zeal and assiduity with which
you have devoted yourself to the task of maturing a
measure for improving the relations between the owners
and occupiers of land in Ireland, and for otherwise
bettering the condition of its agricultural population.
It is my earnest hope that the new law may be productive of benefits commensurate with the care you have
bestowed upon its enactments.

I regret that it has been found impossible to proceed
with many measures on subjects of importance, which
have been, or were prepared to be, submitted to you;
and that, notwithstanding exertions almost unparalleled,
you have been unable adequately to provide the country
with legislation adapted for its growing wants.

It has been my study to use the exceptional powers
confided to me in Ireland by two Acts of this session
with vigilance and firmness, but with discrimination;
while I earnestly desire that the condition of that
country may so improve as to enable me to dispense
with, or to abate, the use of temporary and exceptional
provisions.

Finally, I ask you to join me in imploring the blessing of the Almighty on our united efforts for the
peace, greatness, and happiness of the Empire.

PARLIAMENT X.—SESSION III.

OPENING OF PARLIAMENT BY COMMISSION.

Date.—February 7th, 1882.

The Lords Commissioners were:—The Lord Chancellor; the Lord Steward of the Household; the Lord Chamberlain of the Household; the Earl of Cork; and Lord Monson.

The Cabinet.—First Lord of the Treasury and Chancellor of the Exchequer, Right Hon. William Ewart Gladstone; Lord Chancellor, Right Hon. Lord Selborne; President of the Council, Right Hon. Earl Spencer; Lord of the Privy Seal, Right Hon. Lord Carlingford; Home Secretary, Right Hon. Sir W. V. Harcourt; Foreign Secretary, Right Hon. Earl Granville; Colonial Secretary, Right Hon. Earl of Kimberley; Secretary at War, Right Hon. H. C. E. Childers; Secretary for India, Right Hon. Marquess of Hartington; First Lord of the Admiralty, Right Hon. Earl of Northbrook; Chancellor of the Duchy of Lancaster, Right Hon. John Bright; President of the Board of Trade, Right Hon. Joseph Chamberlain; Chief Secretary for Ireland, Right Hon. W. E. Forster; President of the Local Government Board, Right Hon. J. G. Dodson.

The Queen's Speech.

My Lords and Gentlemen,

It is with much satisfaction that I again invite your advice and assistance in the conduct of public affairs.

I have given my approval to a marriage between my son Prince Leopold, Duke of Albany, and Her Serene Highness Princess Helen of Waldeck and Pyront. I have every reason to believe that this will be a happy union.

I continue in relations of cordial harmony with all foreign Powers.

The treaty for the cession of Thessaly to the Greek Kingdom has now been executed in its main provisions. The transfer of sovereignty and of occupation was effected in a manner honourable to all concerned.

In concert with the President of the French Republic, I have given careful attention to the affairs of Egypt, where existing arrangements have imposed on me special obligations. I shall use my influence to maintain the rights already established, whether by the Firmans of the Sultan, or by various international engagements, in a spirit favourable to the good government of the country, and the prudent development of its institutions.

I have pleasure in informing you that the restoration of peace beyond the North-Western Frontier, together with continued internal tranquillity, plentiful seasons, and increase of the revenue, has enabled my Government in India to resume works of public utility which had been suspended, and to devote its attention to measures for the further improvement of the condition of the people.

The convention with the Transvaal has been ratified by the Representative Assembly; and I have seen no reason to qualify my anticipations of its advantageous working.

I have, however, to regret that, although hostilities have not been renewed in Basutoland, the country still remains in an unsettled condition.

Gentlemen of the House of Commons,

The estimates for the service of the year are in an advanced stage of preparation, and will be promptly submitted to you.

My Lords and Gentlemen,

My communications with France on the subject of a new commercial treaty have not been closed. They will be prosecuted by me, as I have already acquainted you, with a desire to conclude a treaty favourable to extended intercourse between the two nations, to whose close amity I attach so great a value.

The trade of the country, both domestic and foreign, has for some time been improving, and the mildness of the winter season has been eminently suited to farming operations. Better prospects are, I trust, thus opened for the classes immediately concerned in agriculture.

The public revenue, which is greatly, though not always at once, affected by the state of industry and commerce, has not yet exhibited an upward movement in proportion to their increased activity.

The condition of Ireland at this time, as compared with that which I described at the beginning of last year, shows signs of improvement, and encourages the hope that perseverance in the course you have pursued will be rewarded with the happy results which are so much to be desired.

Justice has been administered with greater efficacy; and the intimidation which has been employed to deter occupiers of land from fulfilling their obligations, and from availing themselves of the Act of last session, shows upon the whole a diminished force.

My efforts, through the bounty of Providence, have been favoured by the abundance of the harvest in that portion of the United Kingdom.

In addition to a vigorous exertion of the provisions of the ordinary law, I have not hesitated, under the painful necessity of the case, to employ largely the exceptional powers entrusted to me for the protection of life and property by two Acts of the last session.

You will be invited to deal with proposals for the establishment in the English and Welsh Counties of Local Self-Government, which has so long been enjoyed by the towns; together with enlarged powers of administration, and with financial changes which will give you an opportunity of considering, both as to town and country, what may be the proper extent, and the most equitable and provident form, of contribution from Imperial taxes in relief of local charges.

These proposals, in so far as they are financial, will apply to the whole of Great Britain. It will be necessary to reserve the case of Ireland for a separate consideration.

In connection with the general subject of local administration, I have directed a measure to be prepared and submitted to you for the reform of the ancient and distinguished Corporation of London, and the extension of municipal government to the metropolis at large.

Bills will again be laid before you with which, during the last session, notwithstanding the length of its duration and your unwearied labours, it was found impossible to proceed. I refer particularly to those concerning bankruptcy, the repression of corrupt practices at elections, and the conservancy of rivers and prevention of floods.

Measures will also be proposed to you with respect to a criminal code and to the consolidation and amendment of the laws affecting patents.

The interests of some portions of the United Kingdom have suffered peculiarly of late years, from the extreme pressure of the public business on your time and strength ; but I trust that, during this session, you may be able to consider Bills which will be presented to you in relation to the law of entail and to educational endowments in Scotland, and to improved means of education in Wales.

I commend these and other subjects with confidence to your care ; and it is my earnest prayer that your wisdom and energy may, under the blessing of God, prove equal to the varied and increasing needs of this extended Empire.

Mover of Address in the Lords, Earl of Fingall.
Seconder „ „ Lord Wenlock.
Mover of Address in the Commons, Hon. Edward
Marjoribanks.
Seconder „ „ Mr. J. F. B.
Firth.

INDEX.

ERRATA.

Page 124, line 5, *for* D'Eresby *read* De Eresby.

Page 151, line 22, *for* August *read* April.

Page 247, line 9, *for* Huntley *read* Huntly.

Page 346, col. 2, line 15, *omit* D'Eresby, Lord W.

LONDON:

PRINTED BY W. H. ALLEN AND CO., 13 WATERLOO PLACE, S.W.

January, 1882.

BOOKS, &c.,

ISSUED BY

MESSRS. W. H. ALLEN & Co.,

𝕻𝖚𝖇𝖑𝖎𝖘𝖍𝖊𝖗𝖘 & 𝕷𝖎𝖙𝖊𝖗𝖆𝖗𝖞 𝕬𝖌𝖊𝖓𝖙𝖘 𝖙𝖔 𝖙𝖍𝖊 𝕴𝖓𝖉𝖎𝖆 𝕺𝖋𝖋𝖎𝖈𝖊,

COMPRISING

MISCELLANEOUS PUBLICATIONS IN GENERAL
LITERATURE.

DICTIONARIES, GRAMMARS, AND TEXT BOOKS
IN EASTERN LANGUAGES.

MILITARY WORKS, INCLUDING THOSE ISSUED
BY THE GOVERNMENT.

INDIAN AND MILITARY LAW.

MAPS OF INDIA, &c.

13, WATERLOO PLACE, LONDON, S.W.

Tree and Serpent Worship;

Or, Illustrations of Mythology and Art in India in the First
and Fourth Centuries after Christ, from the Sculptures of the
Buddhist Topes at Sanchi and Amravati. Prepared at the
India Museum, under the authority of the Secretary of State
for India in Council. Second edition, Revised, Corrected, and
in great part Re-written. By JAMES FERGUSSON, Esq., F.R.S.,
F.R.A.S. Super-royal 4to. 100 plates and 31 engravings,
pp. 270. Price £5 5s.

Illustrations of Ancient Buildings in Kashmir.

Prepared at the Indian Museum under the authority of the
Secretary of State for India in Council. From Photographs,
Plans, and Drawings taken by Order of the Government of
India. By HENRY HARDY COLE, LIEUT. R.E., Superintendent
Archæological Survey of India, North-West Provinces. In
One vol.; half-bound, Quarto. Fifty-eight plates. £3 10s.

The Illustrations in this work have been produced in Carbon from
the original negatives, and are therefore permanent.

Pharmacopœia of India.

Prepared under the Authority of the Secretary of State for
India. By EDWARD JOHN WARING, M.D. Assisted by a
Committee appointed for the Purpose. 8vo. 6s.

The Stupa of Bharhut. A Buddhist Monument.

Ornamented with numerous Sculptures illustrative of Buddhist
Legend and History in the Third Century B.C. By ALEX-
ANDER CUNNINGHAM, C.S.I., C.I.E., Major-General, Royal
Engineers (Bengal Retired); Director-General Archæological
Survey of India. 4to. Fifty-seven Plates. Cloth gilt.
£3 3s.

Archælogical Survey of Western India.

Report of the First Season's Operations in the Belgâm and Kaladgi Districts. January to May, 1874. Prepared at the India Museum and Published under the Authoiity of the Secretary of State for India in Council. By JAMES BURGESS, Author of the "Rock Temples of Elephanta," &c., &c., and Editor of "The Indian Antiquary." Half-bound. Quarto. 58 Plates and Woodcuts. £2 2s.

Archæological Survey of Western India. Vol. II.

Report on the Antiquities of Kâthiâwâd and Kachh, being the result of the Second Season's Operations of the Archæological Survey of Western India. 1874–75. By JAMES BURGESS, F.R.G.S , M.R.A.S., &c., Archæological Surveyor and Reporter to Government, Western India. 1876. Half-bound. Quarto Seventy-four Plates and Woodcuts. £3 3s.

Archæological Survey of Western India. Vol. III.

Report on the Antiquities in the Bidar and Aurungabad Districts in the Territory of H.H. the Nizam of Haidarabad, being the result of the Third Season's Operations of the Archæological Survey of Western India. 1875–1876. By JAMES BURGESS, F.R.G.S., M.R.A.S., Membre de la Societé Asiatique, &c., Archæological Surveyor and Reporter to Government, Western India. Half-bound. Quarto. Sixty-six Plates and Woodcuts. £2 2s.

Illustrations of Buildings near Muttra and Agra,

Showing the Mixed Hindu-Mahomedan Style of Upper India Prepared at the India Museum under the authority of the Secretary of State for India in Council, from Photographs, Plans, and Drawings taken by Order of the Government of India. By HENRY HARDY COLE, Lieut. R.E., late Superintendent Archæological Survey of India, North-West Provinces 4to. With Photographs and Plates. £3 10s.

The Cave Temples of India.

By JAMES FERGUSON, D.C.L., F.R.A.S., V.P.R.A.S., and JAMES BURGESS, F.R.G.S., M.R.A.S., &c. Printed nd Published by. Order of Her Majesty's Secretary of State, &c. Royal 8vo. With Photographs and Woodcuts. £2 2s.

Aberigh-Mackay (G.) Twenty-one Days in India.
Being the Tour of Sir Ali Baba, K.C.B. By George
Aberigh-Mackay. Post 8vo. 4s.

Adam W. (late of Calcutta) Theories of History.
An Inquiry into the Theories of History,—Chance,—Law,—
Will. With Special Reference to the Principle of Positive
Philosophy. By William Adam. 8vo. 15s.

Akbar. An Eastern Romance
By Dr. P. A. S. Van Limburg-Brouwer. Translated from
the Dutch by M. M. With Notes and Introductory Life of
the Emperor Akbar, by Clements R. Markham, C.B., F.R.S.
Crown 8vo. 10s. 6d.

Alberg (A.) Snowdrops: Idylls for Children.
From the Swedish of Zach Topelius. By Albert Alberg,
Author of "Whisperings in the Wood." 3s. 6d.

—— **Whisperings in the Wood:** Finland Idylls for Children.
From the Swedish of Zach Topelius. By Albert Alberg,
Author of "Fabled Stories from the Zoo," and Editor of
"Chit-Chat by Puck," "Rose Leaves," and "Woodland
Notes." 3s. 6d.

Allen's Series.
1.—Ansted's World We Live In. 2s.
2.—Ansted's Earth's History. 2s.
3.—Ansted's 2000 Examination Questions in Physical Geography. 2s.
4.—Geography of India. (See page 10.) 2s.
5.—Ansted's Elements of Physiography. 1s. 4d.
6.—Hall's Trigonometry. (See page 11.) 2s.
7.—Wollaston's Elementary Indian Reader. 1s. (See p. 36.)

Ameer Ali. The Personal Law of the Mahommedans (ac-
cor ing to all the Schools). Together with a Comparative
Sketch of the Law of Inheritance among the Sunnis and
Shiahs. By Syed Ameer Ali, Moulvi, M.A., LL.B., Barrister-
at-Law, and Presidency Magistrate at Calcutta. 8vo. 15s.

Anderson (Ed. L.) How to Ride and School a Horse.
With a System of Horse Gymnastics. By Edward L.
Anderson. Cr. 8vo. 2s. 6d.

Anderson (P.) The English in Western India.
8vo. 14s.

Andrew (W. P.) India and Her Neighbours.
By W. P. ANDREW, Author of "Our Scientific Frontier,"
"The Indus and Its Provinces," "Memoir of the Euphrates
Route." With Two Maps. 8vo. 15s.

—— **Our Scientific Frontier.**
With Sketch-Map and Appendix. 8vo. 6s.

Ansted (D. T.) Physical Geography.
By Professor D. T. ANSTED, M.A., F.R.S., &c. Fifth
Edition. Post 8vo., with Illustrative Maps. 7s.
CONTENTS:—PART I.—INTRODUCTION.—The Earth as a Planet.
—Physical Forces.—The Succession of Rocks. PART II.—
EARTH.—Land.—Mountains.—Hills and Valleys.—Plateaux
and Low Plains. PART III.—WATER.—The Ocean.—Rivers.
—Lakes and Waterfalls.—The Phenomena of Ice.—Springs.
PART IV.—AIR.—The Atmosphere. Winds and Storms.—
Dew, Clouds, and Rain.—Climate and Weather. PART V.—
FIRE.—Volcanoes and Volcanic Phenomena.—Earthquakes.
PART VI.—LIFE.—The Distribution of Plants in the different
Countries of the Earth.—The Distribution of Animals on the
Earth.—The Distribution of Plants and Animals in Time.—
Effects of Human Agency on Inanimate Nature.
"The Book is both valuable and comprehensive, and deserves a wide
circulation."—*Observer*.

—— **Elements of Physiography.**
For the use of Science Schools. Fcap. 8vo. 1s. 4d.

—— **The World We Live In.**
Or First Lessons in Physical Geography. For the use of
Schools and Students. By D. T. ANSTED, M.A., F.R.S., &c.
Fcap. 2s. 25th Thousand, with Illustrations.

—— **and Latham (R. G.) Channel Islands. Jersey, Guernsey,**
Alderney, Sark, &c.
THE CHANNEL ISLANDS. Containing: PART I.—Physical
Geography. PART II.—Natural History. PART III.—Civil His-
tory. PART IV.—Economics and Trade. By DAVID THOMAS
ANSTED, M.A., F.R.S., and ROBERT GORDON LATHAM, M.A.,
M.D., F.R.S. New and Cheaper Edition in one handsome
8vo. Volume, with 72 Illustrations on Wood by Vizetelly,
Loudon, Nicholls, and Hart ; with Map. 8vo. 16s.
"This is a really valuable work. A book which will long remain the
standard authority on the subject. No one who has been to the Channel
Islands, or who purposes going there will be insensible of its value."—
Saturday Review.
"It is the produce of many hands and every hand a good one."

Ansted (D. T.) The Earth's History.
Or, First Lessons in Geology. For the use of Schools and Students. By D. T. ANSTED. Third Thousand. Fcap. 2s.

—— **Two Thousand Examination Questions** in Physical Geography. pp. 180. Price 2s.

—— **Water, and Water Supply.**
Chiefly with reference to the British Islands. Part I.— Surface Waters. 8vo. With Maps. 18s.

Archer (Capt. J. H. Laurence) Commentaries on the Punjaub Campaign—1848-49, including some additions to the History of the Second Sikh War, from original sources. By Capt. J. H. LAWRENCE-ARCHER, Bengal H. P. Cr. 8vo. 8s.

Army and Navy Calendar for the Financial Year 1882-83.
Being a Compendium of General Information relating to the Army, Navy, Militia, and Volunteers, and containing Maps, Plans, Tabulated Statements, Abstracts, &c. Compiled from authentic sources. 2s. 6d.

Army and Navy Magazine.
Vols. I. and II. are issued, each containing Six Cabinet Photographs of Celebrated Officers. Volumes 7s. 6d. each.

Aynsley (Mrs.) Our Visit to Hindustan, Kashmir, and Ladakh.
By Mrs. J. C. MURRAY AYNSLEY. 8vo. 14s.

Bellew (Capt.) Memoirs of a Griffin ; or, A Cadet's First Year in India. By Captain BELLEW. Illustrated from Designs by the Author. A New Edition. Cr. 8vo. 10s. 6d.

Bernay (Dr. A. J.) Students' Chemistry.
Being the Seventh Edition of Household Chemistry, or the Science of Home Life. By ALBERT J. BERNAYS, PH. DR. F.C.S., Prof. of Chemistry and Practical Chemistry at St. Thomas' Hospital, Medical, and Surgical College. Crown 8vo. 5s. 6d.

Blanchard (S.) Yesterday and To-day in India.
By SIDNEY LAMAN BLANCHARD. Post 8vo. 6s.
CONTENTS.—Outward Bound.—The Old Times and the New.— Domestic Life.—Houses and Bungalows.—Indian Servants.— The Great Shoe Question.—The Garrison Hack.—The Long Bow in India.—Mrs. Dulcimer's Shipwreck.—A Traveller's Tale, told in a Dark Bungalow.—Punch in India.—Anglo-Indian Literature.—Christmas in India.—The Seasons in Calcutta.—Farmers in Muslin.—Homeward Bound.—India as it Is.

Blenkinsopp (Rev. E. L.) Doctrine of Development in the Bible and in the Church. By REV. E. L. BLENKINSOPP, M.A., Rector of Springthorp. 2nd edition. 12mo. 6s.

Boileau (Major-General J. T.) A New and Complete Set of Traverse Tables, showing the Differences of Latitude and the Departures to every Minute of the Quadrant and to Five Places of Decimals. Together with a Table of the lengths of each Degree of Latitude and corresponding Degree of Longitude from the Equator to the Poles; with other Tables useful to the Surveyor and Engineer. Fourth Edition, thoroughly revised and corrected by the Author. Royal 8vo. 12s. London, 1876.

Boulger (D. C.) History of China. By DEMETRIUS CHARLES BOULGER, Author of " England and Russia in Central Asia," &c. 8vo. vol. I. With Portrait. 18s.

—— **England and Russia in Central Asia.** With Appendices and Two Maps, one being the latest Russian Official Map of Central Asia. 2 vols. 8vo. 36s.

—— **Central Asian Portraits;** or the Celebrities of the Khanates and the Neighbouring States. By DEMETRIUS CHARLES BOULGER, M.R.A.S. Crown 8vo. 7s. 6d.

—— **The Life of Yakoob Beg,** Athalik Ghazi and Badaulet, Ameer of Kashgar. By DEMETRIUS CHARLES BOULGER, M.R.A.S. 8vo. With Map and Appendix. 16s.

Bowring (Sir J.) Flowery Scroll. A Chinese Novel. Translated and Illustrated with Notes by SIR J. BOWRING. late H.B.M. Plenipo. China. Post 8vo. 10s. 6d.

Boyd (R. Nelson) Chili and the Chilians, during the War 1879–80. By R. NELSON BOYD, F.R.G.S., F.G.S., Author of Coal Mines Inspection. Cloth, Illustrated. Cr. 8vo. 10s. 6d.

—— **Coal Mines Inspection:** Its History and Results. 8vo. 14s.

Bradshaw (John) The Poetical Works of John Milton, with Notes, explanatory and philological. By JOHN BRADSHAW, LL.D., Inspector of Schools, Madras. 2 vols., post 8vo. 12s. 6d

Brandis' Forest Flora of North-Western and Central India. By DR. BRANDIS, Inspector General of Forests to the Government of India. Text and Plates. £2 18s.

Briggs (Gen. J.) India and Europe Compared. Post 8vo. 7s.

Bright (W.) Red Book for Sergeants.
Fifth and Revised Edition, 1880. By W. BRIGHT, late Colour-Sergeant, 19th Middlesex R.V. Fcap. interleaved. 1s.

Browne (J. W.) Hardware; How to Buy it for Foreign Markets. 8vo. 10s. 6d.

Buckle (the late Capt. E.) Bengal Artillery.
A Memoir of the Services of the Bengal Artillery from the formation of the Corps. By the late CAPT. E. BUCKLE, Assist.-Adjut. Gen. Ben. Art. Edit. by SIR J. W. KAYE. 8vo. Lond, 1852. 10s.

Buckley (R. B.) The Irrigation Works of India, and their Financial Results. Being a brief History and Description of the Irrigation Works of India, and of the Profits and Losses they have caused to the State. By ROBERT B. BUCKLEY, A M.I.C.E., Executive Engineer of the Public Works Department of India. 8vo. With Map and Appendix. 9s.

Burke (P.) Celebrated Naval and Military Trials.
By PETER BURKE, Serjeant-at-Law. Author of " Celebrated Trials connected with the Aristocracy." Post 8vo. 10s. 6d.

By the Tiber.
By the Author of " Signor Monaldini's Niece." 2 vols. 21s.

Carlyle (Thomas), Memoirs of the Life and Writings of,
With Personal Reminiscences and Selections from his Private Letters to numerous Correspondents. Edited by RICHARD HERNE SHEPHERD, Assisted by CHARLES N. WILLIAMSON. 2 Vols. With Portrait and Illustrations. Crown 8vo. 21s.

Challenge of Barletta (The).
By MASSIMO D'AZEGLIO. Rendered into English by Lady LOUISA MAGENIS. 2 vols. Crown 8vo. 21s.

Collette (C. H.) The Roman Breviary.
A Critical and Historical Review, with Copious Classified Extracts. By CHARLES HASTINGS COLLETTE. 2nd Edition. Revised and enlarged. 8vo. 5s.

—— Henry VIII.
An Historical Sketch as affecting the Reformation in England. By CHARLES HASTINGS COLLETTE. Post 8vo. 6s.

Colquhoun (Major J. A. S.) With the Kurrum Force in the Caubul Campaign of 1878–79. By Major J. A. S. COLQU-HOUN, R.A. With Illustrations from the Author's Drawings, and two Maps. 8vo. 16s.

Cooper's Hill College. Calendar of the Royal Indian Engineering College, Cooper's Hill. Published by authority in January each year. 5s.

CONTENTS.—Staff of the College ; Prospectus for the Year ; Table of Marks ; Syllabus of Course of Study ; Leave and Pension Rules of Indian Service ; Class and Prize Lists ; Past Students serving in India ; Entrance Examination Papers, &c.

Corbet (M. E.) A Pleasure Trip to India, during the Visit of H.R.H. the Prince of Wales, and afterwards to Ceylon. By Mrs. CORBET. Illustrated with Photos. Crown 8vo. 7s. 6d.

Crosland (Mrs. N.) Stories of the City of London ; Retold for Youthful Readers. By Mrs. NEWTON CROSLAND. With ten Illustrations. Cr. 8vo. 6s.

These Stories range from the early days of Old London Bridge and the Settlement of the Knights Templars in England to the time of the Gordon Riots ; with incidents in the Life of Brunel in relation to the Thames Tunnel ; narrated from Personal recollections.

Cruise of H.M.S. "Galatea," Captain H.R.H. the Duke of Edinburgh, K.G., in 1867 —1868. By the REV. JOHN MILNER, B.A., Chaplain ; and OSWALD W. BRIERLY. Illustrated by a Photograph of H.R.H. the Duke of Edinburgh ; and by Chromo-Lithographs and Graphotypes from Sketches taken on the spot by O. W. BRIERLY. 8vo. 16s.

Cunningham (H. S.) British India, and its Rulers. By H. S. CUNNINGHAM, M.A., one of the Judges of the High Court of Calcutta, and late Member of the Famine Commission. 10s. 6d.

Daumas (E.) Horses of the Sahara, and the Manners of the Desert. By E. DAUMAS, General of the Division Commanding at Bordeaux, Senator, &c., &c. With Commentaries by the Emir Abd-el-Kadir (Authorized Edition). 8vo. 6s.

"We have rarely read a work giving a more picturesque and, at the same time, practical account of the manners and customs of a people, than this book on the Arabs and their horses."—*Edinburgh Courant.*

Deighton (K.) Shakespeare's King Henry the Fifth. With Notes and an Introduction. By K. DEIGHTON, Principal of Agra College. Crown 8vo. 5s.

Destruction of Life by Snakes, Hydrophobia, &c., in Western India. By an EX-COMMISSIONER. Fcap. 2s. 6d.

Dickins, (F. V.) Chiushingura : or the Loyal League. A Japanese Romance. Translated by FREDERICK V. DICKINS, Sc.B., of the Middle Temple, Barrister-at-Law. With Notes and an Appendix containing a Metrical Version of the Ballad of Takasako, and a specimen of the Original Text in Japanese character. Illustrated by numerous Engravings on Wood, drawn and executed by Japanese artists and printed on Japanese paper. 8vo. 10s. 6d.

Doran (Dr. J.) "Their Majesties Servants":
Annals of the English Stage. Actors, Authors, and Audiences From Thomas Betterton to Edmund Kean. By Dr. DORAN, F.S.A., Author of "Table Traits," "Lives of the Queens of England of the House of Hanover." &c. Post 8vo. 6s.

"Every page of the work is barbed with wit, and will make its way point foremost. . . . . . provides entertainment for the most diverse tastes."—*Daily News.*

Drury (Col. H.) The Useful Plants of India,
With Notices of their chief value in Commerce, Medicine, and the Arts. By COLONEL HEBER DRURY. Second Edition, with Additions and Corrections. Royal 8vo. 16s.

Dwight (H. O.) Turkish Life in War Time.
By HENRY O. DWIGHT. Crown 8vo. 12s.

Edwards (G. Sutherland) A Female Nihilist.
By ERNEST LAVIGNE. Translated from the French by G. SUTHERLAND EDWARDS. Crown 8vo. 9s.

Edwards (H. S.) The Lyrical Drama: Essays on Subjects, Composers, and Executants of Modern Opera. By H. SUTHERLAND EDWARDS, Author of "The Russians at Home and Abroad," &c. Two vols. Crown 8vo. 21s.

—— **The Russians At Home and the Russians Abroad.**
Sketches, Unpolitical and Political, of Russian Life under Alexander II. By H. SUTHERLAND EDWARDS. 2 vols. Crown 8vo. 21s.

Ensor (F. Sydney) Incidents of a Journey through Nubia
to Darfoor. By F. SYDNEY ENSOR, C.E. 10s. 6d.

Eyre, (Major-General Sir V.), K.C.S.I., C.B. The Kabul In-
surrection of 1841–42. Revised and corrected from Lieut. Eyre's Original Manuscript. Edited by Colonel G. B. MALLESON, C.S.I. Crown 8vo., with Map and Illustrations. 9s.

Fearon (A.) Kenneth Trelawny.
By ALEC FEARON. Author of "Touch not the Nettle." 2 vols. Crown 8vo. 21s.

Forbes (Capt. C. J. F. S.) Comparative Grammar of the
Languages of Further India. A Fragment; and other Essays,
the Literary Remains of Captain C. J. F. S. FORBES, of the
British Burma Commission. Author of " British Burma and
its People: Sketches of Native Manners, Customs, and Religion." 6s.

Fraser (Lieut.-Col. G. T.) Records of Sport and Military
Life in Western India. By the late Lieut.-Colonel G. T.
Fraser, formerly of the 1st Bombay Fusiliers, and more recently attached to the Staff of H.M.'s Indian Army. With
an Introduction by Colonel G. B. MALLESON, C.S.I. 7s. 6d.

Garrick (H. B. W.) Mansukhi and Sundar Singh.
A Hindu Tale. Hindustani and English. With 24 Illustrations. By H. B. W. GARRICK. 4to. 1s. 6d.

Gazetteers of India.
Thornton, 4 vols., 8vo. £2 16s.
„ 8vo. 21s.
„ (N.W.P., &c.) 2 vols., 8vo. 25s.

Gazetteer of Southern India.
With the Tenasserim Provinces and Singapore. Compiled
from original and authentic sources. Accompanied by an
Atlas, including plans of all the principal towns and canton-
ments. Royal 8vo. with 4to. Atlas. £3 3s.

Geography of India.
Comprising an account of British India, and the various states
enclosed and adjoining. Fcap. pp. 250. 2s.

Geological Papers on Western India.
Including Cutch, Scinde, and the south-east coast of Arabia.
To which is added a Summary of the Geology of India gene-
rally. Edited for the Government by HENRY J. CARTER,
Assistant Surgeon, Bombay Army. Royal 8vo. with folio
Atlas of maps and plates; half-bound. £2 2s.

Gillmore (Parker) Encounters with Wild Beasts.
By PARKER GILLMORE, Author of " The Great Thirst
Land," "A Ride Through Hostile Africa," &c. With Ten
full-page Illustrations. Cr. 8vo. 7s. 6d.

—— Prairie and Forest. A description of the Game of
North America, with Personal Adventures in its Pursuit.
By PARKER GILLMORE (Ubique). With Thirty-Seven
Illustrations. Crown 8vo. 7s. 6d.

Glyn (A. C.) History of Civilization in the Fifth Century.
Translated by permission from the French of A. Frederic
Ozanam, late Professor of Foreign Literature to the Faculty
of Letters at Paris. By ASHBY C. GLYN, B.A., of the Inner
Temple, Barrister-at-Law. 2 vols., post 8vo. £1 1s.

Goldstucker (Prof. Theodore), The late. The Literary Remains of. With a Memoir. 2 vols. 8vo. 21s.

Graham (Alex.) Genealogical and Chronological Tables,
illustrative of Indian History. 4to. 5s.

Grant (Jas.) Derval Hampton : A Story of the Sea.
By JAMES GRANT, Author of the " Romance of War," &c.
2 vols. Crown 8vo. 21s.

Greene (F. V.) The Russian Army and its Campaigns in
Turkey in 1877–1878. By F. V. GREENE, First Lieutenant
in the Corps of Engineers, U.S. Army, and lately Military
Attaché to the United States Legation at St. Petersburg. 8vo.
With Atlas. 32s. Second Edition.

—— **Sketches of Army Life in Russia.**
Crown 8vo. 9s.

Griffith (Ralph T. H.) Birth of the War God.
A Poem. By KALIDASA. Translated from the Sanscrit into
English Verse. By RALPH T. H. GRIFFITH. 8vo. 5s.

Hall (E. H.) Lands of Plenty, for Health, Sport, and Profit
British North America. A Book for all Travellers and
Settlers. By E. HEPPLE HALL, F.S.S. Crown 8vo., with
Maps. 6s.

Hall's Trigonometry.
The Elements of Plane and Spherical Trigonometry. With an
Appendix, containing the solution of the Problems in Nautical
Astronomy. For the use of Schools. By the REV. T. G.
HALL, M.A., Professor of Mathematics in King's College,
London. 12mo. 2s.

Hancock (E. C.) The Amateur Pottery and Glass Painter.
With Directions for Gilding, Chasing, Burnishing, Bronzing,
and Groundlaying. By E. CAMPBELL HANCOCK. Illustrated
with Chromo-Lithographs and numerous Woodcuts. Fourth
Edition. 8vo. 6s.

—— **Copies for China Painters.**
By E. CAMPBELL HANCOCK. With Fourteen Chromo-Lithographs and other Illustrations. 8vo. 10s.

Handbook of Reference to the Maps of India.

Giving the Lat. and Long. of places of note. 18mo. 3s 6d.

₊ *This will be found a valuable Companion to Messrs. Allen & Cos.'*
Maps of India.

Harcourt (Maj. A. F. P.) Down by the Drawle.

By MAJOR A. F. P. HARCOURT, Bengal Staff Corps, author of
" Kooloo, Lahoul, and Spiti," " The Shakespeare Argosy," &c.
2 Vols. in one, crown 8vo. 6s.

Hensman (Howard) The Afghan War, 1879-80.

Being a complete Narrative of the Capture of Cabul, the Siege
of Sherpur, the Battle of Ahmed Khel, the brilliant March to
Candahar, and the Defeat of Ayub Khan, with the Operations
on the Helmund, and the Settlement with Abdur Rahman
Khan. By HOWARD HENSMAN, Special Correspondent of the
" Pioneer " (Allahabad) and the " Daily News " (London).
8vo. With Maps. 21s.

General Sir Frederick Roberts writes in regard to the
letters now re-published:—

"Allow me to congratulate you most cordially on the admirable manner in which you have placed before the public the account of our march
from Cabul, and the operations of 31st August and 1st September around
Candahar. *Nothing could be more accurate or graphic.* I thought your
description of the fight at Charasai was one that any soldier might have
been proud of writing ; but your recent letters are, if possible, even better."

Holden (E. S.) Sir William Herschel. His Life and Works.

By EDWARD S. HOLDEN, United States Naval Observatory
Washington. Cr. 8vo. 6s.

Holland.

By Edmondo de Amicis. Translated from the Italian by
CAROLINE TILTON. Crown 8vo. 10s. 6d.

Hough (Lieut.-Col. W.) Precedents in Military Law.

8vo. cloth. 25s

Hughes (Rev. T. P.) Notes on Muhammadanism.

Second Edition, Revised and Enlarged. Fcap. 8vo. 6s.

Hutton (J.) Thugs and Dacoits of India.

A Popular Account of the Thugs and Dacoits, the Hereditary
Garotters and Gang Robbers of India. By JAMES HUTTON.
Post 8vo. 5s.

India Directory (The).

For the Guidance of Commanders of Steamers and Sailing
Vessels. Founded upon the Work of the late CAPTAIN JAMES
HORSBURGH, F.R.S.

PART I.—The East Indies, and Interjacent Ports of Africa
and South America. Revised, Extended, and Illustrated with

Charts of Winds, Currents, Passages, Variation, and Tides. By COMMANDER ALFRED DUNDAS TAYLOR, F.R.G.S., Superintendent of Marine Surveys to the Government of India. £1 18s.

PART II.—The China Sea, with the Ports of Java, Australia and Japan and the Indian Archipelago Harbours, as well as those of New Zealand. Illustrated with Charts of the Winds, Currents, Passages, &c. By the same. (*In preparation.*)

Indian and Military Law.

Mahommedan Law of Inheritance, &c. A Manual of the Mahommedan Law of Inheritance and Contract ; comprising the Doctrine of the Soonee and Sheea Schools, and based upon the text of Sir H. W. MACNAGHTEN's Principles and Precedents, together with the Decisions of the Privy Council and High Courts of the Presidencies in India. For the use of Schools and Students. By STANDISH GROVE GRADY, Barrister-at-Law, Reader of Hindoo, Mahommedan, and Indian Law to the Inns of Court. 8vo. 14s.

Hedaya, or Guide, a Commentary on the Mussulman Laws, translated by order of the Governor-General and Council of Bengal. By CHARLES HAMILTON. Second Edition, with Preface and Index by STANDISH GROVE GRADY. 8vo. £1 15s.

Institutes of Menu in English. The Institutes of Hindu Law or the Ordinances of Menu, according to Gloss of Collucca. Comprising the Indian System of Duties, Religious and Civil, verbally translated from the Original, with a Preface by SIR WILLIAM JONES, and collated with the Sanscrit Text by GRAVES CHAMNEY HAUGHTON, M.A., F.R.S., Professor of Hindu Literature in the East India College. New edition, with Preface and Index by STANDISH G. GRADY, Barrister-at-Law, and Reader of Hindu, Mahommedan, and Indian Law to the Inns of Court. 8vo., cloth. 12s.

Indian Code of Criminal Procedure. Being Act X. of 1872, Passed by the Governor-General of India in Council on the 25th of April, 1872. 8vo. 12s.

Indian Code of Civil Procedure. Being Act X. of 1877. 8vo. 6s.

Indian Code of Civil Procedure. In the form of Questions and Answers, with Explanatory and Illustrative Notes. By ANGELO J. LEWIS, Barrister-at-law. 12mo. 12s. 6d.

Indian Penal Code. In the Form of Questions and Answers. With Explanatory and Illustrative Notes. BY ANGELO J. LEWIS, Barrister-at-Law. Post 8vo. 7s. 6d.

Hindu Law. Defence of the Daya Bhaga. Notice of the Case on Prosoono Coomar Tajore's Will. Judgment of the Judicial Committee of the Privy Council. Examination of such Judgment. By JOHN COCHRANE, Barrister-at-Law. Royal 8vo. 20s.

Law and Customs of Hindu Castes, within the Dekhan Provinces subject to the Presidency of Bombay, chiefly affecting Civil Suits. By ARTHUR STEELE. Royal 8vo. £1 1s.

Moohummudan Law of Inheritance. (See page 29.)

Chart of Hindu Inheritance. With an Explanatory Treatise, By Almaric Rumsey. 8vo. 6s. 6d.

Manual of Military Law. For all ranks of the Army, Militia and Volunteer Services. By Colonel J. K. Pipon, Assist. Adjutant General at Head Quarters, & J. F. Collier, Esq., of the Inner Temple, Barrister-at-Law. Third and Revised Edition. Pocket size. 5s.

Precedents in Military Law; including the Practice of Courts-Martial; the Mode of Conducting Trials; the Duties of Officers at Military Courts of Inquests, Courts of Inquiry, Courts of Requests, &c., &c. The following are a portion of the Contents:— 1. Military Law. 2. Martial Law. 3. Courts-Martial. 4. Courts of Inquiry. 5. Courts of Inquest. 6. Courts of Request. 7. Forms of Courts-Martial. 8. Precedents of Military Law. 9. Trials of Arson to Rape (Alphabetically arranged.) 10. Rebellions. 11. Riots. 12. Miscellaneous. By Lieut.-Col. W. Hough, late Deputy Judge-Advocate-General, Bengal Army, and Author of several Works on Courts-Martial. One thick 8vo. vol. 25s.

The Practice of Courts Martial. By Hough & Long. Thick 8vo. London, 1825. 26s.

Indian Criminal Law and Procedure,

Including the Procedure in the High Courts, as well as that in the Courts not established by Royal Charter; with Forms of Charges and Notes on Evidence, illustrated by a large number of English Cases, and Cases decided in the High Courts of India; and an Appendix of selected Acts passed by the Legislative Council relating to Criminal matters. By M. H. Starling, Esq., LL.B. & F. B. Constable, M.A. Third edition. 8vo. £2 2s.

Indian Infanticide.

Its Origin, Progress, and Suppression. By John Cave-Brown, M.A. 8vo. 5s.

Irwin (H. C.) The Garden of India; or, Chapters on Oudh

History and Affairs. By H. C. Irwin, B.A. Oxon., Bengal Civil Service. 8vo. 12s.

Jackson (Lt.-Col. B.) Military Surveying, &c. 8vo. 14s.

(See page 24).

Jackson (Lowis D'A.) Hydraulic Manual and Working

Tables, Hydraulic and Indian Meteorological Statistics. Published under the patronage of the Right Honourable the Secretary of State for India. By Lowis D'A. Jackson. 8vo. 28s.

—— Canal and Culvert Tables.

Based on the Formula of Kutter, under a Modified Classification, with Explanatory Text and Examples. By Lowis

D'A. JACKSON, A.M.I.C.E., author of "Hydraulic Manual and Statistics," &c. Roy. 8vo. 28s.

Jackson (L. D'A.) Pocket Logarithms and other Tables for Ordinary Calculations of Quantity, Cost, Interest, Annuities, Assurance, and Angular Functions, obtaining Results correct in the Fourth figure. By LOWIS D'A. JACKSON. Cloth, 2s. 6d.; leather, 3s. 6d.

—— **Accented Four-Figure Logarithms, and other Tables.** For purposes both of Ordinary and of Trigonometrical Calculation, and for the Correction of Altitudes and Lunar Distances. Arranged and accented by LOWIS D'A. JACKSON, A.M.I.C.E., Author of "Canal and Culvert Tables," "Hydraulic Manual," &c. Crown 8vo. 9s.

James (A. G. F. Eliot) Indian Industries. By A. G. F. ELIOT JAMES, Author of "A Guide to Indian Household Management," &c. Crown 8vo. 9s.

CONTENTS:—Indian Agriculture; Beer; Cacao; Carpets; Cereals; Chemicals; Cinchona; Coffee; Cotton; Drugs; Dyeing and Colouring Materials; Fibrous Substances; Forestry; Hides; Skins and Horns; Gums and Resins; Irrigation; Ivory; Mining; Oils; Opium; Paper; Pottery; Ryots; Seeds; Silk; Spices; Sugar; Tea; Tobacco; Wood; Wool. Table of Exports. Index.

Jerrold (Blanchard) at Home in Paris. 2 Vols. Post 8vo. 16s.

Joyner (Mrs.) Cyprus: Historical and Descriptive. Adapted from the German of Herr FRANZ VON LÖHER. With much additional matter. By Mrs. A. BATSON JOYNER. Crown 8vo. With 2 Maps. 10s. 6d.

Kaye (Sir J. W.) The Sepoy War in India. A History of the Sepoy War in India, 1857—1858. By Sir JOHN WILLIAM KAYE, Author of "The History of the War in Afghanistan." Vol. I., 8vo. 18s. Vol. II. £1. Vol. III. £1.

CONTENTS OF VOL. I. :—BOOK I.—INTRODUCTORY.—The Conquest of the Punjab and Pegu.—The "Right of Lapse."—The Annexation of Oude.—Progress of Englishism. BOOK II.—The SEPOY ARMY: ITS RISE, PROGRESS, AND DECLINE.—Early History of the Native Army.—Deteriorating Influences.—The Sindh Mutinies.—The Punjaub Mutinies. Discipline of the Bengal Army. BOOK III.—THE OUTBREAK OF THE MUTINY.— Lord Canning and his Council.—The Oude Administration and the Persian War.—The Rising of the Storm.—The First Mutiny.—Progress of Mutiny.—Excitement in Upper India.— Bursting of the Storm.—APPENDIX.

CONTENTS OF VOL II.:—BOOK IV.—THE RISING IN THE NORTH-WEST.— The Delhi History.—The Outbreak at Meerut. —The Seizure of Delhi.—Calcutta in May.—Last Days of General Anson.—The March upon Delhi. BOOK V.—PRO-GRESS OF REBELLION IN UPPER INDIA.—Benares and Allahabad.—Cawnpore.—The March to Cawnpore.—Re-occupation of Cawnpore. BOOK VI.—THE PUNJAB AND DELHI.—First Conflicts in the Punjab.—Peshawur and Rawul Pinder.—Progress of Events in the Punjab.—Delhi.—First Weeks of the Siege.—Progress of the Siege.—The Last Succours from the Punjab.

CONTENTS OF VOL III.:—BOOK VII.—BENGAL, BEHAR, AND THE NORTH-WEST PROVINCES.—At the Seat of Government.—The Insurrection in Behar.—The Siege of Arrah.—Behar and Bengal. BOOK VIII.—MUTINY AND REBELLION IN THE NORTH-WEST PROVINCES.—Agra in May.—Insurrection in the Districts.—Bearing of the Native Chiefs.—Agra in June, July, August and September. BOOK IX.—LUCKNOW AND DELHI.—Rebellion in Oude.—Revolt in the Districts.—Lucknow in June and July.—The siege and Capture of Delhi.

(For continuation, *see* " History of the Indian Mutiny," by Colonel G. B. MALLESON, p. 19.)

Kaye (Sir J. W.) History of the War in Afghanistan.
New edition. 3 Vols. Crown 8vo. £1. 6s.

—— **H. St. G. Tucker's Life and Correspondence.**
8vo. 10s.

—— **Memorials of Indian Governments.**
By H. ST. GEORGE TUCKER. 8vo. 10s.

Keatinge (Mrs.) English Homes in India.
By MRS. KEATINGE. Part I.—The Three Loves. Part II.— The Wrong Turning. Two vols., Post 8vo. 16s.

Keene (H. G.) Mogul Empire.
From the death of Aurungzeb to the overthrow of the Mahratta Power, by HENRY GEORGE KEENE, B.C.S. Second edition. With Map. 8vo. 10s. 6d.

This Work fills up a blank between the ending of Elphinstone's and the commencement of Thornton's Histories.

—— **Administration in India.**
Post 8vo. 5s.

—— **Peepul Leaves.**
Poems written in India. Post 8vo. 5s.

Keene (H. G.). The Turks in India.
Historical Chapters on the Administration of Hindostan by
the Chugtai Tartar, Babar, and his Descendants. 12s. 6d.

Latham (Dr. R. G.) Russian and Turk,
From a Geographical, Ethnological, and Historical Point of
View. 8vo. 18s.

Laurie (Col. W. F. B.) Our Burmese Wars and Relations
with Burma. With a Summary of Events from 1826 to
1879, including a Sketch of King Theebau's Progress. With
various Local, Statistical, and Commercial Information. By
Colonel W. F. B. LAURIE, Author of "Rangoon," "Narrative
of the Second Burmese War,"&c. 8vo. With Plans and Map.
16s.

—— **Ashe Pyee, the Superior Country**; or the great attrac-
tions of Burma to British Enterprise and Commerce. By
Col. W. F. B. LAURIE, Author of "Our Burmese Wars
and Relations with Burma." Crown 8vo. 5s.

Lee (F. G.) The Church under Queen Elizabeth.
An Historical Sketch. By the Rev. F. G. LEE, D.D. Two
Vols., Crown 8vo. 21s.

—— **Reginald Barentyne**; or Liberty Without Limit. A
Tale of the Times. By FREDERICK GEORGE LEE. With
Portrait of the Author. Crown 8vo. 10s. 6d.

—— **The Words from the Cross**: Seven Sermons for Lent,
Passion-Tide, and Holy Week. By the Rev. F. G. LEE, D.D.
Third Edition revised. Fcap. 3s. 6d.

—— **Order Out of Chaos.** Two Sermons.
By the Rev. FREDERICK GEORGE LEE, D.D. Fcap. 2s. 6d.

Lee's (Dr. W. N.) Drain of Silver to the East.
Post 8vo. 8s.

Le Messurier (Maj. A.) Kandahar in 1879.
Being the Diary of Major A. LE MESSURIER, R.E., Brigade
Major R.E. with the Quetta Column. Crown 8vo. 8s.

Lewin (T. H.) Wild Races of the South Eastern Frontier of
India. Including an Account of the Loshai Country. By Capt.
T. H. LEWIN, Dep. Comm. of Hill Tracts. Post 8vo. 10s. 6d.

Lewis (A. J.) Indian Penal Code
In the Form of Questions and Answers. With Explanatory
and Illustrative Notes. By ANGELO J. LEWIS. Post 8vo. 7s. 6d.

Lewis (A. J.) Indian Code of Civil Procedure.
In the Form of Questions and Answers. With Explanatory
and Illustrative Notes. By ANGELO J. LEWIS. Post 8vo. 12s. 6d.

Liancourt's and Pincott's Primitive and Universal Laws of
the Formation and development of language ; a Rational and
Inductive System founded on the Natural Basis of Onomatops.
8vo. 12s. 6d.

Lockwood (Ed.) Natural History, Sport and Travel.
By EDWARD LOCKWOOD, Bengal Civil Service, late Magistrate
of Monghyr. Crown 8vo. With numerous Illustrations. 9s.

Lovell (Vice-Adm.) Personal Narrative of Events from
1799 to 1815. With Anecdotes. By the late Vice-Adm. WM.
STANHOPE LOVELL, R.N., K.H. Second edition. Crown 8vo. 4s.

Lupton (J. I.) The Horse, as he Was, as he Is, and as he
Ought to Be. By JAMES IRVINE LUPTON, F.R.C.V.S., Author
of "The External Anatomy of the Horse," &c. &c. Illustrated. 3s. 6d.

MacGregor (Col. C. M.) Narrative of a Journey through
the Province of Khorassan and on the N. W. Frontier of
Afghanistan in 1875. By Colonel C. M. MACGREGOR,
C.S.I., C.I.E., Bengal Staff Corps. 2 vols. 8vo. With
map and numerous illustrations. 30s.

Mackay (C.) Luck, and what came of it. A Tale of our
Times. By CHARLES MACKAY, LL.D. Three vols. 31s. 6d.

Maggs (J.) Round Europe with the Crowd.
Crown 8vo. 5s.

Magenis (Lady Louisa) The Challenge of Barletta. By Massimo D'Azeglio. Rendered into English by Lady LOUISA
MAGENIS. 2 vols., crown 8vo. 21s.

Malleson (Col. G. B.) Final French Struggles in India
and on the Indian Seas. Including an Account of the
Capture of the Isles of France and Bourbon, and Sketches
of the most eminent Foreign Adventurers in India up to
the period of that Capture. With an Appendix containing
an Account of the Expedition from India to Egypt in 1801.
By Colonel G. B. MALLESON, C.S.I. Crown 8vo. 10s. 6d.

—— **History of Afghanistan,** from the Earliest Period to
the Outbreak of the War of 1878. 8vo. Second Edition.
With Map. 18s.

—— **Herat: The Garden and Granary of Central Asia.**
With Map and Index. 8vo. 8s.

Malleson (Col. G. B.) History of the Indian Mutiny,
1857–1858, commencing from the close of the Second
Volume of Sir John Kaye's History of the Sepoy War.
Vol. I. 8vo. With Map. 20s.

CONTENTS.—Calcutta in May and June.—William Tayler
and Vincent Eyre.—How Bihar and Calcutta were saved.—
Mr. Colvin and Agra.—Jhansi and Bandalkhand.—Colonel
Durand and Holkar.—Sir George Lawrence and Rajputana.—
Brigadier Polwhele's great battle and its results.—Bareli,
Rohilkhand, and Farakhabad.—The relation of the annexa-
tion of Oudh to the Mutiny.—Sir Henry Lawrence and the
Mutiny in Oudh.—The siege of Lakhnao.—The first relief of
Lakhnao.

VOL. II.—The Storming of Delhi, the Relief of Lucknow, the Two Battles of Cawnpore, the Campaign in
Rohilkhand, and the movements of the several Columns
in the N.W. Provinces, the Azimgurh District, and on the
Eastern and South-Eastern Frontiers. 8vo. With 4 Plans.
20s.

VOL. III.—Bombay in 1857. Lord Elphinstone. March
of Woodburn's Column. Mr. Seton-Karr and the Southern
Maratha Country. Mr. Forjett and Bombay. Asirgarh. Sir
Henry Durand. March of Stuart's Column. Holkar and Durand.
Malwa Campaign. Haidarabad. Major C. Davidson and Salar
Jang. Sagar and Narbadi Territory. Sir Robert Hamilton and
Sir Hugh Rose. Central India Campaign. Whitlock and Kirwi.
Sir Hugh Rose and Gwaliar. Le Grand Jacob and Western
India. Lord Canning's Oudh policy. Last Campaign in, and
pacification of, Oudh. Sir Robert Napier, Smith, Michell, and
Tantia Topi. Civil Districts during the Mutiny. Minor
Actions at Out-stations. Conclusion. 8vo. With Plans. 20s.

Manning (Mrs.) Ancient and Mediæval India.
Being the History, Religion, Laws, Caste, Manners and
Customs, Language, Literature, Poetry, Philosophy, Astronomy,
Algebra, Medicine, Architecture, Manufactures, Commerce,
&c., of the Hindus, taken from their writings. Amongst the
works consulted and gleaned from may be named the Rig Veda,
Sama Veda, Yajur Veda, Sathapatha Brahmana, Bhagavat
Gita, The Puranas, Code of Manu, Code of Yajnavalkya,
Mitakshara, Daya Bhaga, Mahabharata, Atriya, Charaka,
Susruta, Ramayana, Raghu Vansa, Bhattikavya, Sakuntala,
Vikramorvasi, Malati and Madhava, Mudra Rakshasa, Ratna-

vali. Kumara Sambhava, Prabodha, Chandrodaya, Megha Duta, Gita Govinda, Panchatantra, Hitopadesa, Katha Sarit, Sagara, Ketala, Pancnavinsati, Dasa Kumara Charita, &c. By Mrs. Manning, with Illustrations. 2 vols., 8vo. 30s.

Marvin (Chas.) Merv, the Queen of the World and the Scourge of the Men-stealing Turcomans. By Charles Marvin, author of " The Disastrous Turcoman Campaign," and " Grodekoff's Ride to Herat." With Portraits and Maps. 8vo. 18s.

—— **Colonel Grodekoff's Ride from Samarcand to Herat,** through Balkh and the Uzbek States of Afghan Turkestan. With his own March-route from the Oxus to Herat. By Charles Marvin. Crown 8vo. With Portrait. 8s.

—— **The Eye-Witnesses' Account of the Disastrous Russian** Campaign against the Akhal Tekke Turcomans : Describing the March across the Burning Desert, the Storming of Den-geel Tepe, and the Disastrous Retreat to the Caspian. By Charles Marvin. With numerous Maps and Plans. 8vo. 18s.

Matson (Nellie) Hilda Desmond, or Riches and Poverty. Crown 8vo. 10s. 6d.

Mayhew (Edward) Illustrated Horse Doctor. Being an Accurate and Detailed Account, accompanied by more than 400 Pictorial Representations, characteristic of the various Diseases to which the Equine Race are subjected; together with the latest Mode of Treatment, and all the re-quisite Prescriptions written in Plain English By Edward Mayhew, M.R.C.V.S. 8vo. 18s. 6d.

CONTENTS.—The Brain and Nervous System.—The Eyes.— The Mouth.—The Nostrils.—The Throat.—The Chest and its contents.—The Stomach, Liver, &c.—The Abdomen.—The Urinary Organs.—The Skin.—Specific Diseases.—Limbs.— The Feet.—Injuries.—Operations.

"The book contains nearly 600 pages of valuable matter, which reflects great credit on its author, and, owing to its practical details, the result of deep scientific research, deserves a place in the library of medical, veterinary, and non-professional readers."—*Field.*

"The book furnishes at once the bane and the antidote, as the drawings show the horse not only suffering from every kind of disease, but in the different stages of it, while the alphabetical summary at the end gives the cause, symptoms and treatment of each."—*Illustrated London News.*

—— **Illustrated Horse Management.** Containing descriptive remarks upon Anatomy, Medicine, Shoeing, Teeth, Food, Vices, Stables; likewise a plain account of the situation, nature, and value of the various points; together with comments on grooms, dealers, breeders, breakers, and trainers; Embellished with more than 400 engravings from original designs made expressly for this work. By E. MAYHEW. A new Edition, revised and improved by J. I. LUPTON. M.R.C.V.S. 8vo. 12s.

CONTENTS.—The body of the horse anatomically considered. PHYSIC.—The mode of administering it, and minor operations. SHOEING.—Its origin, its uses, and its varieties. THE TEETH. —Their natural growth, and the abuses to which they are liable.

FOOD.—The fittest time for feeding, and the kind of food which the horse naturally consumes. The evils which are occasioned by modern stables. The faults inseparable from stables. The so-called "incapacitating vices," which are the results of injury or of disease. Stables as they should be. GROOMS.—Their prejudices, their injuries, and their duties. POINTS.—Their relative importance and where to look for their development. BREEDING.—Its inconsistencies and its disappointments. BREAKING AND TRAINING.—Their errors and their results.

Mayhew (Henry) German Life and Manners.
As seen in Saxony. With an account of Town Life—Village Life—Fashionable Life—Married Life—School and University Life, &c. Illustrated with Songs and Pictures of the Student Customs at the University of Jena. By HENRY MAYHEW, 2 vols., 8vo., with numerous illustrations. 18s.

A Popular Edition of the above. With illustrations. Cr. 8vo. 7s.
"Full of original thought and observation, and may be studied with profit by both German and English—especially by the German."*Athenæum.*

McCarthy (T. A.) An Easy System of Calisthenics and Drilling. Including Light Dumb-Bell and Indian Club Exercises. By T. A. McCARTHY, Chief Instructor at Mr. Moss's Gymnasium, Brighton. Fcap. 1s. 6d.

McCosh (J.) Advice to Officers in India.
By JOHN McCosh, M.D. Post 8vo. 8s.

Meadow (T.) Notes on China.
Desultory Notes on the Government and People of China and on the Chinese Language. By T. T. MEADOWS. 8vo. 9s.

Menzies (S.) Turkey Old and New: Historical, Geographical, and Statistical. By SUTHERLAND MENZIES. With Map and numerous Illustrations. 2 vols., 8vo. 32s.

Military Works—chiefly issued by the Government.

Field Exercises and Evolutions of Infantry. Pocket edition, 1s.

Queen's Regulations and Orders for the Army.   Corrected to 1881. 8vo. 3s. 6d. Interleaved, 5s. 6d. Pocket Edition, 1s. 6d.

Musketry Regulations, as used at Hythe. 1s.

Dress Regulations for the Army. (Reprinting.)

Infantry Sword Exercise. 1875. 6d.

Infantry Bugle Sounds. 6d.

Handbook of Battalion Drill. By Lieut. H. C. SLACK. 2s ; or with Company Drill, 2s. 6d.

Handbook of Brigade Drill. By Lieut. H. C. SLACK. 3s.

Red Book for Sergeants. By WILLIAM BRIGHT, Colour-Sergeant, 37th Middlesex R.V. 1s.

Handbook of Company Drill ; also of Skirmishing, Battalion, and Shelter.Trench Drill. By Lieut. CHARLES SLACK. 1s.

Elementary and Battalion Drill. Condensed and Illustrated, together with duties of Company Officers, Markers, &c., in Battalion. By Captain MALTON. 2s. 6d.

Cavalry Regulations. For the Instruction, Formations, and Movements of Cavalry. Royal 8vo. 4s. 6d.

Manual of Artillery Exercises, 1873. 8vo. 5s.

Manual of Field Artillery Exercises. 1877. 3s.

Standing Orders for Royal Artillery. 8vo, 3s.

Principles and Practice of Modern Artillery. By Lt.-Col. C. H. OWEN, R.A. 8vo. Illustrated. 15s.

Artillerist's Manual and British Soldiers' Compendium. By Major F. A. GRIFFITHS. 11th Edition. 5s.

Compendium of Artillery Exercises—Smooth Bore, Field, and Garrison Artillery for Reserve Forces. By Captain J. M. McKenzie. 3s. 6d.

Principles of Gunnery. By JOHN T. HYDE, M.A., late Professor of Fortification and Artillery, Royal Indian Military College, Addiscombe. Second edition, revised and enlarged. With many Plates and Cuts, and Photograph of Armstrong Gun. Royal 8vo. 14s.

Notes on Gunnery. By Captain Goodeve. Revised Edition. 1s.

Text Book of the Construction and Manufacture of Rifled Ordnance in the British Service. By STONEY & JONES. Second Edition. Paper, 3s. 6d., Cloth, 4s. 6d.

Treatise on Fortification and Artillery. By Major HECTOR STRAITH. Revised and re-arranged by THOMAS COOK, R.N., by JOHN T. HYDE, M.A. 7th Edition. Royal 8vo. Illustrated and Four Hundred Plans, Cuts, &c. £2 2s.

Military Surveying and Field Sketching. The Various
Methods of Contouring, Levelling, Sketching without Instruments,
Scale of Shade, Examples in Military Drawing, &c., &c., &c. As at
present taught in the Military Colleges. By Major W. H. RICHARDS,
55th Regiment, Chief Garrison Instructor in India, Late Instructor in Military Surveying, Royal Military College, Sandhurst.
Second Edition, Revised and Corrected. 12s.

Treatise on Military Surveying; including Sketching in the
Field, Plan-Drawing, Levelling, Military Reconnaissance, &c. By
Lieut.-Col. BASIL JACKSON, late of the Royal Staff Corps. The
Fifth Edition. 8vo. Illustrated by Plans, &c. 14s.

Instruction in Military Engineering. Vol. 1., Part III. 4s.

Elementary Principles of Fortification. A Text-Book for
Military Examinations. By J. T. HYDE, M.A. Royal 8vo. With
numerous Plans and Illustrations. 10s. 6d.

Military Train Manual. 1s.

The Sappers' Manual. Compiled for the use of Engineer
Volunteer Corps. By Col. W. A. FRANKLAND, R.E. With
numerous Illustrations. 2s.

Ammunition. A descriptive treatise on the different Projectiles
Charges, Fuzes, Rockets, &c., at present in use for Land and Sea
Service, and on other war stores manufactured in the Royal
Laboratory. 6s.

Hand-book on the Manufacture and Proof of Gunpowder. as
carried on at the Royal Gunpowder Factory, Waltham Abbey. 5s.

Regulations for the Training of Troops for service in the Field
and for the conduct of Peace Manœuvres. 2s.

Hand-book Dictionary for the Militia and Volunteer Services,
Containing a variety of useful information, Alphabetically arranged.
Pocket size, 3s. 6d. ; by post, 3s. 8d.

Gymnastic Exercises, System of Fencing, and Exercises for
the Regulation Clubs. In one volume. Crown 8vo. 1877. 2s.

Text-Book on the Theory and Motion of Projectiles; the History, Manufacture, and Explosive Force of Gunpowder; the History
of Small Arms. For Officers sent to School of Musketry. 1s. 6d.

Notes on Ammunition. 4th Edition. 1877. 2s. 6d.

Regulations and Instructions for Encampments. 6d.

Rules for the Conduct of the War Game. 2s.

Medical Regulations for the Army, Instructions for the Army,
Comprising duties of Officers, Attendants, and Nurses, &c. 1s. 6d.

Purveyors' Regulations and Instructions, for Guidance of
Officers of Purveyors' Department of the Army. 3s.

Priced Vocabulary of Stores used in Her Majesty's Service. 4s.

Transport of Sick and Wounded Troops. By DR. LONGMORE. 5s.

Precedents in Military Law. By LT-COL. W. HOUGH. 8vo. 25s.

The Practice of Courts-Martial, by HOUGH & LONG. 8vo. 26s.

Manual of Military Law. For all ranks of the Army, Militia, and Volunteer Services. By Colonel J. K. PIPON, and J. F. COLLIER, Esq. Third and Revised Edition. Pocket size. 5s.

Regulations applicable to the European Officer in India. Containing Staff Corps Rules, Staff Salaries, Commands, Furlough and Retirement Regulations, &c. By GEORGE E. COCHRANE, late Assistant Military Secretary, India Office. 1 vol., post 8vo. 7s. 6d.

Reserve Force; Guide to Examinations, for the use of Captains and Subalterns of Infantry, Militia, and Rifle Volunteers, and for Serjeants of Volunteers. By Capt. G. H. GREAVES. 2nd edit. 2s.

The Military Encyclopædia ; referring exclusively to the Military Sciences, Memoirs of distinguished Soldiers, and the Narratives of Remarkable Battles. By J. H. STOCQUELER. 8vo. 12s.

The Operations of War Explained and Illustrated. By Col. HAMLEY. New Edition Revised, with Plates. Royal 8vo. 30s.

Lessons of War. As taught by the Great Masters and Others ; Selected and Arranged from the various operations in War. By FRANCE JAMES SOADY, Lieut.-Col., R.A. Royal 8vo. 21s.

The Surgeon's Pocket Book, an Essay on the best Treatment of Wounded in War. By Surgeon Major J. H. PORTER. 7s. 6d.

A Precis of Modern Tactics. By COLONEL HOME. 8vo. 8s. 6d.

Armed Strength of Austria. By Capt. COOKE. 2 pts. £1 2s.

Armed Strength of Denmark. 3s.

Armed Strength of Russia. Translated from the German. 7s.

Armed Strength of Sweden and Norway. 3s. 6d.

Armed Strength of Italy. 5s. 6d.

Armed Strength of Germany. Part I. 8s. 6d.

The Franco-German War of 1870—71. By CAPT. C. H. CLARKE. Vol. I. £1 6s. Sixth Section. 5s. Seventh Section 6s. Eighth Section. 3s. Ninth Section. 4s. 6d. Tenth Section. 6s. Eleventh Section. 5s. 3d. Twelfth Section. 4s. 6d.

The Campaign of 1866 in Germany. Royal 8vo. With Atlas, 21s.

Celebrated Naval and Military Trials. By PETER BURKE. Post 8vo., cloth. 10s. 6d.

Military Sketches. By SIR LASCELLES WRAXALL. Post 8vo. 6s.

Military Life of the Duke of Wellington. By JACKSON and SCOTT. 2 Vols. 8vo. Maps, Plans, &c. 12s.

Single Stick Exercise of the Aldershot Gymnasium. 6d.

Treatise on Military Carriages, and other Manufactures of the Royal Carriage Department. 5s.

Steppe Campaign Lectures. 2s.

Manual of Instructions for Army Surgeons. 1s.

Regulations for Army Hospital Corps. 9d.

Manual of Instructions for Non-Commissioned Officers, Army Hospital Corps. 2s.

Handbook for Military Artificers. 3s.

Instructions for the use of Auxiliary Cavalry. 2s. 6d.

Equipment Regulations for the Army. 5s. 6d.

Statute Law relating to the Army. 1s. 3d.

Regulations for Commissariat and Ordnance Department 2s.

Regulations for the Commissariat Department. 1s. 6d.

Regulations for the Ordnance Department. 1s. 6d.

Artillerist's Handbook of Reference for the use of the Royal and Reserve Artillery, by WILL and DALTON. 5s.

An Essay on the Principles and Construction of Military Bridges, by SIR HOWARD DOUGLAS. 1853. 15s.

Mill's History of British India,
With Notes and Continuation. By H. H. WILSON. 9 vols. cr. 8vo. £2 10s.

Mitchinson (A. W.) The Expiring Continent; A Narrative of Travel in Senegambia, with Observations on Native Character; Present Condition and Future Prospects of Africa and Colonisation. By ALEX. WILL. MITCHINSON. With Sixteen full-page Illustrations and Map. 8vo. 18s.

Mitford (Maj. R. C. W.) To Caubul with the Cavalry Brigade. A Narrative of Personal Experiences with the Force under General Sir F. S. Roberts, G.C.B. With Map and Illustrations from Sketches by the Author. By Major R. C. W. MITFORD, 14th Bengal Lancers. 8vo. Second Edition. 9s.

Muller's (Max) Rig-Veda-Sanhita.
The Sacred Hymns of the Brahmins; together with the Commentary of Sayanacharya. Published under the Patronage of the Right Honourable the Secretary of State for India in Council. 6 vols., 4to. £2 10s. per volume.

Mysteries of the Vatican;
Or Crimes of the Papacy. From the German of DR. THEODORE
GREISENGER. 2 Vols. post 8vo. 21s.

Neville (Ralph) The Squire's Heir.
By RALPH NEVILLE, Author of "Lloyd Pennant." Two
Vols. 21s.

Nicholson (Capt. H. W.) From Sword to Share; or, a Fortune
in Five Years at Hawaii. By Capt. H. WHALLEY NICHOLSON.
Crown 8vo. With Map and Photographs. 12s. 6d.

Nirgis and Bismillah.
NIRGIS; a Tale of the Indian Mutiny, from the Diary of a
Slave Girl: and BISMILLAH; or, Happy Days in Cashmere.
By HAFIZ ALLARD. Post 8vo. 10s. 6d.

Norris-Newman (C. L.) In Zululand with the British,
throughout the War of 1879. By CHARLES L.; NORRIS-
NEWMAN, Special Correspondent of the London "Standard,"
Cape Town "Standard and Mail," and the "Times" of Natal.
With Plans and Four Portraits. 8vo. 16s.

Notes on the North Western Provinces of India.
By a District Officer. 2nd Edition. Post 8vo., cloth. 5s.
    CONTENTS.—Area and Population.—Soils.—Crops.—Irriga-
tion.—Rent.—Rates.—Land Tenures.

O'Donoghue (Mrs. P.) Ladies on Horseback.
Learning, Park Riding, and Hunting. With Notes upon Cos-
tume, and numerous Anecdotes. By Mrs. POWER O'DONOGHUE,
Authoress of "The Knave of Clubs," "Horses and Horsemen,"
"Grandfather's Hunter," "One in Ten Thousand," &c. &c.
Cr. 8vo. With Portrait. 5s.

Oldfield (H. A.) Sketches from Nipal, Historiral and Descriptive ; with Anecdotes of the Court Life and Wild Sports of the
Country in the time of Maharaja Jang Bahadur, G.C.B.; to
which is added an Essay on Nipalese Buddhism, and Illustrations of Religious Monuments, Architecture, and Scenery,
from the Author's own Drawings. By the late HENRY AM-
BROSE OLDFIELD, M.D., of H. M.'s Indian Army, many years
Resident at Khatmandu. Two vols. 8vo. 36s.

Osborne (Mrs. W.) Pilgrimage to Mecca (A).
By the Nawab Sikandar Begum of Bhopal. Translated from
the Original Urdu. By MRS. WILLOUGHBY OSBORNE. Followed

by a Sketch of the History of Bhopal. By COL. WILLOUGHBY-OSBORNE, C.B. With Photographs, and dedicated, by permission, to HER MAJESTY, QUEEN VICTORIA. Post 8vo. £1. 1s.
This is a highly important book, not only for its literary merit, and the information it contains, but also from the fact of its being the first work written by an Indian lady, and that lady a Queen.

Owen (Sidney) India on the Eve of the British Conquest.
A Historical Sketch. By SIDNEY OWEN, M.A. Reader in Indian Law and History in the University of Oxford. Formerly Professor of History in the Elphinstone College, Bombay. Post 8vo. 8s.

Oxenham (Rev. H. N.) Catholic Eschatology and Universalism.
An Essay on the Doctrine of Future Retribution. Second Edition, revised and enlarged. Crown 8vo. 7s. 6d.

—— Catholic Doctrine of the Atonement.
An Historical Inquiry into its Development in the Church, with an Introduction on the Principle of Theological Development. By H. NUTCOMBE OXENHAM, M.A. 3rd Edition and Enlarged. 8vo. 14s.
"It is one of the ablest and probably one of the most charmingly written treatises on the subject which exists in our language."—*Times.*

—— The First Age of Christianity and the Church.
By JOHN IGNATIUS DÖLLINGER, D.D., Professor of Ecclesiastical History in the University of Munich, &c., &c. Translated from the German bv HENRY NUTCOMBE OXENHAM, M.A., late Scholar of Baliol College, Oxford. Third Edition. 2 vols. Crown 8vo. 18s.

Ozanam's (A. F.) Civilisation in the Fifth Century.
From the French. By The Hon. A. C. GLYN. 2 Vols., post 8vo. 21s.

Pebody (Charles) Authors at Work.
Francis Jeffrey—Sir Walter Scott—Robert Burns—Charles Lamb—R. B. Sheridan—Sydney Smith—Macaulay—Byron Wordsworth—Tom Moore—Sir James Mackintosh. Post 8vo. 10s. 6d.

Pelly (Sir Lewis). The Miracle Play of Hasan and Husain.
Collected from Oral Tradition by Colonel Sir LEWIS PELLY, K.C.B., K.C.S.I., formerly serving in Persia as Secretary of Legation, and Political Resident in the Persian Gulf. Revised, with Explanatory Notes, by ARTHUR N. WOLLASTON, H.M. Indian (Home) Service, Translator of Anwar-i-Suhaili, &c. 2 Vols. royal 8vo. 32s.

Pincott (F.) Analytical Index to Sir JOHN KAYE's History of the Sepoy War, and Col. G. B. MALLESON's History of the Indian Mutiny. (Combined in one volume.) By FREDERIC PINCOTT, M.R.A.S. 8vo. 10s. 6d.

Pipon and Collier's Manual of Military Law.
By Colonel J. K. PIPON, and J. F. COLLIER, Esq., of the Inner Temple, Barrister-at-Law. 5s.

Pollock (Field Marshal Sir George) Life & Correspondence.
By C. R. Low. 8vo. With portrait. 18s.

Pope (G. U.) Text-book of Indian History; with Geographical Notes, Genealogical Tables, Examination Questions, and Chronological, Biographical, Geographical, and General Indexes. For the use of Schools, Colleges, and Private Students. By the Rev. G. U. POPE, D.D., Principal of Bishop Cotton's Grammar School and College, Bangalore; Fellow of the Madras University. Third Edition, thoroughly revised. Fcap. 4to. 12s.

Practice of Courts Martial.
By HOUGH & LONG. 8vo. London. 1825. 26s.

Prichard's Chronicles of Budgepore, &c.
Or Sketches of Life in Upper India. 2 Vols., Foolscap 8vo. 12s.

Prinsep (H. T.) Historical Results.
Deducible from Recent Discoveries in Affghanistan. By H. T. PRINSEP. 8vo. Lond. 1844. 15s.

—— **Tibet, Tartary, and Mongolia.**
By HENRY T. PRINSEP, Esq. Second edition. Post 8vo. 5s.

—— **Political and Military Transactions in India.**
2 Vols. 8vo. London, 1825. 18s.

Richards (Major W. H.) Military Surveying, &c.
12s. (See page 22.)

Rowe (R.) Picked up in the Streets; or, Struggles for Life among the London Poor. By RICHARD ROWE, " Good Words " Commissioner, Author of "Jack Afloat and Ashore," &c. Crown 8vo. Illustrated. 6s.

Rumsey (Almaric) Moohummudan Law of Inheritance, and Rights and Relations affecting it. Sunni Doctrine. Comprising, together with much collateral information, the substance, greatly expanded, of the author's " Chart of Family Inheritance." By ALMARIC RUMSEY, of Lincoln's Inn, Bar-

rister-at-Law, Professor of Indian Jurisprudence at King's
College, London. Author of "A Chart of Hindu Family
Inheritance." 8vo. 12s.

Rumsey (Almaric) A Chart of Hindu Family Inheritance.
Second Edition, much enlarged. 8vo. 6s. 6d.

Sachau (Dr. C. Ed.) The Chronology of Ancient Nations. An
English Version of the Arabic Text of the Athar-ut Bâkiya of
Albîrûnî, or "Vestiges of the Past." Collected and reduced
to writing by the Author in A.H. 390-1, A.D. 1,000. Trans-
lated and Edited, with Notes and Index, by Dr. C. EDWARD
SACHAU, Professor in the Royal University of Berlin. Pub-
lished for the Oriental Translation Fund of Great Britain and
Ireland. Royal 8vo. 42s.

Sanderson (G. P.) Thirteen Years among the Wild
Beasts of India; their Haunts and Habits, from Personal
Observation; with an account of the Modes of Capturing and
Taming Wild Elephants. By G. P. SANDERSON, Officer in
Charge of the Government Elephant Keddahs at Mysore.
With 21 full page Illustrations and three Maps. Second
Edition. Fcp. 4to. £1 5s.

Sewell (R.) Analytical History of India.
From the earliest times to the Abolition of the East India
Company in 1858. By ROBERT SEWELL, Madras Civil Service.
Post 8vo. 8s.

*** The object of this work is to supply the want which has
been felt by students for a condensed outline of Indian History
which would serve at once to recall the memory and guide the
eye, while at the same time it has been attempted to render it
interesting to the general reader by preserving a medium
between a bare analysis and a complete history.

Shadow of a Life (The) A Girl's Story.
By BERYL HOPE. 3 vols., post 8vo. 31s. 6d.

Sherer (J. W.) The Conjuror's Daughter.
A Tale. By J. W. SHERER, C.S.I. With Illustrations by
Alf. T. Elwes and J. Jellicoe. Cr. 8vo. 6s.

—— Who is Mary?
A Cabinet Novel, in one volume. By J. W. SHERER, Esq.,
C.S.I. 10s. 6d.

Signor Monaldini's Niece.
A Novel of Italian Life. Crown 8vo. 6s.

Simpson (H. T.) Archæologia Adelensis; or, a History of the Parish of Adel, in the West Riding of Yorkshire. Being an attempt to delineate its Past and Present Associations, Archæological, Topographical, and Scriptural. By HENRY TRAILL SIMPSON, M.A., late Rector of Adel. With numerous etchings by W. LLOYD FERGUSON. Roy. 8vo. 21s.

Small (Rev. G.) A Dictionary of Naval Terms, English and Hindustani. For the use of Nautical Men trading to India, &c. By Rev. G. SMALL, Interpreter to the Strangers' Home for Asiatics. Fcap. 2s. 6d.

Solymos (B.) Desert Life. Recollections of an Expedition in the Soudan. By B. SOLYMOS (B. E. FALKONBERG), Civil Engineer. 8vo. 15s.

Starling (M. H.) Indian Criminal Law and Procedure. Third edition. 8vo. £2 2s. See page 15.

Steele (A.) Law and Customs of Hindu Castes. BY ARTHUR STEELE. Royal 8vo. £1. 1s. (See page 14.)

Stent (G. C.) Entombed Alive, And other Songs and Ballads. (From the Chinese.) By GEORGE CARTER STENT, M.R.A.S., of the Chinese Imperial Maritime Customs Service, author of " Chinese and English Vocabulary," " Chinese and English Pocket Dictionary," " The Jade Chaplet," &c. Crown 8vo. With four Illustrations. 9s.

Stothard (R. T.) The A B C of Art. Being a system of delineating forms and objects in nature necessary for the attainments of a draughtsman. By ROBERT T. STOTHARD, F.S.A., late H.D.S.A. Fcap. 1s.

Swinnerton (Rev. C.) The Afghan War. Gough's Action at Futtehabad. By the Rev. C. SWINNERTON, Chaplain in the Field with the First Division, Peshawur Valley Field Force. With Frontispiece and Two Plans. Crown 8vo. 5s.

Tayler (W.) Thirty-eight Years in India, from Juganath to the Himalaya Mountains. By WILLIAM TAYLER, Esq., Retired B.C.S., late Commissioner of Patna. In 2 vols.

Contains a memoir of the life of Mr. William Tayler, from 1829 to 1867—during the Government of eight Governors General—from Lord William Bentinck to Lord Lawrence, comprising numerous incidents and adventures, official, personal, tragic, and comic, " from grave to gay, from lively to severe " throughout that period. The first volume contains a hundred illustrations, reproduced by Mr. Tayler himself, from original sketches taken by him on the spot, in Bengal, Behar, N.W. Provinces, Darjeeling, Nipal, and Simla. Vol. I. 25s. (Vol. II. in the press).

Thomson's Lunar and Horary Tables.
For New and Concise Methods of Performing the Calculations necessary for ascertaining the Longitude by Lunar Observations, or Chronometers ; with directions for acquiring a knowledge of the Principal Fixed Stars and finding the Latitude of them. By DAVID THOMSON. Sixty-fifth edit. Royal 8vo. 10s.

Thornton (P. M.) Foreign Secretaries of the Nineteenth Century. By PERCY M. THORNTON.
Contains—Memoirs of Lord Grenville, Lord Hawkesbury, Lord Harrowby, Lord Mulgrave, C. J. Fox, Lord Howick, George Canning, Lord Bathurst, Lord Wellesley (together with estimate of his Indian Rule by Col. G. B. Malleson, C.S.I.), Lord Castlereagh, Lord Dudley, Lord Aberdeen, and Lord Palmerston. Also, Extracts from Lord Bexley's Papers, including lithographed letters of Lords Castlereagh and Canning, which, bearing on important points of public policy, have never yet been published ; together with other important information culled from private and other sources. With Ten Portraits, and a View shewing Interior of the old House of Lords. (Second Edition.) 2 vols. 8vo. 32s. 6d.

Thornton's Gazetteer of India.
Compiled chiefly from the records at the India Office. By EDWARD THORNTON. 1 vol., 8vo., pp. 1015. With Map. 21s.
  ₊ *The chief objects in view in compiling this Gazetteer are:—*
1st. *To fix the relative position of the various cities, towns, and villages with as much precision as possible, and to exhibit with the greatest practicable brevity all that is known respecting them ; and*
2ndly. *To note the various countries, provinces, or territorial divisions, and to describe the physical characteristics of each, together with their statistical, social, and political circumstances.*
   To these are added minute descriptions of the principal rivers and chains of mountains ; thus presenting to the reader, within a brief compass, a mass of information which cannot otherwise be obtained, except from a multiplicity of volumes and manuscript records.
The Library Edition.
   4 vols., 8vo. Notes, Marginal References, and Map. £2 16s.

Thornton (E.) Gazetteer of the Punjaub, Affghanistan, &c.
Gazetteer of the Countries adjacent to India, on the northwest, including Scinde, Affghanistan, Beloochistan, the Punjaub, and the neighbouring States. By EDWARD THORNTON, Esq. 2 vols. 8vo. £1 5s.

Thornton's History of India.

The History of the British Empire in India, by Edward Thornton, Esq. Containing a Copious Glossary of Indian Terms, and a Complete Chronological Index of Events, to aid the Aspirant for Public Examinations. Third edition. 1 vol. 8vo. With Map. 12s.

₊ *The Library Edition of the above in 6 volumes, 8vo., may be had, price £2 8s.*

Thornton (T.) East India Calculator.

By T. THORNTON. 8vo. London, 1823. 10s.

—— **History of the Punjaub,**

And of the Rise, Progress, and Present Condition of the Sikhs. By T. THORNTON. 2 Vols. Post 8vo. 8s.

Tilley (H. A.) Japan, the Amoor and the Pacific.

With notices of other Places, comprised in a Voyage of Circumnavigation in the Imperial Russian Corvette *Rynda*, in 1858–1860. By HENRY A. TILLEY. Eight Illustrations. 8vo. 16s.

Tod (Col. Jas.) Travels in Western India.

Embracing a visit to the Sacred Mounts of the Jains, and the most Celebrated Shrines of Hindu Faith between Rajpootana and the Indus, with an account of the Ancient City of Nehrwalla. By the late Lieut.-Col. JAMES TOD, Illustrations. Royal 4to. £3 3s.

₊ *This is a companion volume to Colonel Tod's Rajasthan.*

Torrens (W. T. McC.) Reform of Procedure in Parliament

to Clear the Block of Public Business. By W. T. McCULLAGH TORRENS, M.P. Crown 8vo. 6s.

Trimen (Capt. R.) Regiments of the British Army,

Chronologically arranged. Showing their History, Services, Uniform, &c. By Captain R. TRIMEN, late 35th Regiment. 8vo. 10s. 6d.

Trotter (L. J.) History of India.

The History of the British Empire in India, from the Appointment of Lord Hardinge to the Death of Lord Canning (1844 to 1862). By Captain LIONEL JAMES TROTTER, late Bengal Fusiliers. 2 vols. 8vo. 16s. each.

—— **Lord Lawrence.**

A Sketch of his Career. Fcap. 1s. 6d.

—— **Warren Hastings, a Biography.**

By Captain LIONEL JAMES TROTTER, Bengal H. P., author of a "History of India," "Studies in Biography," &c. Crown 8vo. 9s.

Underwood (A. S.) Surgery for Dental Students.
By ARTHUR S. UNDERWOOD, M.R.C.S., L.D.S.E., Assistant
Surgeon to the Dental Hospital of London. 5s.

Vambery (A.) Sketches of Central Asia.
Additional Chapters on My Travels and Adventures, and of the
Ethnology of Central Asia. By Armenius Vambery. 8vo. 16s.
" A valuable guide on almost untrodden ground."—*Athenæum.*

Vibart (Major H. M.) The Military History of the Madras
Engineers and Pioneers. By Major H. M. VIBART, Royal
(late Madras) Engineers. In 2 vols., with numerous Maps
and Plans. Vol. I. 8vo. 32s. (Vol. II. in the Press.)

Victoria Cross (The) An Official Chronicle of Deeds of Per-
sonal Valour achieved in the presence of the Enemy during
the Crimean and Baltic Campaigns and the Indian, Chinese,
New Zealand, and African Wars. From the Institution of the
Order in 1856 to 1880. Edited by ROBERT W. O'BYRNE.
Crown 8vo. With Plate. 5s.

Waring (E. J.) Pharmacopœia of India.
By EDWARD JOHN WARING, M.D., &c. 8vo. 6s. (See page 2.)

Watson (M.) Money.
By JULES TARDIEU. Translated from the French by MAR-
GARET WATSON. Crown 8vo. 7s. 6d.

Watson (Dr. J. F.) and J. W. Kaye, Races and Tribes of
Hindostan. The People of India. A series of Photographic
Illustrations of the Races and Tribes of Hindustan. Prepared
under the Authority of the Government of India, by J. FORBES
WATSON, and JOHN WILLIAM KAYE. The Work contains
about 450 Photographs on mounts, in Eight Volumes, super
royal 4to. £2. 5s. per volume.

Webb (Dr. A.) Pathologia Indica.
Based upon Morbid Specimens from all parts of the Indian
Empire. By ALLAN WEBB, B.M.S. Second Edit. 8vo. 14s.

Wellesley's Despatches.
The Despatches, Minutes, and Correspondence of the Marquis
Wellesley, K.G., during his Administration in India. 5 vols.
8vo. With Portrait, Map, &c. £6. 10s.
    *This work should be perused by all who proceed to India in the
Civil Services.*

Wellington in India.
Military History of the Duke of Wellington in India. 1s.

Wilberforce (E.) Franz Schubert.
A Musical Biography, from the German of Dr. Heinrich Kreisle von Hellborn. By EDWARD WILBERFORCE, Esq., Author of "Social Life in Munich." Post 8vo. 6s.

Wilk's South of India.
3 vols. 4to. £5. 5s.

Wilkins (W. N.) Visual Art; or Nature through the Healthy Eye. With some remarks on Originality and Free Trade, Artistic Copyright, and Durability. By WM. NOY WILKINS, Author of "Art Impressions of Dresden," &c. 8vo. 6s.

Williams (F.) Lives of the English Cardinals.
The Lives of the English Cardinals, from Nicholas Breakspeare (Pope Adrien IV.) to Thomas Wolsey, Cardinal Legate. With Historical Notices of the Papal Court. By FOLKESTONE WILLIAMS. 2 vols., 8vo. 14s.

—— Life, &c., of Bishop Atterbury.
The Memoir and Correspondence of Francis Atterbury, Bishop of Rochester, with his distinguished contemporaries. Compiled chiefly from the Atterbury and Stuart Papers. By FOLKESTONE WILLIAMS, Author of "Lives of the English Cardinals," &c., 2 vols. 8vo. 14s.

Williams (Monier) Indian Wisdom.
Or Examples of the Religious, Philosophical and Ethical Doctrines of the Hindus. With a brief History of the Chief Departments of Sanscrit Literature, and some account of the Past and Present Condition of India, Moral and Intellectual. By MONIER WILLIAMS, M.A., Boden Professor of Sanscrit in in the University of Oxford. Third Edition. 8vo. 15s.

Wilson (H. H.) Glossary of Judicial and Revenue Terms, and of useful Words occurring in Official Documents relating to the Administration of the Government of British India. From the Arabic, Persian, Hindustani, Sanskrit, Hindi, Bengali, Uriya, Marathi, Guzarathi, Telugu, Karnata, Tamil, Malayalam, and other Languages. Compiled and published under the authority of the Hon. the Court of Directors of the E. I. Company. 4to., cloth. £1 10s.

White (S. D.) Indian Reminiscences.
By Colonel S. DEWE' WHITE, late Bengal Staff Corps. 8vo. With 10 Photographs. 14s.

Wollaston (Arthur N.) Anwari Suhaili, or Lights of Canopus.
Commonly known as Kalilah and Damnah, being an adaptation
of the Fables of Bidpai.   Translated from the Persian.   Royal
8vo., 42s.; also in royal 4to., with illuminated borders, designed specially for the work, cloth, extra gilt.   £3 13s. 6d.

—— **Elementary Indian Reader.**
Designed for the use of Students in the Anglo-Vernacular
Schools in India.   Fcap.   1s.

Woolrych (Serjeant W. H.)
Lives of Eminent Serjeants-at-Law of the English Bar.   By
HUMPHRY W. WOOLRYCH, Serjeant-at-Law.   2 vols. 8vo.   30s.

Wraxall (Sir L., Bart.) Caroline Matilda.
Queen of Denmark, Sister of George 3rd.   From Family and
State Papers. By SIR LASCELLES WRAXALL, Bart. 3 vols., 8vo.
18s.

Young (J. R.) Course of Mathematics.
A Course of Elementary Mathematics for the use of candidates
for admission into either of the Military Colleges; of appli-
cants for appointments in the Home or Indian Civil Services;
and of mathematical students generally.   By Professor J. R.
YOUNG.   In one closely-printed volume. 8vo., pp. 648.   12s.

"In the work before us he has digested a complete Elementary
Course, by aid of his long experience as a teacher and writer; and he has
produced a very useful book.   Mr. Young has not allowed his own taste
to rule the distribution, but has adjusted his parts with the skill of a
veteran."—*Athenæum.*

Young (M.) and Trent (R.)   A Home Ruler.
A Story for Girls.   By MINNIE YOUNG and RACHEL TRENT,
Illustrated by C. P. Colnaghi.   Crown 8vo.   3s. 6d.

Works in the Press.

THE HISTORY OF INDIA, AS TOLD BY ITS OWN HISTORIANS;
the Local Muhammadan Dynasties.   Vol. I. Guzerat.   By
John Dowson, M.R.A.S., late Professor of the Staff
College.   Forming a Sequel in two or more volumes to
Sir H. M. Elliott's Original work on the Muhammadan
period of the History of India; already edited, annotated,
and amplified by the same Author.   Published under the
Patronage of H.M.'s Secretary of State for India.

AN INTEGRAL CALCULUS. Simplified for Schools. By W. P. Lynam, Indian Public Works Department.

DIPLOMATIC STUDY OF THE CRIMEAN WAR. Translated from the original as published by the Russian Foreign Office. 2 vols.

ON AND OFF DUTY; being Leaves from an Officer's Note Book. Part I.—Turania; Part II.—Lemuria; Part III. —Columbia. By Captain S. P. Oliver. Crown 8vo. Illustrated.

HISTORY OF SHORTHAND. With an analysis and review of its present condition and prospects at Home and Abroad. By Thomas Anderson, Parliamentary Reporter.

EGYPT: Physical, Political and Strategical; together with an Account of its Engineering Capabilities and Agricultural Resources. By Griffin W. Vyse, late on special duty for H.M.'s Government in Egypt and Afghanistan.

THE PLAYS AND POEMS OF CHARLES DICKENS. Collected and Edited by Richard Herne Shepherd. 2 vols.

THE ENGLISH IN INDIA. New Sketches.. By E. de Valbezen, late Consul General at Calcutta, Minister Plenipotentiary. Translated from the French, with the Author's permission, by a Diplomat.

PIONEERING IN THE FAR EAST, AND JOURNEYS TO CALIFORNIA IN 1849, AND TO THE WHITE SEA IN 1878. By Ludwig Verner Helmes. With Illustrations from original Sketches and Photographs.

FRANZ LIZST: Artist and Man. By L. Ramann. Translated from the German.

ON BOARD A UNION STEAMER. By Captain S. P. Oliver.

SHADOWS OF THE PAST: the Autobiography of Gen. Kenyon. By J. S. Lloyd, Author of " Ruth Everingham," " The Silent Shadow," &c.

THREE FIVE-ACT PLAYS, AND TWELVE DRAMATIC SCENES. Suitable for Recitation and Home Theatricals. By Martin F. Tupper, D.C.L., F.R.S., Author of " Proverbial Philosophy."

AN ILLUSTRATED EDITION OF TWENTY-ONE DAYS IN INDIA. Being the Tour of Sir Ali Baba, K.C.B. By George Aberigh Mackay.

QUEER PEOPLE. From the Swedish of "Leah." By Albert Alberg. 2 vols.

THE QUEEN'S SPEECHES IN PARLIAMENT. From her Accession to 1882 inclusive. Being a Compendium of English History during the present Reign as told from the Throne, with complete Index. Edited and Compiled By F. Sydney Ensor.

THE JESUITS. A Complete History of public and private proceedings from the foundation of the Order to the present time. By Theodor Greussinger.

ACCENTED FIVE-FIGURE LOGARITHMS of the numbers from 1 to 99999 without Differences. Arranged and Accented by Lowis D'A. Jackson.

PRIVATE THEATRICALS. Being a Practical Guide for the Home Stage, both before and behind the Curtain. By an Old Stager. Illustrated with Suggestions for Scenes after designs by Shirley Hodson.

WITH THE BOERS IN THE TRANSVAAL. By C. L. Norris-Newman, Author of "In Zululand with the British." 8vo. With Map and Plans.

Oriental Works in the Press.

A Hindi Manual. By FREDERIC PINCOTT, M.R.A.S.

An English-Arabic Dictionary. By DR. STEINGASS.

An Arabic-English Dictionary. By DR. STEINGASS.

An English-Persian Dictionary. Compiled from Original Sources. By ARTHUR N. WOLLASTON, M.R.A.S., Translator of the "Anwar-i-Suhaili."

An English-Hindi Dictionary. By FREDERIC PINCOTT, M.R.A.S.

A Malay, Achinese, French, and English Vocabulary. Prepared by Dr. A. J. W. BIKKERS.

Alif Laila, ba-Zuban-i-Urdu (The Arabian Nights in Hindustani.) Roman Character. Edited by F. PINCOTT, M.R.A.S.

A SELECTION FROM

MESSRS. ALLEN'S CATALOGUE

OF BOOKS IN THE EASTERN LANGUAGES, &c.

HINDUSTANI, HINDI, &c.

[Dr. Forbes's Works are used as Class Books in the Colleges and Schools in India.]

Forbes's Hindustani-English Dictionary in the Persian Character, with the Hindi words in Nagari also; and an English Hindustani Dictionary in the English Character; both in one volume. By DUNCAN FORBES, LL.D. Royal 8vo. 42s.

Forbes's Hindustani-English and English Hindustani Dictionary, in the English Character. Royal 8vo. 36s.

Forbes's Smaller Dictionary, Hindustani and English, in the English Character. 12s.

Forbes's Hindustani Grammar, with Specimens of Writing in the Persian and Nagari Characters, Reading Lessons, and Vocabulary. 8vo. 10s. 6d.

Forbes's Hindustani Manual, containing a Compendious Grammar, Exercises for Translation, Dialogues, and Vocabulary, in the Roman Character. New Edition, entirely revised. By J. T. PLATTS. 18mo. 3s. 6d.

Forbes's Bagh o Bahar, in the Persian Character, with a complete Vocabulary. Royal 8vo. 12s. 6d.

Forbes's Bagh o Bahar in English, with Explanatory Notes, illustrative of Eastern Character. 8vo. 8s.

Forbes's Bagh o Bahar, with Vocaby., English Character. 5s.

Forbes's Tota Kahani; or, "Tales of a Parrot," in the Persian Character, with a complete Vocabulary. Royal 8vo. 8s.

Forbes's Baital Pachisi; or, "Twenty-five Tales of a Demon," in the Nagari Character, with a complete Vocabulary. Royal 8vo. 9s.

Forbes's Ikhwanu s Safa; or, "Brothers of Purity," in the Persian Character. Royal 8vo. 12s. 6d.

[For the higher standard for military officers' examinations.]

Forbes's Oriental Penmanship; a Guide to Writing Hindustani in the Persian Character. 4to. 8s.

Platts' Grammar of the Urdu or Hindustani-Language. 8vo. 12s.

Eastwick (Edward B.) The Bagh-o-Bahar—literally translated into English, with copious explanatory notes. 8vo. 10s. 6d.

Small's (Rev. G.) Tota Kahani; or, "Tales of a Parrot." Translated into English. 8vo. 8s.

Platts' J. T., Baital Pachisi; translated into English. 8vo. 8s.

Platts' Ikhwanu S Safa; translated into English. 8vo. 10s. 6d.

Platt's (J. T.), A Hindustani Dictionary. Part I. Royal 8vo. 10s. 6d.

Hindustani Selections, with a Vocabulary of the Words. By James R. Ballantyne. Second Edition. 1845. 5s.

Singhasan Battisi. Translated into Hindi from the Sanscrit. A New Edition. Revised, Corrected, and Accompanied with Copious Notes. By Syed Abdoolah. Royal 8vo. 12s. 6d.

Robertson's Hindustani Vocabulary. 3s. 6d.

Akhlaki Hindi, translated into Urdu, with an Introduction and Notes. By Syed Abdoolah. Royal 8vo. 12s. 6d.

Sakuntala. Translated into Hindi from the Bengali recension of the Sanskrit. Critically edited, with grammatical, idiomatical, and exegetical notes, by Frederic Pincott. 4to. 12s. 6d.

Principles of Persian Caligraphy. Illustrated by Lithographic Plates of the Ta"lik Character, the one usually employed in writing the Persian and the Hindustani. Prepared for the use of the Scottish Naval and Military Academy by James R. Ballantyne. Second Edition. 4to. 3s. 6d.

SANSCRIT.

Haughton's Sanscrit and Bengali Dictionary, in the Bengali Character, with Index, serving as a reversed dictionary. 4to. 30s.

Williams's English-Sanscrit Dictionary. 4to., cloth. £3. 3s.

Williams's Sanskrit-English Dictionary. 4to. £4 14s. 6d.

Wilkin's (Sir Charles) Sanscrit Grammar. 4to. 15s.

Williams's (Monier) Sanscrit Grammar. 8vo. 15s.

Williams's (Monier) Sanscrit Manual; to which is added, a Vocabulary, by A. E. Gough. 18mo. 7s. 6d.

Gough's (A. E.) Key to the Exercises in Williams's Sanscrit Manual. 18mo. 4s.

Williams's (Monier) Sakuntala, with Literal English Translation of all the Metrical Passages, Schemes of the Metres, and copious Critical and Explanatory Notes. Royal 8vo. 21s.

Williams's (Monier) Sakuntala. Translated into English Prose and Verse. Fourth Edition. 8s.

Williams's (Monier) Vikramorvasi. The Text. 8vo. 5s.

Cowell's (E. B.) Translation of the Vikramorvasi. 8vo. 3s. 6d.

Thompson's (J. C.) Bhagavat Gita. Sanscrit Text. 5s.

Haughton's Menu, with English Translation. 2 vols. 4to. 24s.

Johnson's Hitopadesa, with Vocabulary. 15s.

Hitopadesa. A new literal translation from the Sanskrit Text of Prof. F. Johnson. For the use of Students. By Frederic Pincott, M.R.A.S. 6s.

Hitopadesa, Sanscrit, with Bengali and English Trans. 10s. 6d.

Wilson's Megha Duta, with Translation into English Verse, Notes, Illustrations, and a Vocabulary. Royal 8vo. 6s.

PERSIAN.

Richardson's Persian, Arabic, and English Dictionary. Edition of 1852. By F. Johnson. 4to. £4.

Forbes's Persian Grammar, Reading Lessons, and Vocabulary. Royal 8vo. 12s. 6d.

Ibraheem's Persian Grammar, Dialogues, &c. Royal 8vo. 12s. 6d.

Gulistan. Carefully collated with the original MS., with a full Vocabulary. By John Platts, late Inspector of Schools, Central Provinces, India. Royal 8vo. 12s. 6d.

Gulistan. Translated from a revised Text, with Copious Notes. By John Platts. 8vo. 12s. 6d.

Ouseley's Anwari Soheili. 4to. 42s.

Wollaston's (Arthur N.) Translation of the Anvari Soheili. Royal 8vo. £2 2s.

Keene's (Rev. H. G.) First Book of The Anwari Soheili. Persian Text. 8vo. 5s.

Ouseley's (Col.) Akhlaki Mushini. Persian Text. 8vo. 5s.

Keene's (Rev. H. G.) Akhlaki Mushini. Translated into English. 8vo. 3s. 6d.

Clarke's (Captain H. Wilberforce, R.E.) The Persian Manual. A Pocket Companion.

PART I.—A concise Grammar of the Language, with Exercises on its more Prominent Peculiarities, together with a Selection of Useful Phrases, Dialogues, and Subjects for Translation into Persian.

PART II.—A Vocabulary of Useful Words, English and Persian, showing at the same time the difference of idiom between the two Languages. 18mo. 7s. 6d.

The Bústán. By Shaikh Muslihu-d-Dín Sa'di Shírází. Translated for the first time into Prose, with Explanatory Notes and Index. By Captain H. Wilberforce Clarke, R.E. 8vo. With Portrait. 30s.

A Translation of Robinson Crusoe into the Persián Language. Roman Character. Edited by T. W. H. Tolbort, Bengal Civil Service. Cr. 8vo. 7s.

BENGALI.

Haughton's Bengali, Sanscrit, and English Dictionary, adapted for Students in either language; to which is added an Index, serving as a reversed dictionary. 4to. 30s.

Forbes's Bengali Grammar, with Phrases and dialogues. Royal 8vo. 12s. 6d.

Forbes's Bengali Reader, with a Translation and Vocabulary Royal 8vo. 12s. 6d.

Nabo Nari. 12mo. 7s.

ARABIC.

Richardson's Arabic, Persian and English Dictionary. Edition of 1852. By F. JOHNSON. 4to., cloth. £4.

Forbes's Arabic Grammar, intended more especially for the use of young men preparing for the East India Civil Service, and also for the use of self instructing students in general. Royal 8vo., cloth. 18s.

Palmer's Arabic Grammar. 8vo. 18s.

Forbes's Arabic Reading Lessons, consisting of Easy Extracts from the best Authors, with Vocabulary. Royal 8vo., cloth. 15s.

The Arabic Manual. Comprising a condensed Grammar of both Classical and Modern Arabic; Reading Lessons and Exercises, with Analyses and a Vocabulary of useful Words. By Prof. E. H. PALMER, M.A., &c., Author of " A Grammar of the Arabic Language." Fcap. 7s. 6d.

TELOOGOO.

Brown's Dictionary, reversed; with a Dictionary of the Mixed Dialects used in Teloogoo. 3 vols. in 2, royal 8vo. £5.

Campbell's Dictionary. Royal 8vo. 30s.

Brown's Reader. 8vo. 2 vols. 14s.

Brown's Dialogues, Teloogoo and English. 8vo. 5s. 6d.

Pancha Tantra. 8s.

Percival's English-Teloogoo Dictionary. 10s. 6d.

TAMIL.

Rottler's Dictionary, Tamil and English. 4to. 42s.

Babington's Grammar (High Dialect). 4to. 12s.

Percival's Tamil Dictionary. 2 vols. 10s. 6d.

GUZRATTEE.

Mavor's Spelling, Guzrattee and English. 7s, 6d.

Shapuaji Edalji's Dictionary, Guzrattee and English. 21s.

MAHRATTA.

Molesworth's Dictionary, Mahratta and English. 4to. 42s.

Molesworth's Dictionary, English and Mahratta. 4to. 42s.

Esop's Fables. 12mo. 2s. 6d.

Fifth Reading Book. 7s.

A Grammar of the Mahratta Language. For the use of the
East India College at Hayleybury. By JAMES R. BALLANTYNE, of
the Scottish Naval and Military Academy. 4to. 5s.

MALAY.

Marsden's Grammar. 4to. £1 1s.

CHINESE.

Morrison's Dictionary. 6 vols. 4to. £10.

Marshman's—Clavis Sinica, a Chinese Grammar. 4to. £2 2s.

Morrison's View of China, for Philological purposes ; containing a
Sketch of Chinese Chronology, Geography, Government, Religion and
Customs, designed for those who study the Chinese language. 4to. 6s.

PUS'HTO.

The Pushto Manual. Comprising a Concise Grammar ; Exercises and Dialogues ; Familiar Phrases, Proverbs, and Vocabulary. By
Major H. G. RAVERTY, Bombay Infantry (Retired). Author of the
Pus'hto Grammar, Dictionary, Selections Prose and Poetical, Selections
from the Poetry of the Afgháns (English Translation), Æsop's Fables,
&c. &c. Fcap. 5s.

MISCELLANEOUS.

Reeve's English-Carnatica and Carnatica-English Dictionary.
2 vols. (Very slightly damaged). £8.

Collett's Malayalam Reader. 8vo. 12s. 6d.

Esop's Fables in Carnatica. 8vo. bound. 12s. 6d.

A Turkish Manual, comprising a Condensed Grammar with
Idiomatic Phrases, Exercises and Dialogues, and Vocabulary. By
Captain C. F. MACKENZIE, late of H.M.'s Consular Service. 6s.

W. H. ALLEN & CO.'S ORIENTAL MANUALS.

Forbes's Hindustani Manual, containing a Compendious Grammar, Exercises for Translation, Dialogues, and Vocabulary, in the Roman Character. New edition, entirely revised. By J. T. PLATTS, 18mo. 3s. 6d.

Williams's (Monier) Sanskrit Manual; to which is added, a Vocabulary, by A. E. GOUGH. 18mo. 7s. 6d.

Gough's (A. E.) Key to the Exercises in Williams's Sanscrit Manual. 18mo. 4s.

The Arabic Manual. Comprising a condensed Grammar of both Classical and Modern Arabic; Reading Lessons and Exercises, with Analyses and a Vocabulary of useful Words. By Prof. E. H. PALMER, M.A., &c., Author of "A Grammar of the Arabic Language." Fcap. 7s. 6d.

A Turkish Manual, comprising a Condensed Grammar with Idiomatic Phrases, Exercises and Dialogues, and Vocabulary. By Captain C. F. MACKENZIE, late of H.M.'s Consular Service. 6s.

Clarke's (Capt. H. W., R.E.) The Persian Manual, containing a concise Grammar, with Exercises, useful Phrases, Dialogues, and Subjects for Translation into Persian; also a Vocabulary of Useful Words, English and Persian. 18mo. 7s. 6d.

The Pushto Manual. Comprising a Concise Grammar; Exercises and Dialogues; Familiar Phrases, Proverbs, and Vocabulary. By Major H. G. RAVERTY, Bombay Infantry (Retired). Fcap. 5s.

A RELIEVO MAP OF INDIA.

BY HENRY F. BRION.

In Frame, 21s.

"A map of this kind brings before us such a picture of the surface of a given country as no ordinary map could ever do. To the mind's eye of the average Englishman, India consists of 'the plains' and 'the hills,' chiefly of the former, the hills being limited to the Himalayas and the Nilgiris. The new map will at least enable him to correct his notions of Indian geography. It combines the usual features of a good plain map of the country on a scale of 150 miles to the inch, with a faithful representation of all the uneven surfaces, modelled on a scale thirty-two times the horizontal one; thus bringing out into clear relief the comparative heights and outlines of all the hill-ranges, and showing broad tracts of uneven ground, of intermingled hill and valley, which a common map of the same size would hardly indicate, except to a very practised eye. The plains of Upper India are reduced to their true proportions; the Central Provinces, Malwa, and Western Bengal reveal their actual ruggedness at a glance; and Southern India, from the Vindhyas to Cape Comorin, proclaims its real height above the sea-level. To the historical as well as the geographical student such a map is an obvious and important aid in tracing the course of past campaigns, in realising the conditions under which successive races carried their arms and settlements through the Peninsula, and in comprehending the difference of race, climate, and physical surroundings which make up our Indian Empire. Set in a neat frame of maplewood, the map seems to attract the eye like a prettily-coloured picture, and its price, a guinea, should place it within the reach of all who care to combine the useful with the ornamental."—*Home News.*

MAPS OF INDIA, etc.

Messrs. Allen & Co.'s Maps of India were revised and much improved during 1876, with especial reference to the existing Administrative Divisions, Railways, &c.

District Map of India; corrected to 1876;
Divided into Collectorates with the Telegraphs and Railways from Government surveys. On six sheets—size, 5ft. 6in. high; 5ft. 8in. wide, £2; in a case, £2 12s. 6d.; or, rollers, varn., £3 3s.

A General Map of India; corrected to 1876;
Compiled chiefly from surveys executed by order of the Government of India. On six sheets—size, 5 ft. 3 in. wide; 5 ft. 4 in. high, £2; or, on cloth, in case, £2 12s. 6d.; or, rollers, varn., £3 3s.

Map of India; corrected to 1876;
From the most recent Authorities. On two sheets—size, 2 ft. 10in. wide; 3 ft. 3 in. high, 16s.; or, on cloth, in a case, £1 1s.

Map of the Routes in India; corrected to 1874;
With Tables of Distances between the principal Towns and Military Stations On one sheet—size, 2 ft. 3 in. wide; 2 ft. 9 in. high, 9s.; or, on cloth, in a case, 12s.

Map of the Western Provinces of Hindoostan,
The Punjab, Cabool, Scinde, Bhawulpore, &c., including all the States between Candahar and Allahabad. On four sheets—size, 4 ft. 4in. wide; 4 ft. 2 in. high, 30s.; or, in case, £2; rollers, varnished, £2 10s.

Map of India and China, Burmah, Siam, the Malay Peninsula, and the Empire of Anam.
On two sheets—size, 4 ft. 3 in. wide; 3 ft. 4 in. high, 16s.; or, on cloth, in a case, £1 5s.

Map of the Steam Communication and Overland Routes
between England, India, China, and Australia. In a case, 14s.; on rollers, and varnished, 18s.

Map of China,
From the most Authentic Sources of Information. One large sheet—size, 2 ft. 7 in. wide; 2 ft. 2 in. high, 6s.; or, on cloth, in case, 8s.

Map of the World;
On Mercator's Projection, showing the Tracts of the Early Navigators, the Currents of the Ocean, the Principal Lines of great Circle Sailing, and the most recent discoveries. On four sheets—size, 6ft. 2 in. wide; 4 ft. 3 in. high, £2; on cloth, in a case, £2 10s : or, with rollers, and varnished, £3.

Handbook of Reference to the Maps of India.
Giving the Latitude and Longitude of places of note. 18mo. 3s. 6d.

Russian Official Map of Central Asia.
Compiled in accordance with the Discoveries and Surveys of Russian Staff Officers up to the close of the year 1877. In 2 Sheets. 10s. 6d., or in cloth case, 14s.

Published on the arrival of every Mail from India.   Subscription 26s. per annum, post free, specimen copy, 6d.

ALLEN'S INDIAN MAIL,

AND

Official Gazette

FROM

INDIA, CHINA, AND ALL PARTS OF THE EAST.

ALLEN's INDIAN MAIL contains the fullest and most authentic Reports of all important Occurrences in the Countries to which it is devoted, compiled chiefly from private and exclusive sources. It has been pronounced by the Press in general to be *indispensable* to all who have Friends or Relatives in the East, as affording the only *correct* information regarding the Services, Movements of Troops, Shipping, and all events of Domestic and individual interest.

The subjoined list of the usual Contents will show the importance and variety of the information concentrated in ALLEN's INDIAN MAIL.

Summary and Review of Eastern News.

Precis of Public Intelligence	Shipping—Arrival of Ships
Selections from the Indian Press	„ „ Passengers
Movements of Troops	„ Departure of Ships
The Government Gazette	„ „ Passengers
Courts Martial	Commercial—State of the Markets
Domestic Intelligence—Births	„ Indian Securities
„ „ Marriages	„ Freights
„ „ Deaths	&c. &c. &c.

Home Intelligence relating to India, &c.

Original Articles	Arrival reported in England
Miscellaneous Information	Departures „ „
Appointments, List of Furloughs, Extensions, &c.	Shipping—Arrival of Ships
„ Civil	„ „ Passengers
„ Military	„ Departure of Ships
„ Ecclesiastical and	„ „ Passengers
„ Marine	„ Vessel spoken with
	&c. &c. &c.

Review of Wooks on the East.—and Notices of all affairs connected with India and the Services.

Each year an INDEX is furnished, to enable Subscribers to bind up the Volume which forms a complete

ASIATIC ANNUAL REGISTER AND LIBRARY OF REFERENCE.

LONDON: WM. H. ALLEN & Co., 13, WATERLOO PLACE, S.W.

(PUBLISHERS TO THE INDIA OFFICE),

To whom Communications for the Editor, and Advertisements are requested to be addressed.

Subscription, 32s. per annum.   Postage Free.   Or in
Monthly Parts, price 3s.

PRÉCIS OF OFFICIAL PAPERS,

BEING

ABSTRACTS OF ALL PARLIAMENTARY RETURNS

DIRECTED TO BE PRINTED BY

BOTH HOUSES OF PARLIAMENT.

"Messrs. Allen have commenced the publication of a most useful work, the need of which has been felt for a long time, though until now no one has had the courage to attempt it. . . . . . The *précis* is very well done."—*Journal of the Statistical Society*, June, 1880.

"There is no doubt as to the value of most parliamentary publications, but few persons have the time or inclination to wade through them, and thus much valuable matter is missed, but in this *précis* Messrs. Allen and Co. give an outline of just what is required."—*Iron Trade Review.*

"Messrs. Allen & Co.'s book is composed of abstracts of all returns directed to be printed by either or both of the Houses of Parliament, and the work has evidently been done by practised *précis* writers who understand how to reach the important features of Government papers."—*Liverpool Daily Courier.*

"This is a publication which supplies a great want. We gladly welcome this work, both for reading and for reference."—*United Service Gazette.*

"The papers are carefully condensed."—*British Mail.*

"In the case of statistical returns it is especially good."—*Cambridge Chronicle.*

"This is not a Blue-book; but none of them can exceed it in value. Every business man will have it upon the desk corner for reference, and it should be found on the table of every public reading room and private library."—*Western Times.*

"A most useful work of reference."—*The Railway News.*

"This is a very important work, and its perusal will place readers on a far higher intellectual level and acquaintance with the parliamentary papers than most embryo members of Parliament possess."—*Finance Chronicle and Insurance Circular.*

"This serial is calculated to be of much service."—*Iron.*

"The above contains a vast amount of valuable information and statistics."—*Sunday Times.*

"We scarcely need add that it is a valuable work."—*Herapath's Railway Journal.*

"As a book of reference, promises to be of inestimable value to public men, journalists, economists, historical students, and, indeed, all who are interested in national progress and contemporary politics."—*The Statist.*

"The difficult work of summarising is extremely well executed. Both paper and type are good."—*Broad Arrow.*

"An excellent publication."—*The Farmer.*

"Messrs. Allen & Co. earn the gratitude of all who require to keep themselves acquainted with the contents of parliamentary papers by the publication of this *précis.* The compilation has been made with discretion, and will be found extremely valuable and useful for reference."—*Dundee Advertiser.*

"As a handy work of reference, and a means of saving time and labour, it will be highly appreciated."—*Allen's Indian Mail.*

"The utility of the *précis* is very considerably heightened by an admirable table of contents numerically and alphabetically arranged."—*The Railway News and Joint Stock Journal.*

"The *précis* of official papers will give new value to the parliamentary returns."—*Liverpool Courier.*

"Nous croyons rendre service au public et à ceux de nos confreres qui ne la connaitraient pas, en leur signalent cette publication nouvelle."—*Moniteur des Interêts Materiels,* Brussels.

LONDON : **W. H. ALLEN & CO., 13, WATERLOO-PLACE.**

www.ingramcontent.com/pod-product-compliance
Lightning Source LLC
Chambersburg PA
CBHW032315280326
41932CB00009B/822